CIVILISING CAPITALISM
The Labor Movement in New South Wales 1870-1900

Bede Nairn

AUSTRALIAN NATIONAL UNIVERSITY PRESS
CANBERRA 1973

First published in Australia 1973

Printed in New Zealand for the Australian National University Press, Canberra

United Kingdom, Europe, Middle East, Africa and Caribbean: Angus & Robertson (U.K.) Ltd, London

North, South, and Central America: International Scholarly Book Services, Inc., Portland, Oregon

Southeast Asia: Angus & Robertson (S.E. Asia) Pty Ltd, Singapore

Japan: United Publishers Services Ltd, Tokyo

Library of Congress Catalog Card no. 72-94970

ISBN 0 7081 0486 X

This book is dedicated to the memory
of John Christian Watson (1867–1941)
the first Labor prime minister of Australia.

Acknowledgments

Librarians are essential for the writing of history. I have to thank all those who have helped me in the Library of New South Wales, including those in the Mitchell Library and the Dixson Library, and in the Australian National Library.

My thanks are due, too, to my colleagues in the Australian Dictionary of Biography section of the department of history in the Australian National University; particularly to Douglas Pike whose understanding encouragement reflects his refined and extensive scholarship; to Nan Phillips, tireless and efficient; to Martha Rutledge whose knowledge of the work of Edmund Barton has been of great use to me, though it is not responsible for the views I express in this book; and to Ruth Frappell who has a comprehensive knowledge of the resources of the Mitchell Library.

In their own way typists are as invaluable to historians as librarians. I have to express my gratitude for the uncomplaining and capable co-operation of Jean Nairn, Margaret Crago and Dorothy Smith.

Contents

Cartoons

All cartoons reproduced by permission of *The Bulletin*

Drawing by Lionel Lindsay on dedication page reproduced by permission
from the *Australian Worker,* 30 April 1904.

Abbreviations

ADB	:	*Australian Dictionary of Biography*
ALF	:	Australian(asian) Labor Federation
AS	:	*Australian Star*
AWU	:	Australian Workers' Union
DT	:	*Daily Telegraph*
FSA	:	Free Selectors' Association
HS	:	*Historical Studies,* University of Melbourne
JRAHS	:	*Journal of the Royal Australian Historical Society*
LEL	:	Labor Electoral League
ML	:	Mitchell Library, Sydney
NL	:	National Library, Canberra
PD	:	*Parliamentary Debates,* Series 1, New South Wales
PLL	:	Political Labor League
SMH	:	*Sydney Morning Herald*
TLC	:	Trades and Labor Council of New South Wales
WMDA	:	Working Mens' Defence Association

A note on the spelling of Labor

By 1900 in all official Party usage the spelling was almost invariably 'Labor', applying both to the Labor Party and the Labor movement (trade unions): these forms have been used in this book from 1870. From an early stage the *Daily Telegraph* used 'Labor' (or 'labor'), but the *Sydney Morning Herald* retained 'Labour' (or 'labour') up to 1900 and beyond: the most common popular spelling in the 1890s was 'Labour' (or 'labour') and this is reflected in many direct quotations in this book.

Labor Party was the implied official synonym of the Labor Electoral League from 1891 to 1895, and of the Political Labor League from 1895 (June) to 1900. Where 'Labor' and 'Party' are used alone in this book, they stand for Labor Party, except that occasionally 'Labor' on its own stands for Labor movement: the meaning is clear from the text.

Introduction

The New South Wales Labor Party, founded in 1891, was indigenous to its colonial society: a truism, but one that has to be stated, for some theorists, of various political hues, write of it as if, in some extraordinary way, it should have been independent of its society.

New South Wales, founded in 1788, was the oldest of the Australian colonies. In the beginning it was a prison settlement, with the governor, in theory, and often in practice, an autocratic ruler subject only to controls exercised by the British government, 12,000 miles away. Not until the 1820s, when a charter of justice was given to the colony and a Legislative Council established, did the penal forms begin to dissolve, slowly, because the Council was appointed by the governor and its main task was to advise him. By the 1830s a broad social separation had been clarified: those who were ex-convicts and the children of convicts on one hand, and those who were free settlers and their children on the other hand. The cleavage cut across tendencies to divide the colonists simply into masters and servants, or employers and employees, and was complicated by the success in business and on the land of many ex-convicts. The social composition was further confused by the aspirations of the native-born, who had a common love of country that, at the level of achievement at least, blurred, and at times even obliterated, their parental origins, bond or free. This strong patriotic strand was clearly manifest in the 1830s in the public career of William Charles Wentworth and merged significantly into the whig-liberal current that was conditioning demands for self-government and improvements in the system of trial by jury. In the late 1820s Wentworth, himself a son of a convict mother, had taken a leading part in the struggle against Governor Darling for freedom of the press.

The governors of the 1830s and 1840s, Bourke, Gipps, FitzRoy, were responsive to the changed conditions, and they were assisted notably by John Hubert Plunkett, their chief law officer, an Irish Roman Catholic, who had an ingrained respect for the rule of law.[1] Plunkett was the chief architect of the Church Act 1836, which substantially placed all Christian denominations in the colony on an equal footing, but which was also seen by all colonists as a charter of social equality.[2] Given Plun-

kett's race and religion, his very career as one of the two top public
servants provided clear evidence of the open nature of the colonial
society. Nevertheless, despite the comparatively favourable climate, in
the 1830s continued pressure had to be maintained on the British government to obtain self-government, and the reformed Legislative Council in
1842 was only partly representative, with twenty-four of its thirty-six
seats elected on a restricted franchise.

The struggles of the colonists continued in the 1840s when the three
main issues were the need for increased self-government, the rights of
land squatters to some form of security of tenure, and resistance to
British attempts to restore the transportation of convicts that had been
abolished in 1840. These were large questions that involved the whole
colony, including the working class; each one dictated confrontation with
the British government, but there was also considerable division of
opinion within the colony on them. Public debate was extensive, especially on squatting and transportation, and when the decade closed
the government had virtually yielded to popular demands on all three
problems. In the early 1850s discussion was centred on the need for full
self-government, and in 1851–4 narrowed down to the details of a
system of responsible government based on two Houses of parliament. In
1856 the parliamentary system began. The colonists of New South Wales
had been conditioned by a generation of political agitation, much of
which included high level debate, to solve fundamental constitutional
problems. Unlike the other Australian colonies, with the partial exception
of Tasmania, virtually no concession had been made gratuitously to New
South Wales by the British government.

The drawn-out constitutional struggle and Wentworth's leading part in
it had enlivened local patriotism. The leading politician of the 1850s
was Charles Cowper who had come to the colony in 1809 at the age of
two. He certainly regarded himself as a New South Welshman, as did
practically all of the other major politicians of the responsible government era in the nineteenth century. Between 1856 and 1900 there were
thirteen separate premiers (some of them in office more than once) and
nine of them, including Cowper, were well formed in the colonial mould,
although only two were born in New South Wales: James Squire Farnell,
premier in 1877, descended on his mother's side from a convict, was
born in Sydney in 1825; George Dibbs, premier in 1885, 1889 and 1891,
was born in Sydney in 1834. William John Lyne, premier in 1899 was
born in Tasmania in 1844 and came to New South Wales in 1875. Of
the rest John Robertson, born in England, came to the colony in 1820,
aged four; James Martin, born in Ireland, arrived in 1820, aged one;
William Forster's parents were married in Sydney in 1816, he was born
in India in 1818 and returned to New South Wales with his parents in
1829. A partial exception among the nine 'colonial' premiers was Henry

Parkes who was twenty-four when he arrived in Sydney in 1839; he had been influenced by radical politics in England; against that, with great energy and much skill he threw himself into colonial politics and was a prominent leader in the anti-transportation movement in the late 1840s and in the campaign for a liberal constitution in the early 1850s. He was rightly regarded as a 'colonial'. The remaining 'colonial' premier was George Reid, who figures very largely in this book; Reid was born in Scotland in 1845 and was brought to New South Wales seven years later. Through these men, especially Robertson, who died in 1891, and Parkes, who died in 1896, the great constitutional contests of the pre-responsible government era were kept alive until 1900.

The association of the native-born with the winning of constitutional freedom was consolidated in the 1850s by a trio of brilliant lawyer-politicians, William Bede Dalley, born in Sydney in 1831; Daniel Deniehy, born in Sydney in 1828; and Richard Driver, born at Cabramatta in 1829. Dalley and Deniehy were also talented essayists and literary critics, and the fact that they were Catholics reflected the flowering of an open liberal democratic society. The sectarian bitterness noted by historians did not really begin in New South Wales until about the middle 1860s, when Irish Catholic bishops and Irish Protestant clergymen decided to fight Ireland's battles overseas, and disturbed the tolerant religious equilibrium attained in the colony. These Christians were fortuitously aided in their disruptive work by the attempt of a mad Catholic Irishman to assassinate the Duke of Edinburgh, Queen Victoria's son, in Sydney in 1868. Dalley, especially, came to exemplify the vigour, richness and humanity of colonial society. Both his father and mother had been transported to New South Wales, but before he was thirty he had made his mark as a leading barrister, a scintillating orator and a successful politician; by the 1880s he had become one of the greatest men in the colony, witty, generous, and, above all, humane, with a vision of a united Australia; in 1886 ill-health caused him to refuse the chief justiceship.

Dalley, Deniehy and Driver reinforced the older liberals to ensure that the New South Wales constitution was the most democratic possible in 1855; they also helped to continue the fight to improve it by changes to facilitate amendments, and to introduce manhood suffrage and voting by secret ballot. The three young nativists were part of the vague liberal coalition opposed to a conservative group that consisted chiefly of the great pastoralists, some city magnates, and the high officials of the old colonial order. With Robertson's Land Acts of 1861 the liberals' triumph was virtually complete. The objective of these acts was to break the monopoly of the pastoralist lessees by allowing farmers to select land and settle on it before it was surveyed. In the 1860s with Robertson, Forster, Martin and Parkes to the fore the liberals were successful in abolishing state aid to churches and in reforming the educational system. They also embarked on vigorous extension of the railways. The prosperity and contentedness of New South Wales seemed to have resulted from their insight and persistence.

If political freedom, religious toleration and educational reform were the politics of the liberals, free trade was their fiscal policy. Their political triumph set the seal on free trade and most New South Welshmen became ardent supporters of it. Martin was an interesting exception. Free trade came to be seen as a necessary part of liberalism; it was based on the primacy of the pastoral industry, with Sydney becoming one of the great ports of the Pacific Ocean through which flowed huge exports of wool, and in return many and varied commodities were received from all parts of the world. As the colony had vast deposits of coal and sufficient amounts of iron ore and other raw materials, some significant local manufacturing also developed without any protective tariff. By the 1880s, New South Wales was second only to Victoria in population and national income; by the end of the decade the mother colony's economy began to outstrip all the rest and early in the 1890s its population became the largest. To most New South Welshmen this result seemed part of the natural order, a deserved reward for their success in transforming against great odds a penal settlement into a model of democratic liberalism. To many of them as the 1880s ended, mounting demands for Federation sounded like cries for financial help from the protectionist southern colonies, rather than calls for national union.

Capitalism was fundamental to New South Wales as, indeed, it was to all the Australian colonies. It could not have been otherwise as they were offshoots of the greatest capitalist society in the world, Britain. But it was a modified capitalism, conditioned by the powerful role of the government from the very foundation of the settlement, and by the pressures exerted by a pioneering frontier society. Private property in land was taken for granted, commerce thrived from Governor King's time (1800–6) as merchants strove for profits, and Governor Macquarie's encouragement of John Dickson in 1813–15 helped the beginning of light manufacturing. Capitalism in New South Wales in the nineteenth century was never uncontrolled, never free from criticism; and, to a degree because of these restraints, its survival was never in doubt. In its curbed form it seemed to be part of the constitutional struggles of the 1830s and 1840s; it became synonymous with the liberalism that was believed to be making the colony great and prosperous. Robertson's land policy, with widespread support, was seen as a necessary check to keep the capitalism of the pastoralists within bounds. The distant might of Britain provided constant evidence of the efficacy of the system.

Not without some tension, trade unions fitted into this colonial society from the 1830s; but essentially they were accepted without demur, and

trade unionists could not have conceived that it might have been otherwise. It seems that no union had a continuous history for more than four
or five years prior to 1850, but some eighteen were formed, and undertook the usual range of activities of workers' combinations, including
strikes; they were part of the way in which capitalism was curbed. After
1850, unions took on a permanent form, surviving and developing in
harmony with economic growth. By 1871 when the Trades and Labor
Council (TLC) was formed in Sydney, there were probably fifteen
permanent unions in the metropolitan area and at least one, the Coal-
Miners', in Newcastle. Within twenty years the number of unions in the
colony, most of them in Sydney, had reached about 100. With their
assistance, the TLC was able to keep capitalism under reasonable
restraint, but by 1891 its control was weakening.

The growth of trade unions was not only a tribute to the industrial
leadership of the TLC, it also reflected the economic expansion that had
taken New South Wales ahead of the other Australian colonies. This
great development had out-stripped the sanctions of the liberal society
built up over a century by New South Welshmen. In particular, the
parliamentary system, adequate for a pastoral-commercial economy,
could not adjust easily to the modern needs of a society in which agriculture and industry were assuming increasing significance. Signs of disintegration were clearly discernible from about 1885, when, for the first time,
the validity of free trade came under strong and persistent attack from
protection devotees, some of whom were even elected to parliament.
Indications of deep social malaise enshrouded the extraordinary patriotic
excesses of many citizens of Sydney at the time of Queen Victoria's
golden jubilee in 1887, and elements of decay in the legal system were
revealed in 1886–7 by the circumstances surrounding the trial and
hanging of several youths in what was known as the Mount Rennie rape
case. At the general election of 1887 Parkes, now aged seventy-two, made
a prodigious come-back to become premier (for the fourth time) on the
cry of 'save liberalism and free trade'; but within two years his government had fallen, to be succeeded by a brittle ministry led by Dibbs that
lasted less than two months. Parkes returned in 1889 to head a government which, two years later, was still marking time. Dalley had died in
1888, Robertson died in 1891. Parkes, the last of the pre-1856 liberals
was visibly failing, and in 1890 his condition was aggravated by an
accident in which he suffered a badly broken leg. In this situation in
1891 New South Wales had to make rational judgments about Federation.

The year before, capitalism had had an unprecedented triumph over
the trade unions in the great maritime strike, which, centred in New
South Wales, affected virtually the whole continent. The pastoralists had
been vitally involved in the strike, and in 1891 they followed up their

success by a savage confrontation with the shearing unions in which the men were not only defeated, but also humiliated. Essential parts of the system that had maintained a vital social equilibrium in the colony had been disturbed. Now society's problem was not simply to restrain capitalism but to civilise it. In addition the social and political balance had to be restated and restored in modern terms. With the essential aid of George Reid the New South Wales Labor Party undertook this daunting task. The Party was founded by the TLC in 1891; with its support George Reid became premier at the head of a reformed liberal-free trade group in 1894. By the end of 1899 colonial society had been resuscitated and the political system renovated, and New South Wales had examined Federation in great detail and had accepted it.

Under the guidance of the TLC the Labor Party had developed naturally out of trade unionism. By 1891 unions were an integral social institution, with the vital task of maintaining and improving the quality of life, the living standards and the industrial conditions of the working class. This corporate role was understood and appreciated by the whole colony and was nicely symbolised by various fraternal functions, including annual banquets, at which it was not unusual for the premier, cabinet ministers, and occasionally even the governor, to attend. The TLC naturally sent its commiserations to Parkes when he broke his leg. Neither the unions nor the Council considered that this social adhesion made them in any sense inferior to any other section of the community. They valued the freedoms they shared with all other colonists, freedom of speech, of assembly, of the press; they appreciated the rule of law, the democratic parliamentary system, their open society. As all these boons seemed to stem from the British Crown, they were prepared in return to combine loyalty to 'home', as some of them called Britain, with an intense local patriotism. The TLC, as the representative of the trade unions, was intent on upholding a balanced society in order to maintain what they regarded as the normal rights of the working class, which included the right to improve their lot. When communal balance was manifestly upset in the middle 1880s, the Council started to grope its way towards a remedy. By the time of the unions' defeat in the martime strike the Council had determined that the needs of the times demanded direct parliamentary intervention by Labor. The alternative of an unnecessary and unwinnable social revolution did not occur to it, if only because, after 1871, its major industrial work had been associated with both direct and indirect political action. Capitalism could be civilised by variations on the themes the Council had used to keep it in check.

The Labor Party invited all radicals to help it in the task of restoring and modernising New South Wales. Many of them, including some trade unionists, did not agree that the solution was simply to renovate an old system, but rather to replace it with a new one, although they were uncertain of its form. This group, some of them, had the best of intentions; but most of them were socialist elitists, blinded by their frustrations to the deeply rooted humane values of colonial society, and ultimately seeking their inspiration from alien sources whose understanding of human freedom was demonstrably and dangerously defective. The Labor Party was prepared to accept what it regarded as the best of socialism, but it rejected a policy of organising a socialist state that seemed as if it would inevitably and irretrievably distort hard-won liberty. Labor people weighed the confused promise of an alien earthly paradise against its high price, which included the constriction of the human spirit, and decided to continue their efforts for betterment in the society to which they belonged. The Party was helped to come to this conclusion by the minority status of the organised socialists, and the overwhelming evidence that almost all the people of New South Wales wanted improvements from within the system they cherished. By 1900 the Labor Party was a mass democratic radical party, naturally conditioned by the society from which it had emerged, and made well aware, both from within and from without, that it had to attack the problems of rural as well as urban regeneration in New South Wales, and that it had a vital part to play in a federated Australia.

From his personal belief in the values of colonial society, George Reid had reached similar conclusions to those of the TLC. But Reid's vision, sharp and revitalising as it was, could only be limited by the exigencies of his own political career. He did not have a detailed policy of reform, or a permanent party apparatus to ensure a momentum that would compensate for his inevitable loss of impetus in the face of very great opposition. And Reid found that, with the help of the Labor Party, he had to 'pick up Federation from the gutter' where the protectionist government of Dibbs and Edmund Barton had left it in 1894. The problems of national union gradually absorbed his immense energies, and his reforming zeal slowly faded. But Reid's 1894–5 attack on 'the classes', the entrenched property, financial and public service interests, provided necessary help for the work of the Labor Party. The events of 1899 when Labor removed Reid from office showed conclusively that the Party had ultimate control over him; but he had provided the personal prestige, the political skill and the essential link with the past that had made far-reaching changes possible. It is one of the great ironies of Australian history that Reid's efforts for reform in New South Wales, and for Federation, should have cost him the honour of being Australia's first prime minister.

I   *The Power of the Trades and Labor Council*

The New South Wales Trades and Labor Council met for the first time on 25 May 1871 with delegates from six out of a probable fifteen trade unions in Sydney.[1] The foundation of the TLC was remotely affected by the formation of the London Trades Council in 1860 and the British Trade Union Congress in 1868. More immediately it was connected with the Eight Hour System Extension and General Short Hour League which operated in Sydney from August 1869 to May 1871.[2]

Francis Burdett Dixon was the first deputy chairman of the League, its secretary for a time, and its most active member. A stonemason born in Yorkshire in 1832, he came to Australia in 1859; until his death in 1884, Dixon was the outstanding leader of the Labor movement in New South Wales.[3] At the eight-hour League's meeting on 13 October 1870 he

> stated that in the event of another election in Sydney it would be highly necessary that the Conference [League] should be prepared to act in any part that it might be called upon, and he very much wished to see a better organisation in the form of a Trades Council.

In March 1871 a group of trade unionists, centred in the Amalgamated Society of Engineers, circularised other unions in Sydney about the need for a trades council.[4] Two months later the TLC's inaugural meeting followed.

Dixon's speech of October 1870 reflected a basic tenet of the New South Wales Labor movement: that industrial action and political action were complementary. It was not a doctrine unanimously and consistently held, much less grounded in ideology and perfectly developed. It was a persistent, pragmatic belief that accompanied the strivings of wage earners to improve their material conditions, above all in the 1870s and 1880s to reduce their hours of work, and also to increase wages. At the 1860 general election the notion had encouraged some coalminers to organise the success of T. Lewis in Northumberland, and some engineers and others the win of D. C. Dalgleish (1827–70) in West Sydney.[5] Between 1870 and 1891 the idea of political action waxed and waned, at times articulated compellingly by Labor leaders and assented to, at other times questioned and temporarily discarded. A good guide to the extent of support for political action was the degree of success of industrial action by the trade unions at any particular time. At no time were industrial and political action clearly demarcated, nor was a clear-cut division possible. By the middle 1870s political action came to be defined as direct political action, with some kind of parliamentary delegates somehow representing Labor. In 1891 the movement was prepared to try to put the idea into practice on a big scale. As it was the need for a universal eight-hour day that sparked off Labor's parliamentary aspirations in 1869–74, so it was in 1889–91.

Intervention in politics automatically involved acceptance of the community practices, grounded in 'the Constitution', formally enacted in the 1855 Constitution Act of the Imperial Parliament, the statutory basis of the colonial parliamentary system. And 'the Constitution' included 'the rule of law' and other aspects of the British system of government. The British connection was emphasised by the presence of the governor of the colony, still powerful, and, significantly, an Imperial official. The natural social integration of the TLC was illustrated in May 1872 when W. Edmunds was permitted to address it to 'suggest . . . the advisability of the Council endeavoring to bring forward a candidate to represent the working classes in the event of an election'.[6] In November the Council resolved to do its utmost to defeat the mayor of Sydney, M. Chapman, in the city council elections, because of his opposition to the eight hours, and to support W. Camb, who favoured it. In October the following year Dixon 'at some length' moved that the Council 'take into consideration the advisability of bringing before [its] societies the propriety of direct labor representation in the Legislature of the Colony'. The proposal was carried unanimously.[7]

Before any serious action could be taken on Dixon's motion the Council became embroiled in disputes in the iron trades over the eight hours. Following a strike the benefit had been grudgingly conceded in some shops in December 1873, but the following month a wider strike broke out after a disagreement over meal breaks. The retention of the eight hours was also in question. Dixon was now secretary of the TLC and the successful conclusion of the strike in March 1874 was a triumph for his strong and diplomatic leadership.[8] Dixon's achievement mirrored the rising power of the TLC, which influenced the formation of some seventeen new unions in 1874, ten of which joined the Council to give it by the end of the year twenty-five affiliations out of some forty-one unions in the colony. They all sought the eight-hour day. Within the existing social framework the TLC had evoked a degree of working class self-realisation and solidarity.

Henry Parkes formed his first government in May 1872. In 1873 the ministry was seriously weakened by the resignation of Attorney-General Edward Butler, aggrieved by Parkes's failure to redeem a pledge to make him chief justice. From April 1874 the government was under

attack on a variety of constitutional grounds because of the promise of
the governor, Sir Hercules Robinson, to release from prison Frank
Gardiner, a bushranger who in 1864 had been sentenced to thirty-two
years. Gardiner's discharge in June intensified the political excitement
and Parkes barely survived a virtual vote of censure. But his government
fell in November after he had laid on the table of the Legislative
Assembly an Executive Council minute in which Robinson had made
some provocative statements about those responsible for the 'clamour'
against his exercise of the prerogative of mercy.

On the TLC the confidence and self-assurance of the delegates facilitated Dixon's political designs. Concurrently with the June parliamentary
crisis his motion was carried, that the Council 'considers it expedient and
highly desirable that Labor should be directly represented in Parliament'.[9]
The same night, Angus Cameron (1847–96) arrived as the delegate of
the Progressive Carpenters and Joiners, and Jacob Garrard (1846–1931)
of the Amalgamated Society of Engineers: both strongly supported
Dixon. They were destined to become prominent parliamentarians.[10] On
24 June Cameron succeeded in getting a committee of seven appointed,
including Dixon and himself, to 'draw up a scheme' to implement the
decision to go into politics. His speech summed up the complex combination of the pressures driving Labor into the parliamentary arena and
the inhibitions pulling them back from it: 'in some very eloquent remarks
he urged the working men to help themselves'; he denied that Labor
intervention involved 'class legislation'; he stressed the need for funds
and for the support of those who were not members of trade unions.[11]
Cameron took it for granted that Labor was anchored to its society and
that the TLC planned to improve the parliamentary system.

The TLC committee's discussions revealed the residual differences of
opinion about the political experiment. When its report was examined
'clause by clause' on 28 July, Cameron tried unsuccessfully to have it
referred back for reconsideration. Most interest was displayed in the
method of selection of Labor's parliamentary candidates, as to whether
they should be chosen by the affiliated unions or by the TLC. Eventually,
on the motion of Cameron and Garrard, the Council was given the task.
The scrutiny continued on 5 August when Dixon urged that finality be
reached 'as it was very possible that a dissolution of Parliament might
take place as early as September'. After Garrard had moved that the
Council decide on the electorates and select four candidates from the
number nominated by affiliated unions, the amended report was adopted.
The Committee now had the problem of rallying the support of unions
to the scheme.[12]

The process by which delegates reached the TLC ensured that they
were, for the most part, able and experienced trade unionists. They were
leaders of unions, their education furthered in debate, in keeping books

of record, in trying to balance income and expenditure. While Dixon was the outstanding general leader, his social awareness, and Cameron's and Garrard's, reflected a quality present in the great majority. But this insight, so well illustrated by the decision to go into politics, was tempered by the immediate need to ensure the survival of each individual union. A TLC delegate had a dual role: to take care of his union's interests, and to develop the wider aims of the Labor movement. At times it was easy to harmonise these roles, at times difficult, sometimes even impossible. So the class solidarity extracted and nurtured by the TLC, tenacious, comforting and determinative as it may have been, was neither explicit nor stable. The parliamentary scheme of 1874 accentuated the internal strains of Labor fellow-feeling. As citizens, the TLC delegates accepted the contemporary political system, but as unionists, they were trying to mend it. Parkes and John Robertson were emerging as the great parliamentarians of the 1870s, both had deep roots in the colony's political history, both were commanding men, masters of the familiar constitutional approach to politics. When Cameron denied that Labor in politics meant 'class legislation', he was affirming the approved view that parliament represented an indivisible society; that the factions of members coalescing uneasily around Parkes and Robertson in the Legislative Assembly, together with the members of the Legislative Council, would make laws that would neither unduly benefit nor hinder any group in the colony. Despite this, Cameron had also urged the working class to help themselves by getting one of their members into parliament: their success would challenge the view of a classless parliament. The events surrounding the TLC's 1874 attempt to organise Labor representation in parliament exposed the innate conflicts in the movement's view of the way in which it should operate in New South Wales society. These cleavages were not closed, but rather re-emphasised, and widened when the Parliamentary Labor Party was founded in 1891.

The 1874 parliamentary plan not only raised the question of the relationship of the Labor movement to society, it also brought into the open the issue of the nature of the connection between the TLC and its affiliated unions. There was no chance of the Council imposing its will on the unions unless they were agreeable. Unions could disaffiliate at any time, and several did so between 1871 and 1894, when the Council was temporarily disbanded because of a severe economic depression. Unions adhered to the social formulas of a classless Parliament and often argued that discussions of politics achieved no purpose and even weakened industrial action. To a degree these opinions were sincerely held and were occasionally proved correct. Unions strove to keep their industrial objectives clearly before them; and their aims were simple. It was by no means apparent to all unions that parliamentary action could help to lower hours and increase wages, especially as orthodox economic doctrine held that wages and working hours should be fixed by the free play of supply and demand. Of course, the TLC's political ambitions showed that many unionists, taking a radical and perhaps clearer view, could perceive politics as a valuable adjunct to industrial action, and were prepared to challenge orthodox economics. There was often a gap between the articulation of implied basic Labor opinion by the Council and the wary judgments of individual unions. Limited finance sharpened their discrimination. There was no payment of members of parliament in New South Wales until 1891, so any successful Labor candidate in 1874 would need a subsidy; and, moreover, money was needed for electoral campaigning.

Garrard and Cameron hoped that Council would agree to ask each affiliated union for £10 each for 'election expenses', but in August 1874 the TLC discreetly decided to ask the unions 'whether they [were] prepared to join in this [political movement] and to what extent they would contribute to its support'.[13] Two thousand copies of a circular were distributed widely, to non-affiliated as well as affiliated unions and to many individuals. The text acknowledged the social origins of the parliamentary plan, and reflected Dixon's thinking when it stressed that the New South Wales constitution gave opportunities for the development of manufacturing industries; this was the first explicit suggestion of the Council's bias towards fiscal protection, which was another of Labor's basic doctrines, though, like political action, it did not have unanimous or constant support: and protection ran counter to majority colonial opinion which upheld free trade. The circular also stated that a 'Labor Representation Fund' would be set up to receive donations, and that the Council would support successful candidates, 'so long as his or their actions are not in direct opposition to the view of Council'.[14] The pressure of union autonomy prevented an attempt to have affiliated unions submit details of the electorates in which all their members were qualified to vote,[15] but a permanent electoral committee, including Dixon, Cameron and Garrard, was set up on 28 October to superintend the details of the whole project. Parliament was dissolved on 26 November. Elections were to be held over the period 8 December 1874 to 12 January 1875, the kind of arrangement that applied up to and including the general election of 1891: it enabled certain property owners to vote in several electorates and gave the ministry some chance to influence the result of the elections by fixing the timetable to favour its supporters.

Despite high hopes of four candidates being run for several seats, only one, Cameron, contested the elections; he lost in East Sydney on 9 December, but won in West Sydney on 16 December. These seats covered the inner city area, and each returned four members. The difficulty of raising sufficient funds for campaigning and for the salaries of any successful candidates was the obvious reason for the lack of starters, but there were at least two powerful secondary causes, both of which were to condition the growth of the parliamentary Labor Party in the 1890s. The TLC was almost entirely a city institution, though by 1874 there were some active coal mining unions in the Hunter River district and that year they had close contacts with the TLC,[16] and there were some small, isolated country unions in correspondence with it. Indeed the decision to seek parliamentary representation had been conditioned by radical urban thought, shaped in tough conflicts with city employers, brought to a head by failure to achieve a widespread eight-hour day. Dixon, Cameron and Garrard were typical city radical workers. The debate about political action and its resolution owed nothing to the experience of country workers. Inevitably the Council concentrated on city seats where nearly all of its delegates and most Labor voters worked and lived. There was no chance of success even in suburban areas. This was a situation that had to be changed for a big-scale Labor representation. The transformation in the 1890s showed the power of the bush unions, which were founded from 1886; they introduced new themes into the development of working class solidarity. Trade unionism in the 1870s, despite its power, was a minority movement, narrowly located.

The other reason for only one Labor candidate being run related to the nature of colonial politics. The TLC's electoral committee soon found that it had to come to terms with the existing system. In being forced to contest only East Sydney and West Sydney the Council found itself campaigning in the traditional top seats, in which all of the familiar political issues were concentrated. And they were seats that attracted the top politicians: Parkes ran for East Sydney, Robertson for West Sydney. It was impossible for political observers to isolate one question as the main election issue; the implications of the Gardiner case were hardly discussed, but the need to maintain free trade and for basic educational reform were prominent. The educational question was to develop as the most important political problem of the 1870s. The labor question, simplified in the form of the crusade for the eight-hour day, attracted little attention outside the unions. There was a trade union vote in each electorate, especially in West Sydney, but it was not entirely at the TLC's disposal: the electorate committee soon realised that it would be hard put to win one seat, and to do this it needed support outside the Labor movement.

At Cameron's first meeting in East Sydney he said while 'he stood . . . as an earnest and bona fide advocate for the rights of labour . . . [yet] . . . he wished it to be distinctly understood that he disclaimed any connection with any aggressive action towards the employers of labour'; he instanced the success of T. Burt and A. Macdonald as working class representatives at the 1874 British general elections; he claimed he would not favour any one class against another and that he stood for free, compulsory and secular education. Dixon moved the vote affirming Cameron's fitness to represent East Sydney and J. Garrett, MLA, a prominent supporter of Robertson, moved the vote of thanks to the chairman.[17] At Cameron's next meeting, on his platform were J. Greenwood, a leader of the educational reform campaign and G. R. Dibbs, prominent in that movement and in city business. Cameron again made a general appeal from his working class base and complained that 'he found the greatest difficulty in getting his meetings advertised, and could only account for it on the supposition that the billsticker had been got at'.[18] Cameron's billposting problem revealed that Labor could expect no undue favours at any level of electioneering.

Parkes topped the poll at East Sydney with 3829 votes, J. Macintosh, another experienced politician, was second with 3651, A. Stuart, a wealthy businessman entering Parliament for the first time, third with 3083 and J. Davies, a chief Orangeman and head of many wowser organisations fourth with 2394 votes.[19] Cameron did creditably to come fifth with 2189 votes. There were eight other candidates including W. Forster, who had been premier in 1859–60 and 'Jimmie' Pawsey, an aged negro who added to the gaiety of several city elections in the 1860s and 1870s. The *Sydney Morning Herald* complimented Cameron as 'a young man of considerable promise', and added that he had gained votes from Education League members and supporters and from many non-working class people who wanted to see Labor represented in parliament.[20] With a Council sub-committee of six in charge of details, Cameron began his contest for West Sydney at once. He ran a similar campaign to that in East Sydney, and a correspondent in the *Herald* sounded a sour note by doubting Cameron's independence and stating that the trade unions ruled 'with a rod of iron'.[21] Cameron gained the fourth seat against eight well-known colonists most of whom were practised politicians. Robertson came first, Dibbs second, and H. C. Dangar third.[22]

The cost of the electoral campaigns to the TLC was £53.0.4 for East Sydney and £64.19.0 for West Sydney.[23] Funds were raised from non-affiliated as well as affiliated unions and from the public. The restless nature of Labor solidarity was again revealed when a delegate, W. Miller, took exception to 'certain portions' of the report to the TLC of the West Sydney campaign balance sheet; he said it cast 'severe and undeserved reflections upon [certain delegates]'.[24] The new parliament opened on 27 January 1875 and by then the Council had adopted a voluntary scheme whereby each affiliated union paid 1/- per quarter per member towards Cameron's salary. He resigned as secretary of the Council and from 18 December 1874 was paid £3 per week 'plus bonus of £2 for expenses incurred by that gentleman'. His salary was raised to £5 per week, payable monthly, from 1 February 1875 and £3.3.0 was reimbursed to him 'towards membership of refreshment rooms'.[25]

The TLC's parliamentary plan included financial support for successful candidates 'so long as his or their actions were not in direct opposition to [its] views'. With the strong monetary bond there was an implied pledge in this condition, but it gave Cameron considerable freedom; it was a novel compromise with the existing parliamentary system, and had some portentous implications. Parliament did not meet until the late afternoon, usually four o'clock, to facilitate the attendance of the many city professional and businessmen who were members of the Legislative Assembly, and of members who lived in the suburbs. But the meetings usually went on until late at night and all-night sittings were common. These arrangements made it virtually impossible for Cameron to continue to work at his trade. He had to conform to the Council's control or find some other source of income. On the other hand, the TLC had no chance of erecting formal machinery to decide on political principles that would guide Cameron's actions. The control it exercised over Cameron was related to the sagacity of a few interested and capable leaders, chiefly Dixon, and to the pressure of unforeseen events that generated excitement from time to time. But the experiment was a vital one, both for the Labor movement and for the New South Wales parliament. No MLA had ever been in quite the same position as Cameron, and none in the 1874 Parliament was even remotely placed as he was. He owed his success mainly to a permanent organisation outside parliament, and to a degree he was answerable to it. He was an independent member in the traditional style, but with a vital difference. In many ways his career as a Labor representative was the pattern of the parliamentary Labor Party of 1891.

Naturally, Cameron was impressed with his new role as MLA. It was a realisation of a congenial dream. Despite the ritual of disrespectful remarks passed about them, members of parliament were accepted as among the really important men of the colony, distant from but similar to the great models at Westminster. But Cameron was resourceful and had graduated from a hard school; he was not overcome by his surroundings and he had to reaffirm his reputation among his working class supporters. The *Evening News* soon tried to bring him back to the field: 'That exemplary young member, Mr. Cameron took occasion, yesterday to read his honourable colleagues a lesson on their manners . . . [but] surely, even a 'son of toil' may behave like a gentleman without always talking about it'.[26] This type of external pressure reinforced the inside influences at work to make Cameron conform fully to the system. Meanwhile, he was active and vocal as became a man known as the 'stentorian carpenter'. He advocated payment of members, sought to clean up Sydney's lodging houses, sought better protection of animals and relentlessly pleaded for legislation for the eight-hour day. He started the shift of the gaze of the somewhat dilettante radicalism that occasionally blinked in Parliament to

a new view of the role of the state in social and industrial problems, and
so introduced a new type of radicalism there. On the eight-hour day the
Herald was alive to the dangers of Cameron's mission, and warned that
'the community at large has not demanded any such state interference
between capital and labor'.[27]

Cameron was only one of seventy-two members of the Legislative
Assembly and the keen edge of his reformism depended on moral support and guidance from the TLC, and, above all, on its financial help.
The dice were loaded substantially in favour of Parliament absorbing
him. The Council had to concentrate on the continual flow of industrial
problems brought before it; with no time or special political knowledge
to give to Cameron, it was soon finding it hard to keep up his salary. In
April 1875 the Boilermakers' Union complained about the way in which,
to the detriment of locally made products, he had handled in Parliament
the question of badly manufactured English locomotives. Dixon defended
him and the union's delegate was satisfied.[28] Cameron attended Council
on 17 June and gave an account of his parliamentary work; he was given
approval to go to individual unions' meetings if he were invited. In June
and July the Council was trying to ensure that three backsliding unions
continued their subscriptions to the parliamentary fund.[29] By September
the finance scheme was seen to be inadequate and it was announced
that 'extra efforts would be necessary' to keep Cameron's salary at £5
per week.[30] Disenchantment was beginning to set in with the unions.
Legislation for the eight hours was as far off as ever. An attempt failed in
October to amend the system of unions' subscriptions, but the urgency of
the problem forced it through the following month.[31] The new scheme
provided for weekly payments by unions, according to numbers of members, to produce an income of £6 per week. Most of the unions would
have nothing to do with it.

Cameron was determined to keep his salary intact. At the end of
1875 he outlined to the TLC what he planned for 1876, especially a
brake on assisted immigration and modifications to the agreements
validating bill, which sought to ratify employment agreements made in
Britain between colonial masters and intending immigrants. He also
stressed how he was trying to encourage the colonial manufacture of
locomotives in New South Wales.[32] But the financial position was getting
worse and unions' opposition to Cameron's view of the validating bill was
crystallising. On 3 February the Iron Trades Laborers' Union protested
to the TLC about it. Dixon was now the Council's president and for the
first time he openly confronted Cameron. The issue summed up nicely
the point at which the sectional union view of a problem parted company
from the community view, and the inherent ambiguities in the relations
between an industrial organisation and a politician. Dixon reflected union

opinion when he emphasised the dangers to hard-won conditions if employers were allowed to set their own standards on hours and wages in recruitment contracts in Britain. Cameron, moulded by compromising debate, saw the advantages of immigrants being sure of employment on arrival, and how that would prevent the spread of unemployment and act as a check on unrestricted assisted immigration. He exposed a main part of the basic conflict when he denied the Iron Laborers' allegation that he had said 'he was not responsible to the Council, only to the general electors of West Sydney'. But TLC opinion was against him. All the accumulated financial stresses, the factional and personal frustrations, and the fears of unions came to the fore. The Council declared the bill 'detrimental to the interests of the working classes' and requested Cameron to abstain from voting on the question in Parliament.[33] Cameron agreed to conform. A month later the Council refused a request from Cameron's own union to rebuke him, because it said 'only on Trade questions will [it] be justified in attempting to curb [his] political career'.[34]

These events hastened Cameron's thorough assimilation to Parliament. His election campaign speeches in 1874 and the type of his non-TLC supporters showed that on balance he was more of a Robertson man than a Parkes man. These classifications changed subtly, serpentinely and serially in response to the dynamics of the parliamentary system, connected in part with personal friendships and enmities, the allocation of government jobs and funds to specific electorates, and occasionally a particular principle, such as education reform. In due course Cameron would join the Parkes men, but in 1876–9 he belonged to Robertson. His absorption was natural and he had much to contribute to parliament. Thirty-five members of the parliamentary Labor Party faced similar problems in 1891–4, and despite party institutional help unknown to Cameron, most of them were somewhat similarly digested by parliament. On 2 April 1876 Cameron called a public meeting to reassure West Sydney electors that he represented them and not the TLC.[35] On his platform were Robertson, now premier, and three of his senior ministers, including W. B. Dalley, who typified all that was most attractive in the high style, intellect and humanity of colonial society. The *Herald,* which now found Cameron tiresome, commented that his parliamentary colleagues did 'not seem to have acted as if he was a man that could not be got at', and hoped that his independence might now be real:[36] such were the ingenious definitions of 'independence'. Cameron had no violent break with the TLC, where he went on 13 April to express thanks and the wish that he would maintain his relations with the Labor movement. His salary was stopped from 2 April.

The Cameron experience of 1874–6 is a vital part of the whole history of the parliamentary Labor Party in New South Wales. It revealed the compulsive but discordant forces at work driving Labor into politics and the general problems associated with the plunge. Some of the details, of course, were different in the 1890s when Labor entered parliament permanently, and this introduced variations on the main themes. But the substantial nature of Labor's social integration was to remain a basic conditioner of its political activity. The Labor movement had the task of being the pivotal reforming element in society, nevertheless this did not mean that it could detachedly and coldly proceed with its mission. The TLC was a social as well as an industrial institution; trade unions were normal manifestations of the urge for improvement; trade unionists were citizens, with the customary range of human associations and human problems. Labor was shaped by its society even as it actively led it in vital areas of community change. The TLC's chief work was industrial. Its delegates were aware of the overlap between industrial and political questions, and the Council could initiate parliamentary action, but it could not control it. Unions were the primary industrial units, and could perceive the advantages of political action; but were divided and variable on its continuing efficacy, and acutely conscious of its financial cost. In parliament, Labor men were subjected to great and powerful traditions. Parliament was at once the microcosm of society and a very source of both its stability and growth. Although a Labor man was convinced that he represented a movement, he very soon knew also that the movement was but a part, however vital, of a whole. He was obliged to adjust, and often did so without being aware of the process. Cameron was the prototype of the Labor MLA in New South Wales.

The immediate effects of Cameron's default broadened the stream of Labor opinion which held that the movement should steer clear of politics. This meant that the view of parliament as an impartial institution remained practically unimpaired. The new situation also gave the TLC a chance to consolidate its foundational strength as the general Labor organisation. For the balance of the 1870s the Council gained in experience as it developed its techniques of industrial relations reform. Its general objective was to ensure that unions' rules were applied in particular trades and occupations: this involved common agreement on wages and hours. The wage rates sought were variable but general insistence remained on the eight-hour day, so that that goal retained its binding force, strenthened as more unions slowly achieved it. The TLC consolidated the gradual process by which individual unions came to be recognised as the corporate representative of their members; and, more or less concurrently, the Council was being accepted as the general spokesman of the Labor movement. Its status grew as its deputations to members of the Legislative Assembly and ministers increased and were publicised, as its conciliation role with employers developed, both by correspondence and interview, and as its powerful support gave a stamp of approval to strikes, the accepted last resort of unions in an intractable dispute. By 1878, when it took an important part in the seamen's strike,[37] which extended from November to January 1879, the TLC had attained a prominent position in colonial society.

Angus Cameron's election and activities in Parliament encouraged improvers who were seeking to extend the range of legislation. The Free Selectors' Association (FSA) represented country opinion, but its narrow aims concentrated on land reform and blunted its radicalism. In the city, Bathurst and Newcastle, the Working Men's Defence Association (WMDA) used its name to attract some working class assistance; but, founded in June 1877,[1] it was essentially an organisation that sought fiscal protection on the Victorian model, and had middle class support and the backing of some manufacturers. Dixon was a member and was active at a conference in October 1877 dominated by the WMDA but including representatives of the TLC and FSA. Ninian Melville (1843–97), an undertaker whose father was a prominent Orangeman and publican, was chairman of the meeting on the first day; a radical with some working class following, he said that the meeting sought united country and city action for the 1877 general election and subsequent elections. But after the FSA delegates had withdrawn and the TLC had eased out, the Association changed its name to the Political Reform League.[2] Dixon and Melville ran unsuccessfully for the WMDA at East Sydney and Garrard and T. W. White at West Sydney. The episode indicated the continuing interest in politics of Labor men and the guarded attention of the TLC, whose prestige, general progressivism, anti-immigration policy and bias towards protection made it an obvious target for any middle class reforming group. The experience also alerted Dixon to the divisive dangers presented to the Council by the new community approach to politics initiated by groups outside the Labor movement. When the Political Reform League intervened in the 1878–9 seamens' strike, Dixon persuaded the Council to maintain its support of the strike but withdraw from active leadership because 'the matter was now assuming an important political phase' and 'the constituent societies' had not given their consent.[3]

This cautious attitude to non-Labor radicalism stressed the independence of the TLC while yet leaving it the option of renewing its own direct participation in politics. Dixon's articulation of the implied autonomy of the Labor movement was probably his greatest contribution to New

South Wales working class development: the tradition made possible the political separateness of the TLC in the 1880s and the survival of the parliamentary Labor Party in the 1890s. Dixon was president of the first Intercolonial Trade Union Congress organised by the Council in October 1879 during the International Exhibition season in Sydney. The range of topics discussed represented a summary of the 'Labor question', and the debates, of very high quality, showed that legislation was needed in many instances to correct abuses. Although direct parliamentary action was not considered, the political implications of the proceedings were clear, especially when a motion was carried in favour of the 'encourage-ment of native industries'.[4] This particular proposal raised the issue of free trade versus protection, and with the education problem soon to be solved by the 1880 act, the fiscal question was about to begin to shape the colony's primary political division of the 1880s. John Vicars, owner of a textile factory, addressed the Congress on the need to foster local industries: the incident was yet another reminder that, independent as the Labor movement was, it was yet socially involved: on this occasion with the added complications of seeming to take sides on a major political question in association with an employer.

After a decade of rivalry Parkes and Robertson formed a coalition government on 21 December 1878. It lasted until 4 January 1883 and reformed not only education but also the electoral system. The Electoral Act of 1880 provided for seventy-two seats with a scheme of multiple representation that fixed 108 members for the general elections of that year. The change coincided with depressed trade that sharpened the TLC's protection and anti-immigration predilections. At the Council's meeting of 4 March J. R. Talbot (1833–1905), an ironmoulder, com-plained about the use of English iron on the Tamworth bridge; other delegates raised the unemployment and distress of Newcastle miners and the opinion was expressed that 'there would be no remedy unless it was made an election cry at the next general elections'.[5] Against this back-ground the Council executive, headed by W. B. Cole, president, and W. Roylance, secretary, planned to organise a form of direct sponsoring of approved candidates at the general election. There was, however, con-siderable opposition from constituent unions to the scheme, and the complaints were not reduced when Cole and Roylance organised a 'Caucus of Trades' that planned to have non-affiliated unions co-operating with the Council's parliamentary committee. By the time of the elections, November–December, the Stonemasons had disaffiliated after their delegate J. Munroe had reminded the Council of the 'un-wisdom of interfering in Politics and reviewed the past history of the Council to prove his point'.[6] The scheme received its quietus on 2 November when Talbot's motion was carried that 'this Council does not recognise the candidature of Messrs Jacob Garrard, or John Taylor or any other candidate for Parliamentary honours'.[7] The drive to direct political action was not dormant by any means but majority TLC opinion still clearly favoured the building up of industrial strength concurrently with relying on the familiar parliamentary system.

At the 1880 general election Garrard was returned for the new seat of Balmain. Melville had won a by-election at Northumberland in April and retained his seat in November. The new parliament had a majority of members who had not previously sat in parliament; Cameron and Garrard, especially, and Melville formed a leaven of working class radicalism. Nearly all the members of the Legislative Assembly were free traders, but Melville was a confirmed protectionist; he was joined by another, R. C. Luscombe, in 1883, and in 1885 by E. W. O'Sullivan (1846–1910), a printer, who had been president of the TLC in 1883.[8] The missionary protectionist cell made up for its sparseness by much vocal activity inside and outside parliament. Aided by economic depression and the nominal cessation of land sales in 1883, which had been a major source of the colony's income, they were able to stress the need for increased customs duties to balance the budget. There were almost infinite gradations in the argument as to when additional import levies ceased to be revenue producing and became protective and, as excited debate began, 'discriminating protectionists', 'moderate free traders' and other discerning groups of politicians and citizens slowly emerged to shape a loosely defined dual division in the legislature and the colony. From 1885 the old image of parliament as the impartial source of law began to dissolve as some members seemed to become less independent in response to the charismatic liturgy of the fiscal issue. But the debate was a confined one. In some extra-terrestial way it was hoped by the respective protagonists that the introduction of either protection or free trade would solve all the pressing social and economic problems of the colony. In fact reforming legislation, especially on the 'Labor question', virtually dried up, even as tinkering with customs duties in 1884–91 produced a 'mongrel tariff', neither free trade nor protective. TLC delegates could not fail to notice the novel and disordered situation.

Indeed the delegates were forced to respond. In 1881 the Protection and Political Reform League had replaced the Political Reform League as the main propaganda body for protection. In May 1885 as the fiscal debate sympathetically grew in volume with a deepening recession, the League asked the TLC to be represented by its president and secretary at a protection conference. It was approved 12 to 10 after a lively argument in which O'Sullivan and Talbot supported the proposal and John West (1852–1931), a plumber, put the Dixon line of unfettered interest.[9] In August B. R. Wise, a barrister, aged twenty-seven, fresh from Oxford, handsome and protean, the colony's most talented non-

Labor radical, reacted to this middle class resurgence of solicitude for the TLC, by giving with Council approval, an 'impartial lecture' on the 'Principles and Purposes of Trade Unionism'.[10] Wise astutely assessed the social significance of trade unionism and virtually invited the TLC to intervene and clean up the 'political life [of] . . . New South Wales', which he argued was probably the most 'stagnant and unhealthy' of 'any English-speaking community'. He followed this up with a request to the Council to send two representatives to a conference of the Free Trade Association, which he was helping to form in order to modernise the familiar colonial creed and to counter the protectionists' publicity. This time Talbot angrily played on the Council's propensity for protection and prevailed on it to 'erase' the request 'from the books of the Council'.[11] The TLC had no trouble in asserting its independence against free traders. But it could not support protection unequivocally.

The parliament elected in 1885 saw no less than four separate ministries in fourteen months, with budgetary problems dictating a series of crises.[12] Gradually more members came to accept the need for additional customs duties, though very few would go so far as Melville and O'Sullivan and raise the imports to the point at which it was unprofitable to import certain commodities. In fact this would have been self-defeating in most cases because extra revenue was needed. Encouragement to local industries was hardly practical in the 1880s but in the excitement of debate, distinctions were blurred so that any increases in customs duties, especially *ad valorem* imposts, were regarded as protective by a majority of members of the Legislative Assembly and the leading newspapers. The confusion reflected the pressing need for thoroughgoing reforms to modernise the colony's financial system. Property and income taxation were put forward as means to meet the deficit, and eventually in 1886 the Jennings ministry carried a composite income policy based on 5 per cent *ad valorem* duties. Direct taxation had been adumbrated at various times since responsible government had been inaugurated in the colony in 1856, but income from the selling and renting of crown lands and from overseas loans had usually been enough for successive ministries' needs. Whenever balance of payments difficulties had arisen customs duties had been increased, but quickly reduced when the particular financial stringency eased. Parkes had achieved great renown in 1872 by removing existing *ad valorem* duties. Free trade was therefore very beneficial to the middle class and property owners. It meant that for the upkeep of government they had to pay virtually no more than the poorest colonists. Free trade was also identified with constitutional freedom and with the greatness of Britain. Moreover, it did have economic advantages for a colony that exported so much wool. The jobs of many workers depended on it, especially in the Sydney maritime industries. Free trade in New South Wales had deeply rooted support based on a complex web

of vested interest and emotional attachment. Any threat to the policy
was seen as perilous to a congenial and proud life-style.

So Jennings's 1886 financial innovations were said to have 'sneaked in
protection'; they provoked unparalleled controversy in and out of
parliament, in which by implication the very nature of the political
system was in question. The protectionists seized the opportunity to
advance their cause as the abstract argument was strikingly thrown into
relief in September by mounting unemployment and the government's
provision of relief work and rations. That month the protectionists
formed the National Protection Association and in October succeeded
in getting the TLC to appoint two representatives to a conference to
plan a tariff to meet the changed needs of the colony.[13] The dangers to
the Council's political freedom were overlooked by the president W.
Westman when he reported on the success of the conference, and remarked that 'the joint efforts of employer and employee would greatly
advance the cause of those interested in the industries of this country'.[14]
In parliament Parkes organised relentless pressure on the Jennings ministry and it finally gave up in January 1887. Parkes formed a new government, obtained a dissolution and held elections in February.

These events spurred the protectionists to intensify their attempts to
take over the TLC. They formed yet another body, the Protection
Union, which in January gratuitously made seats available on its
executive for the TLC's president and secretary. The Council's debate on
the offer released all the fears of those delegates who were sceptical of
close connections with employers and of those who were opposed to
political entanglements. Although the Protection Union had strong
support from the new president, J. V. Wiley, and Talbot, West's amendment was carried that the offer be refused with thanks because it 'was
outside the objects of the Trades and Labor Council'.[15] The Typographical Society expressed a durable trade union conviction when it
wrote to tell the Council that it considered 'the introduction of [party
politics] . . . is directly opposed to the best interests of trade unionism'.[16]

With the extraordinary political instinct and perception that marked
his long and eminent public career, Parkes made sure at the general
election that 'party politics' meant 'protection *versus* free trade'. This
ingenious tactic did not mean that political parties had emerged from
the parliamentary confusion, though there were some signs that they
were being spawned in the vast sweep of the changing colonial political
tide. Parkes turned seventy-two in 1887; still a master of the old
political system, he had neither the desire nor the vision to inaugurate a
new one. The old system had been shaken. Parkes set out to restore it and
used the new slogans magnificently. Free trade to Parkes 'embodie[d] the
sum of all the blessing that freedom has given the world';[17] he believed,
and got a majority of voters to believe, that all the multitude of pressing

improvements would naturally be added to that faith. At the 1887 elections neither the free traders nor the protectionists defined the basic areas of reform; naturally, neither presented a definite program for progress demanded by the changed conditions. They staked the future of New South Wales on fiscal doctrine, defined vaguely but chanted *crescendo*. Parkes won because, with consummate skill, he linked free trade to colonial tradition, sound government and freedom. He dodged the direct taxation question nimbly, said nothing of industrial reform and easily identified the protectionists with restriction and reaction. Given that the free traders had Wise didactically defining and arguing taxation reform and George H. Reid (1845–1918) in the wings shrewdly reflecting on the temper and needs of the times, Parkes's great success ensured that the protectionists would take a back seat in New South Wales virtually for the rest of the century. His win also forced a somewhat clearer and firmer division in Parliament with many confirmed free traders, notably Dibbs, changing their political coats to adjust their prospects to the new winds of colonial opinion. For the sake of doctrine the radical protectionists were happy to accept Dibbs as their leader and many other conservatives as their colleagues. The eclipse of O'Sullivan and Melville confirmed West's wise assessment of the dangers of middle class political organisations and TLC delegates acknowledged his leadership by making him Council president in September and chairman of the new parliamentary committee.

In 1887 the TLC modernised its rules and procedures following a comprehensive survey between March and June.[18] All trade unions in the colony were invited to take part in the work under the auspices of a 'Conference of All Trades'. A visitor, A. White of the Federated Trades and Labor Organizations of the (United States) Pacific Coast, supplied tangible evidence of the upsurge in the 1880s of international contacts between Labor groups, some of whom, notably socialists and single taxers, were closely connected to middle class radicalism. Although only a few non-affiliated unions attended the Conference, its proceedings manifested the great prestige of the TLC and its adaptation to changing times. The consultations followed the second Intercolonial Trade Union Congress in Melbourne in 1884, the third in Sydney in 1885, and the fourth in Adelaide in 1886, gatherings that reflected both the growing power of unionism and the developing self-consciousness of unionists. They also revealed the widening of working class horizons beyond the confines of particular colonies. An Australian view of industrial problems was emerging to play a part in the incipient national Federation movement from 1887, but it certainly did not obliterate colonial Labor rivalries in the nineteenth century. The Congresses took their name from the British Trade Union Congress and the influence of that body on the colonial meetings was clear in many of the debates, especially in the various proposals to establish a trade union parliamentary committee: the variation in the naming of the sixth Congress at Hobart in 1889 to Trades and Labor Union Congress symbolised both the increasing acceptance of unskilled unions and the essential individuality of the Australian Labor movement.[19]

The debates at the five Labor conventions of the 1880s dissected the 'Labor question', seeking solutions, mainly legislative, for excessive working hours and for protection of union funds; demanding workers' compensation, early closing of shops, inspection of scaffolding and land boilers (steam engines), a system of conciliation, factories and workshop laws and the repeal or amendment of masters and servants' Acts. The social implications of trade union activity permeated discussion of apprenticeship conditions, technical education, the Victorian recidivist bill (1884), assisted British immigration and restriction of entry of Chinese. Contemporary Labor theory was sifted by analyses of the need for co-operation and amalgamation of federation of unions; and the relation of general theory to economics probed by discussion on property and land taxation. Political involvement was laid bare by arguments about one man, one vote, the enfranchisement of seamen and, above all, encouragement of local industries, payment of members and direct representation of Labor in parliament. Together these matters represented practically all of the fundamental political, social and industrial issues confronting New South Wales in the late 1880s: no other group was scrutinising them in such a systematic way. Although the intermittent nature of the congresses and their lack of permanent control inevitably reduced their Australia-wide impact, the knowledge and experience gained by New South Wales unionists at the meetings complemented the socially curative work and the political activity that they were already involved in. Most of them were or had been TLC delegates and their communal vision was sharpened by encounters with unionists from other colonies. They consolidated the pre-eminent position of the TLC in the vanguard of the forces making for reform in the colony as the decade drew to a close.[20]

John Norton (1858–1916), later to achieve some notoriety as the proprietor of the newspaper *Truth,* and as an MLA, was an atypical and not a highly regarded delegate of the TLC, where he represented the Lithgow Miners' Union in the late 1880s, but he was tireless and vocal, with an eye to his own future and an ear to the urgent demands of his followers. He was at the March 1888 Trade Union Congress at Brisbane, again for the Lithgow Miners', and dramatised the habitual discussion of direct parliamentary representation by moving:

  (i) That . . . the various Trades and Labor Councils of Australasia should
      formulate an electoral programme in accordance with the resolutions

come to at this and preceding congresses for support of all interested in labor and the acceptance of Parliamentary candidates.

(ii) That no candidate who does not adhere to the labor programme should receive the support of the Labor Party,

(iii) and this congress congratulates the Trades and Labor Council of South Australia on its success at the recent general elections.[21]

This exhortation was approved at a time when the familiar methods of the TLC were losing some of their effectiveness despite the new rules. W. F. Schey (1856–1913), a railwayman, was elected for Redfern in 1887 as a protectionist. He had been a delegate on the Council and as an MLA co-operated closely with it, especially in its attempts to have an eight-hour day bill passed. In November 1888 he told the Council's parliamentary committee that three bills were essential, eight hours, factories and workshops, and early closing, and advised the committee to write to all members of the Legislative Assembly and Council 'to let [them] know that the working man was watching their action as regards legislating for the Labor Party'.[22] The committee kept up the pressure but nothing came of it.

The TLC was at last coming to realise that the changes wrought on parliament by the fiscal debate were superficial, however much they showed that the old view of a classless, detached legislature was outmoded. Members now had a somewhat different view of their role, but the final control of legislation was still rooted in a system that simply could not cope with the need for pressing reforms. By 1888 the TLC had had a seventeen-year relationship with parliament, fluctuating from the initial direct links provided by Cameron to the active co-operation of Cameron, Garrard, O'Sullivan and Schey and the contacts of many deputations with ministers and other members. In 1880 it had reconsidered direct participation and in 1885–7 had been involved with the outside bodies that had foreshadowed the new approach to politics. Now in 1888–9 the Council implicitly began to review its relations with its society against the background of general advice from inter-colonial Labor conventions and the particular realisation that its most urgent requests were being ignored by parliament. The indications were that the current of Council opinion would revert to the need for direct parliamentary representation, especially as parliament finally passed in September 1889 a measure sought by radicals since 1861, payment of members (Parliamentary Representatives Allowance Act (No. 2) 1889, 53 Vic No. 12).

In this charged atmosphere the TLC again revised its rules from October 1888 to September 1889[23] and in August conferred with the Employers' Union in an unsuccessful attempt to have a board of conciliation established.[24] The day-to-day industrial work was increasing and affiliation of unions grew sympathetically.[25] In September T. J. Houghton (1862–1933), a printer, who was Council's part-time general secretary at £30 a year, reported that he had arranged 'a monster demonstration' in the Sydney Domain on behalf of the London dock strikers. The following month he submitted his resignation 'owing to [the] enormous increase in duties and failing health'. He was persuaded to remain 'with assistance' and in December became the Council's first full-time general secretary. Houghton did a masterly organising job to raise funds for the London strikers and ensured maximum publicity for the Council when he invited speakers, ranging from Cardinal Moran, Julian Salomons, QC, and John Dillon, visiting Irish MP, to Reid, Dibbs, Garrard, O'Sullivan and John Norton to mass meetings in the Domain in September.[26] On 3 October P. J. Brennan (1843–1906) gave notice of a motion for 'Labor candidates' to be run at the next general elections; on 15 October the Council's parliamentary committee discussed it; on 24 October the Council decided to hold a special meeting to consider the motion.[27] On 7 November 'Mr. P. J. Brennan, in a lengthy speech moved, "That the Parliamentary Committee be instructed to consider at [its] next meeting the advisability of bringing forward Labor candidates at the next general elections, and the said Committee draw up a Labor platform and submit same to Council" '.[28]

3   *The Trades*
      and Labor Council Intervenes

Peter Joseph Brennan, originally a ship's steward, was one of the most experienced trade unionists in New South Wales.[1] He had been an active TLC delegate since 1884 and a vice-president when Council was collecting funds for a monument for the grave of F. B. Dixon who died that year. Brennan was firmly in the mainstream of Council tradition with its emphasis on concentration on industrial issues, intervening in politics when necessary and stressing Labor independence at all times. His work on the Council had coincided with the flowering of its social significance and its final acceptance as one of the leading institutions in New South Wales, with the ramifications of 'industrial issues' taking it from leadership of strikes to an influential role in a range of industrial-social, industrial-economic and industrial-political questions, illustrated by work on improvement of lifeboats, conciliation of coalfields disputes and the establishment of a colonial technical education system. All colonists, especially the citizens of Sydney, were aware of the TLC. Its great 1889 public demonstrations for the London dockers were accepted as part of the natural order and Brennan's presence there taken as evidence of the emergence of yet another Labor leader. On the TLC Brennan provided the vital insight to evaluate the converging conditions forcing the Council to reconsider direct participation in politics. At an appropriate time he was consummating a stream of ideas and policies present from the foundation of the TLC in 1871. But he knew there were other opinions on the subject, both within and without the Labor movement. He was soon made aware that they were still potent.

The free trade newspaper *Evening News* attempted to spike the proposal before a decision could be made on it. Mischievously it appealed to traditional Labor objections to direct political activity based on trade union separatism, fears of domination by employer groups, misgivings over costs and fiscal wrangling. 'As the Council', it said, 'is bound not to divide itself into hostile fiscal camps, and will not stand the needful expenses, the money will be found by a manufacturing ring', and went on to advise the Council to abstain 'from disputes on fiscal policy'.[2] On the last point the newspaper illustrated the success of Parkes's coup in having politics limited to arguments about protection and free trade. But this was a delusive division, shakily shaped by pseudo doctrine and emotional verbiage, designed to prop up an outmoded system and doomed to churn out a series of polymorphous, deformed and discontinuous political organisations optimistically regarded as two political parties.[3] Brennan and the TLC planned to get to the heart of the politics demanded by changed colonial conditions by a program for industrial, financial and electoral improvement; and, implicitly, to fashion a real political party with a clear-cut and detailed reforming policy. While Brennan's motion was being considered, the United Laborers' Union wrote to complain about the waste of Council's time on fiscal squabbling, but was promptly told that 'no debates on free trade or protection take place in the Council'. W. G. Higgs (1862–1951), a printer, seized the opportunity in his *Trades and Labour Advocate* to support Brennan's campaign. He criticised the Laborers' and the Seamen's Union, which had also said that politics should be eschewed, in a trenchant article that restated in contemporary terms the traditional inclination of Labor for direct intervention in Parliament. 'Political questions', he said, 'are of the greatest possible importance to trades-unions and their members . . . ; approach the Legislature, go to the fountain head; that is your far superior method of warfare'.[4]

The TLC debate on Brennan's proposals continued throughout December 1889 and January 1890, with delegates patently uncertain and hesitant as if feeling their way downstairs in the dark. Without being fully aware of it, they were pioneering the first modern political party in Australia: ordinary citizens, however alert, they were enmeshed in their society, but they were yet beginning to change it fundamentally. Naturally the party embedded in the core of their aspirations did not spring out perfectly moulded and ready for confident action. Inevitably, the foundation of an enduring parliamentary Labor Party was to be a painful and long process. But the TLC delegates were experienced in colonial mores and aware and proud of the importance of their social role. They instinctively aimed to formulate a new type of political party geared to the independence of the TLC. So Houghton's amendment of 5 December 1889 was rejected: it would have continued the current futile practice of organisations endorsing those parliamentary candidates who glibly agreed to do what they could for them if elected.[5] Eventually Brennan's original motion was passed, 35 to 3, on 30 January 1890.[6] He was elected president of the Council on 6 February.

The Council's parliamentary committee, with Brennan in charge, accordingly went to work on the Labor platform. The news spread and several aspiring parliamentary candidates, attracted by the salary of £300 to be paid from the next parliament (the general election was normally due early in 1892) and the possibility of financial help from the TLC, wrote to the committee seeking encouragement. Brennan soon perceived that a Labor candidate had to be defined, and on 11 March he firmly instigated the groping of the Labor movement to draw up rules that would control the selection of candidates and their activities in parliament, if elected. This revelation was a reversion in part to the parliamentary experiment with Cameron in 1874 but an ominous break with existing political conventions, and a vital variation of the various schemes put forward at the union congresses. On 11 March after Brennan had given 'his views at length on the general question' the committee resolved that 'all Labour Candidates must be financial members of a recognised labour organisation [and] that where deemed inadvisable to run a Labour Candidate any person accepting the Labour Platform and pledging himself to vote in favor of such measures receive the support of the Trades and Labour Council'.[7] This prescription was the beginning of the system of formal pre-selection of candidates who had to be party members firmly pledged to a written program. On 3 April the completed platform was approved by the TLC 'in globo'. Another plank (No. 14) was added by the parliamentary committee on 8 April and a circular was prepared for dispatch to all unions, seeking support for the principle of direct representation of Labor in parliament, for the platform and the definition of a Labor candidate, and 'for a *pro rata* contribution of threepence per member from . . . all labour organisations in the colony'.[8] The platform was:

1. Abolition of plural voting
2. Free and compulsory education
3. Legalisation of the eight-hour system
4. A Workshops and Factories' Act, and the appointment of representative working men as inspectors
5. Greater protection to persons engaged in the mining industry
6. Extension of the franchise to seamen and shearers
7. Extension to seamen of the benefits of the Employers' Liability Act
8. Supervision of land boilers and machinery
9. An elective Upper House
10. Any measure that would secure for the wage-earner a fair and equitable return for his or her labour
11. Amendment of the Masters and Servants Act
12. Amendment of the Masters and Apprentices Act
13. Amendment of the Trades Union Act
14. Invalidation of agreements between master and man made outside the colony.

Ten of the fourteen planks were simple trade union objectives practically all of which had been discussed at the congresses of the 1880s as had the abolition of plural voting ('one man, one vote'). The education plank was in an important sense the starting point of the Labor movement's great interest in quality of life questions, which were seen to be so vital to members of the working class and their children, but which had a far wider scope and, when developed, would bind the movement firmly to the electorate and continually dilute ideology. But the whole platform and its background affirmed Labor's will to be bound to the electorate. At the same time the platform made perfectly clear how the development of New South Wales over a century, particularly economic change in the 1880s, had produced a situation in which industrial legislation was urgently required.

Other political groups, concentrating on single panaceas, were incapable of perceiving the real needs of the times. The unstable and blurred division of Parliament into free traders and protectionists was intensified outside when successive attempts broke down to establish permanent bodies with firm links with members of the Legislative Assembly. Both fiscal groups failed in strenuous efforts from August to October 1889 to compose the confusion by setting up orderly organisations.[9] The tariff confrontation was a disturbed reaction to the manifest need for wide-ranging reform including, indeed, national Federation. Fiscalism reflected the last phase of the old New South Wales colonial order. Essentially politically sterile, it yet helped to prepare the ground for parliamentary solutions. Although the fiscalists, especially the free traders, had deep roots in the colony, they had soaked up the inertia and self-satisfaction of the old parliamentary system and were incapable of breaking out to found a political party. But, of course, following Parkes's lead they learnt how to play party politics.

Under some overseas impulsion two other political bodies, enthusiastic if exiguous, emerged bat-like from the blind alley that colonial politics had reached in 1887–9. Both the Single Tax League and the Australian Socialist League were founded in 1887 as expressions of the contemporary groping for solutions for fundamental social problems; both reflected the deep concern of many colonists with the paradoxical human misery that seemed to deepen as industrial capitalism expanded.[10] The humanity of members of these leagues clashed with their missionary zeal, but this did not prevent them from appealing to a variety of radicals, some of them trade unionists. The Single Tax League had some short-run advantages: the pure theory of its prophet, Henry George,[11] seemed to argue for exclusive taxation on the unearned increment of land values, i.e., the increase in land values arising from the growth of a society; but this tenet was not clear and could be interpreted as simple taxation on land, on a variety of scales and for a variety of purposes; the theory could also be seen as supporting land nationalisation. Hence the Single Tax League gathered to it many country and city improvers, some of them basically opposed one to another, but all seeking reform through 'the single tax'. The benefits of such a tax for city businessmen attracted some, but the essential millenialism of the creed frightened most of them.

The charisma surrounding George also helped the single taxers for a while, especially as his visitation to Australia was forecast from 1888 and eventuated in 1890. But George was an ardent free trader, a bitter opponent of trade unionism and socialism who in his missionary tour became entangled in New South Wales politics. This episode, in conjunction with the confused single-mindedness of the League's adherents, effectively nullified its lasting influence, though it was very active in 1889–93. The Single Tax League had no hope of founding a political party; but it added to the zest of the period 1887-94 by trying to infiltrate the free traders, the TLC and the parliamentary Labor Party, injecting a stream of ideas into the effervescing debates, admittedly mostly limited to land and often muddled: but 'the land question' remained a vital one, and ideas were at a premium.

The organised socialists were a colourful clique, cantankerous and sectarian. Like the single taxers they were moved to thought and action by the hardships of the working class; but, taking their inspiration from variegated British and European sources, often upper middle class, they were more directly opposed to capitalism than were the followers of Henry George. They attracted fewer members of the working class than the single taxers. The socialists had some long-term advantages running for them but their diverse doctrine was based on a hard-core elitism, which in suitable foreign soil would lead to blood-letting and terrorism to perfect mankind, but which in Australia ensured that its confirmed disciples remained in a perpetual and generally disgruntled minority. However, the drift of socialism's economic theory was towards a more rational system of production and distribution, and this provided at once a goal and a spur to its followers and appealed to many generous and humane citizens, most of them in their twenties, who did not take seriously the malevolent implications of the anti-democratic tendency of its social theory. So at the level of economic reform, with some vague social reconstruction as a corollary, socialism had an important inspirational effect not only on members of the Labor movement but also on alert members of the middle class, such as B. R. Wise. Socialism with all its variations and its internationalism had many useful ideas to offer improvers, and as some eminent economists responded to the stimulus it gave to their own analyses, its effects seeped through to modify much colonial thinking about human welfare and the role of the state. But this vast process did not mean that the Australian Socialist League, or any other socialist or similar body, had an influence in New South Wales beyond its diminutive status. The League with fewer than thirty members in 1887–9, and fewer than 100 thereafter, was virtually unknown outside the inner city area of Sydney and a small fraction of Newcastle, and was of considerably less significance than the Single Tax League up to 1894. The prospects of its forming a political party were infinitesimal.

The TLC naturally attracted some single taxers, nearly all members of the Single Tax League, some socialists, some of whom belonged to the Socialist League, and some of those radicals who were both. And Council delegates were probably more influenced by the literature and debate of the swirling reform currents than most colonists. The sincerity and zeal of Henry George showed in his writings which were probably the most popular of the surfeit of regenerative books and pamphlets available. But the very cacophonous medley of the literature reduced its direct impact, though there is no doubt that it helped to predispose many Labor men, including some TLC delegates, to active reform. This jumbled gingering effect was well evoked in 1915 by John Daniel Fitzgerald:

> The fine rhetoric of [George's] 'Progress and Poverty' . . . profoundly influenced us. Gronland's 'Co-operative Commonwealth', which was . . . a popular exposition of Marxism, became popular too. We were keen readers of Carlyle's 'Past and Present' and 'The French Revolution'. Many knew Disraeli's 'Sybil', Kingsley's 'Alton Locke' and Dickens' 'Hard Times' almost by heart. Ruskin attracted and fascinated too. The 'Wealth of Nations' fascinated many . . . I say now that Bellamy's book ['Looking Backwards'] was a revelation to the working classes . . . "Oh! if we could only organize society like that", was the aspiration of thousands . . . whose lot seemed to be ceaseless toil for a bare pittance without leisure, without opportunity . . . [Important, too, was] the steady rise of the 'Bulletin', which had always expressed an ultra-Radical-Socialist policy that carried it to a great circulation and a great influence in the industrial world, and especially among the men in the interior of the continent and the men on the land.[12]

A little later George Black widened the radicals' reading horizon as he looked back to the 1880s, 'that time [when] the theories of most social reformers, political economists, and philosophers, ancient and modern were familiar in our ears as household words'.[13]

Fitzgerald (1862–1922), was a Roman Catholic; originally a printer, he later became a barrister, and a significant town-planner; handsome, Vandyke-bearded, he was generous, witty and good-humoured and probably the best representative of the *fin-de-siècle* colonial radical; devoted to music, art and architecture, he wrote execrable short plays. A TLC delegate in the 1880s, he went through republican, socialist and protectionist phases and was a Labor MLA in 1891–4. Expelled from the Party in 1893, he returned as a Labor candidate in 1910 and became president of the Political Labor League in 1915 and a minister in W. A. Holman's National Government in 1916–20. Fitzgerald was the best example of the young delegates in the late 1880s who kept the TLC in touch with changing intellectual radicalism. His socialism, as with many others, was worn lightly, did not distort his personality and complemented his natural impulse for compassionate reform. Men like Fitzgerald gave a humane tone to socialism that softened its joyless heart and widened its colonial influence. His mention of the *Bulletin* as one of the many cerebral conditioners of the Labor Party underlines the need to seek elsewhere than literature for the mainspring of its source. The *Bulletin* in the late 1880s had still not lost its infantilism, and was only a little more socialist than the *Sydney Morning Herald* and the *Daily Telegraph*. George Black (1854–1936), a journalist, was an able but often cheerless improver, much less attractive and elegant than Fitzgerald, though more successful politically and, in his day, just as good a socialist and republican.

P. J. Brennan belonged to an earlier generation of trade unionists than Fitzgerald and in the 1880s his energies were absorbed by organising new unions and helping to restore ailing ones. Like Fitzgerald he was a Catholic, but trade unionism, rather than single taxism or socialism, was his working creed. Brennan belonged to the majority type of TLC delegate who had made the Council into the powerful and independent institution it had become by 1890. Like Dixon, Brennan had a protectionist bias but, with most Council delegates, he aimed to keep outside forces where they belonged. The 1890 platform hewn by the TLC under Brennan reflected the strength of the pragmatism wrapped up in trade unionism that, in effect, made of it a separate body of flexible doctrine grounded in day-to-day industrial problems and impervious to any other political-social theory. Trade unionism went to the very heart of its colonial industrial-democratic society, conserving personal and political freedom and automatically rejecting any theory that seemed as if it would change the basic nature of its milieu. Of course many unionists embraced revolutionary creeds stemming from papal encyclicals to socialist and anarchist decrees, but most did so in a way that left their unionist loyalties intact. There was always a majority of unionists who could not see any disconcerting qualities in protests such as those received by the TLC from the Coach Builders', United Laborers' and Stereotypers' Unions in 1891 against business of 'semi-political, sectarian, and socialistic character [being] discussed while trade union matters were delayed'.[14] Trade unionism, of course, was the natural foundation of the TLC. It was a base that alone could condition the creation of a parliamentary Labor Party, and it remained essential for its survival. But on its own, unionism could not sustain the Party.

The inherent conflict between trade unionism and politics had been just as much a vital part of the history of the TLC as had been their compatability. The oscillations produced by this dichotomous affinity affected Brennan's strong campaign in 1890 to obtain unions' support for the Labor platform and plans for direct parliamentary intervention. On 10 April, four days before the Council issued its circular seeking funds and approval for political action, the Wharflaborers' Union appealed for help in negotiations with the Steamship Owners' Association regarding 'constant men' and 'smoke-oh'. The TLC decided to arrange a deputation to the Association.[15] This was the beginning of the complex preliminaries of the great maritime strike of August–November.[16] As the waterfront aspects of the disputes widened between April and August and merged with complicated bargaining in the pastoral industry, the TLC was drawn further and further into the vortex of the conflict.[17] The Council's ordinary industrial work increased at the same time.[18] That it could still keep some control of the political project in these arduous circumstances showed the high quality of its administrative system as well as the un-flagging dedication of its delegates, especially the executive officers. But the great pressure pushed trade union matters to the fore and increased Brennan's difficulties in getting approval for parliamentary action.

By the middle of May only seventeen unions had replied to the circular, six being in favour and eleven against;[19] nearly all the unions emphasised the financial problem raised by the proposal. The Young branch of the Shearers' Union asked for the inclusion in the platform of 'Amendment to Land Act', and the Boot Trade Union wanted a plank on the encouragement of native industries. These suggestions indicated both the general interest in the platform and the influences that would seek to widen it. Concurrent with the promotion of the political plan, the TLC in May appointed a sub-committee of five to devise a newspaper. John Christian Watson (1867–1941), a compositor on the *Daily Telegraph,* was one of the five; he had become a delegate in January, representing the Typographical Union.[20] Without the flair of Fitzgerald, Watson had a lot in common with him, including a protectionist bias seasoned with the latest progressive thought absorbed by young radicals with a socialist bent; but Watson had qualities not possessed by Fitzgerald or any other Labor leader of the time, including an effortless ability to relate humanely with practically everyone he knew and an instinctive capacity to instil in others the respect for himself that he had for them. Intelligent and liberal, leadership came naturally to him, the more effective because he could neither patronise nor scorn anyone, reinforced by physical strength, a well-adjusted personality and a down-to-earthness that stopped far short of cynicism. Watson knew something of newspapers, and, from a Presbyterian background, at the age of twenty-three had acquired a practical experience of hard times and an appreciation of just how trade unionism could help to make life a little more than endurable for the working class. Knowing that the Labor platform needed selling, he was just the one to lead the TLC newspaper committee to seize the opportunity to dress it up for modern consumption. The circular advertising 'A Workman's Newspaper' and approved by the Council on 27 June was almost certainly drafted chiefly by him.[21]

The stated 'Objects of the Paper' also summed up nicely the contemporary role of the TLC, 'It is intended that the paper shall be devoted to faithful advocacy of the rights of Labour and the cause of

Trade-unionism *in their most enlightened and liberal sense*' (italics
supplied). The rest of the statement fell naturally into place, including
support for the existing Labor platform and the parliamentary plans, and
current ideas about extension of the role of government in employment,
the federation of labour, national Federation and co-operation; fiscalism
was nailed as a 'side-issue'. On 17 July, Watson, Hart and C. Lindsay
were appointed to rally support for the newspaper; by the end of the
month fourteen unions had replied to their circular, five being for the
paper, nine against it. But the increasing momentum of industrial
business now temporarily pushed aside the campaign for political action
and a newspaper.

On 7 August a deputation came to the TLC from the non-affiliated
Marine Officers' Association and received a warm welcome and unanimous sympathy 'in their present difficulty' with the Shipowners' Association. The same night the Wagga Wagga branch of the Shearers' Union
advised that the 'first lot of non-union shorn wool would reach Sydney
on the following day'. Months of concentrated work on maritime-pastoral
problems had reached a climax. The executive 'was empowered to attend
the proposed conference with the representatives of the maritime bodies'.[22]
The strike broke out on 16 August to involve ten unions in New South
Wales and probably 15,000 unionists when the shearers came out from
24 September to 2 October; as well, there were many unions and some
10,000 unionists on strike in three other colonies; it was the greatest
stoppage of work in Australia up to that time. The TLC executive,
particularly Brennan, was engaged virtually full-time in the struggle
until it was called off on 5 November with the men defeated. Brennan,
Houghton and Talbot were members of the Labor Defence Council,
which controlled the strike in New South Wales, and Brennan was
chairman of the Australian Labor Conference, which sought to co-
ordinate action in all the colonies.

The maritime strike revealed the significant social unity that the
peculiar amalgam of free trade and liberalism had conditioned in New
South Wales and the high regard in which the Labor movement was
held. While, indeed, this strike was on an unprecedented scale, the
colony had been exposed to very many since about 1860 and had come
to accept them as normal, however regrettable. The place of the TLC
in the colony simply expressed this situation. There were of course many
bitter opponents of trade unions, some of them in Parliament and one,
at least, W. McMillan, in the ministry. But Parkes himself, still premier
in 1890, for a political lifetime had preached the doctrine that the state
was neutral in industrial affairs: this was why he opposed legislation for
the eight-hour day and was lukewarm on similar reforms. The general
liberal consensus declared by Parkes was unable to adjust abruptly to
change whereby the state could intervene in industrial matters in a

neutral way. A new province of law and order could not be conceived or produced in a day. But the established ways could lessen the asperities of even the maritime strike and calmly suggest to the Labor movement that there were other, and perhaps better ways to achieve its objectives. The TLC, having painfully come to the same conclusion, was singularly receptive to such advice.

Parkes resoundingly re-affirmed the familiar values by a classic censure of McMillan for his partisan handling of an incident during the strike,[23] and W. G. Higgs's personal vision of 1889 gradually became colonial-wide in 1890: Sir Alfred Stephen, chief justice in 1843–73, Cardinal Moran and the capitalist newspapers reflected a great majority social opinion in agreeing that the legislature provided a field for a 'far superior method of warfare' for Labor. On the TLC from September the free traders, protectionists, single taxers and socialists began to liven up under the stimulus of exciting strike events, all of which slowly paved the way to industrial defeat for Labor. More unions joined the Council. The fresh breezes of modern reformism let in by Fitzgerald, Watson and other young delegates gradually gathered force to consolidate TLC judgment that political action, if not better than industrial action at all times, was a valuable complement to it. Brennan was justified. At the end of 1890 Houghton could triumphantly report:

> To some of you, especially those who have but recently taken your seats, it will appear almost incredible that during the half year just closed the Council has been equally if not more successful than at any period during the 20 years of its existence.[24]

The collapse of the strike had completed the hegemony of the Council. The Maritime Council expired, the Building Trades Council joined the TLC. Late in November the TLC formalised its pinnacle of power by resolving:

> That it be a standing order of this Council that any society or societies not affiliated to the Trades and Labor Council having a dispute or disputes with their employers, and wishing for the support of the Council, before striking must place their dispute or disputes entirely in the hands of the Council, which will thereupon carry out the same in accordance with the rules of the Council. In no case will the Council or societies affiliated support any union not complying with the above.[25]

4 Decisive Action
for a Labor Party

Paradoxically, the maritime strike *débâcle* strengthened the TLC at the very time it was striving to lead Labor into parliament. The reverse swept trade union opinion into unison with colonial belief that politics was the better path. At first the lead-up to the strike and then the first weeks of the great episode drained the Council's energies away from its political plans, then the realisation of defeat re-sharpened delegates' determination and re-invigorated their zeal as they were joined by new union representatives and advised on all sides to go into politics. Brennan renewed his campaign. On 8 October as chairman of the Australian Labor Conference, with W. G. Spence (1846–1926) as secretary, he issued a manifesto that summarised the strikers' case and suggested that Labor attention be given to the need for direct parliamentary represen-tation.[1] At the same time he had the Labor Defence Committee write to the TLC asking that Labor candidates be run at the next elections; the Council referred the request to its parliamentary committee.[2]

In the middle of the ensuing preparations to restore the parliamentary scheme, one of the members for West Sydney died and a by-election was set for 25 October. The Labor Defence Committee and the parliamentary committee conferred with a view to running a Labor candidate. This was an important event in the evolution of the idea of a selected and pledged candidate; it also forecast the difficulties of getting agreement about the mechanics of selection. The two committees agreed that the maritime unions and the TLC should nominate one starter each and that a special selection meeting would be held, consisting of the Council's parliamentary committee and two representatives of each of the maritime unions, with 'each society to sign an agreement accepting such selection as final'.[3] The parliamentary committee held a special meeting on 17 October with five contenders, including Brennan, T. M. Davis (1856–1899) of the Seamen's Union and A. J. Kelly (1854–1913) of the Wharflaborers' Union; each signed a document:

> We, the undersigned, hereby pledge the respective societies represented by us at this meeting to abide by the selection made by this meeting of a candidate to run in the interests of Labor for the constituency of West Sydney at the forthcoming election.[4]

The mercurial aspects of Labor unity were re-affirmed when G. A. Edwards of the Stewards' and Cooks' Union objected to the TLC's having eleven votes to a total eight of the waterfront unions; but Brennan was selected after an exhaustive ballot and very soon found that, despite the pledge, some of the maritime unions preferred A. J. Taylor, a proprietor of the newspaper *Truth*. Brennan withdrew[5] and Taylor won but did nothing for Labor. The incident intensified the TLC's resolution to control the parliamentary scheme and Houghton observed that 'we must strain every nerve in the endeavour to overcome the ungovernable jealousy and paltriness of spirit which appears to permeate some of our own members'.[6]

The parliamentary committee continued its review of the political scheme. By the end of October they had devised a series of questions for prospective Labor candidates and had revised the platform. To the original fourteen planks they added:

15. Prohibition of the sweating system
16. Establishment of a Department of Labor
17. Establishment of a national bank
18. Water conservation and irrigation
19. Elective magistrates
20. Abolition of money deposits in parliamentary elections
21. Extension of the principle of the government as an employer.[7]

Contacts with country centres were illustrated by letters to the mining and pottery unions at Lithgow (Hartley electorate) asking them to confer with the Eskbank Engine Drivers', Firemen's and Cleaners' Association 'to select and assist in the return of a Labor candidate at the next elections'.[8] The general outline was emerging of a political organisation controlled by the TLC: the platform was in good shape, the definition of a Labor candidate decided on, the necessary connections with unions in the local electorates adumbrated, and the need for some kind of a selection pledge clear.

By November the most important missing link in the structure of Labor's political organisation was local electoral branches. As early as June, C. Jones had moved on the Council for a form of constituency unit with control of selection, and in July Fitzgerald had raised the need for 'District Labor Councils'.[9] The decisive move came in the clearer atmosphere on the TLC at the end of November when R. Harris, with Jones seconding, successfully moved that,

> with a view of securing better representation of Labor in Parliament and to effectively organise all that are favourable to the said object, this Council deems it advisable to establish Labor Electoral Leagues in every centre where practicable throughout the colony, and the Parliamentary Committee be instructed to prepare a scheme for the organisation and government of same.[10]

This proposal was part of the inner logic of the whole parliamentary plan, but it was an uncharted area of social action for the TLC, with clear portents of embarrassing problems of control. The Council was primarily an industrial body that had taken a significant part in many transient activities that overlapped with Labor interests, but it had never contemplated the permanent establishment and management of a minimum of seventy-four branches devoted entirely to political affairs. The parliamentary committee handled its commission gingerly and in February 1891 after a long discussion decided to appoint a sub-committee of three, Houghton, F. Cotton and R. Boxall to

> draft a scheme for government of [the] leagues . . . to provide that [they] shall have control of their own funds, select their own candidates in each electorate, and generally to conduct their own business, but in no way to act contrary to the rules laid down by the Parliamentary Committee of the Trades and Labor Council, and that the subscription to same should be 2/- per half year, payable in advance.[11]

Cotton (1857–1942) was one of the most active leaders of the Single Tax League and an energetic permeator of the associations formed by the free traders.[12] He had been a Methodist lay preacher, and a shearer; in 1889 he became a journalist; in 1890 he represented the Wagga Wagga branch of the Shearers' Union on the TLC. Cotton's trade unionism was limited, ideologically flawed by Georgeism and hence suspect on the Council; but he was vocal and tireless and, as with the young men affected by various combinations of colonial free trade-liberalism, protectionism and socialism, he exposed the TLC to reformist pressures; he was a useful delegate. He mixed some vanity with carelessness with the truth and certainly magnified his own role in the long and complex production of a parliamentary Labor Party.[13] Boxall was a very experienced trade unionist of Brennan's generation; in the 1880s he had been president of the Tinsmiths and Sheet-Iron Workers' Union and an executive officer of the TLC. He had protectionist leanings, as did Houghton who was the very model of a meticulous secretary. The parliamentary committee had selected its sub-committee with care. The three men balanced youthful progressivism and union experience; and, above all, they knew how to get on with a job. Their task was obviously not to inaugurate a Labor Party, but rather to review and stabilise all the hard work and thinking that had gone into the idea in the preceding sixteen months, and especially to fit into the general scheme the proposal for electoral leagues. They wasted no time. On 10 March they submitted a 'draft scheme for the formation of Labour Electoral Leagues'. The report was fully debated, revised and finally put into shape as the 'Proposed Platform and Rules of the Labour Electoral League of N.S.W.', for the consideration of the full TLC.[14]

The proposals included a platform, extended from twenty-one to twenty-nine planks, a statement on 'Objects of Association', and rules governing qualification of membership, annual subscription, application of funds, treasurer and trustees, central committee, branches, district canvassing committees, selection of candidates and expenses of parliamentary elections. The novelty of the scheme was emphasised by a rule that prevented members of parliament from holding office in the League and provided that if an officer were elected to parliament he had to resign his post. But the sweep of the project, its whole structure and content, envisaging a type of political organisation previously unknown in the colony, differed clearly from the past fumblings of other groups, notably the fiscalists, to found a political party. Nevertheless it was an articulation by the TLC of ideas and procedures implicit within colonial society, propounded, of course, chiefly by the Labor movement since 1871, but also sketched, however defectively, by political reformers in the 1880s. The TLC was in the final stages of making its unique contribution to the stable parliamentary growth of New South Wales, and indeed Australia, by launching the first modern Australian political party. The parliamentary committee emphasised the Council's founding role by providing that the central committee of the new organisation should be the parliamentary committee 'with the addition of one delegate from each branch', and that the treasurer and trustees of the TLC should control funds raised by the central committee. But the recognition of branch delegates and the appeal in an object of association to all 'democratic and progressive electors' insinuated again the seeds of separatism as well as the wider social implications involved in the vast undertaking.

The platform was an extension of the twenty-one planks already hammered out. The ninth plank 'An Elective Upper House' was omitted, to leave twenty of the previous year's points in the forefront of the new program. The nine new points included three simple but vital additional electoral reforms, one that stressed the right of country selectors in improvements they had made on their holdings, one that favoured local government and decentralisation, one that proposed local control of applications for mineral leases, one in favour of Federation 'upon a national, as opposed to an Imperialistic basis', one in favour of land taxation and one that sought reform in the method of raising municipal revenue. The Federation plank was a response to the exciting and persistent debate that had gradually developed, temporarily retarded by the maritime strike, after Parkes had projected the question into public discussion in October 1889. The selector plank stressed the recognition of the need for a specific country appeal, conditioned by the increased presence of delegates on the TLC from bush unions. The land taxation plank was dressed up in Georgean jargon and transparently reflected Cotton's single taxism. Only one of the original principles had its wording changed: the original No. 2, 'Free and compulsory education' became

'Free, compulsory and technical education, higher as well as elementary, to be extended to all alike', a significant change that summarised the basic conditioning force of the new party: social amelioration. But the texture of the whole Labor platform looked to the future, thrusting at last practically all of the currently demanded reforms into politics in a systematic way. As the 'Objects of Association' put it, the TLC was reaching out for the help of all concerned citizens,

1. To secure for the wealth producers of this colony such legislation as will advance their interests by the return to Parliament of candidates pledged to uphold the platform of this Association.
2. To secure the due enrolment of all members of this Association who may be entitled to a vote in any electorate.
3. To bring all electors who are in favour of democratic and progressive legislation under one common banner, and to thoroughly organise such voters with a view to concerted and effective action at all general elections in the future.[15]

All radicals, whether free trade, protectionist, single tax, socialist or whatever were invited to the feast prepared by the TLC.

The Council lost no time in working over the proposed platform and rules in great detail. Under the new president, W. H. Sharp (1844–1929), a printer, three special meetings were held in March. On 17 March the objects were adopted without alteration as were the first twenty planks, except No. 6 to which 'general laborers' were added to those for whom the franchise was sought; amendments were made to planks 21, 22, 25; the Federation plank, No. 26, had 'Australian colonies' changed to 'Australasian colonies'. Predictably, the land taxation plank, No. 27, provoked lively debate which became so extended that it was adjourned to 24 March, when after a division the original plank was carried 29 to 18. The argument exemplified the strength of the pragmatic trade unionism that conditioned the TLC, and moulded the conformity of the delegates, whatever their world-view, to ensure the attainment of possible gains for the working class and maintain their freedom.[16] Many delegates, protectionists and/or socialists mainly, were bitter opponents of the single taxers and considered that the plank was pure Georgean doctrine. It read:

The recognition in our legislative enactments of the natural and inalienable rights of the whole community to the land—upon which all must live, and from which by labour all wealth is produced—by the taxation of the value, which accrued to land by the presence and needs of the community, irrespective of improvements effected by human exertion.

There was little doubt that Cotton had worded this plank, but it could be interpreted as simply implying a tax on the unimproved value of land and not necessarily a single tax. This is how Houghton took it and the majority of delegates agreed with him. 'Some of the strongest Protectionists on the Council', Houghton later told the *Star,* 'were among the principal supporters of the plank . . . The adoption of [the] plank . . . points to the majority . . . [being] land taxers'.[17] The debate occupied the whole meeting on 24 March and a week later the overhaul was completed with additional amendments and the addition of four planks:

30. That all government contracts and tenders be executed in the colony

31. The stamping of Chinese-made furniture

32. The extension of franchise to policemen and soldiers

33. The abolition of the present defence force, and the establishment of the military system on a purely voluntary basis

To the 'qualification of membership' was added a restriction that 'no person shall be a member of more than one electoral league'; and Fitzgerald manifested the independence of Labor and his own and the movement's adherence to colonial democracy by getting approval for:

1. All candidates to give a written pledge to resign on being called upon to do so by a two-thirds majority of the voters.
2. All Labour members elected to the Legislature to sit on the crossbenches.[18]

On 6 April the parliamentary committee systematised the platform and reduced it to sixteen planks:[19]

1. Electoral reform to provide for the abolition of plural voting; the abolition of money deposits in Parliamentary elections; extension of the franchise to seamen, shearers, and general labourers by means of a provision for the registration of votes; extension of the franchise to policemen and soldiers; abolition of the six months residential clause as a qualification for the exercise of the franchise; single-member electorates and equal electoral districts on adult population basis; all Parliamentary elections to be held on one day, and that day to be a public holiday; and all public houses to be closed during the hours of polling.
2. Free, compulsory and technical education, higher as well as elementary, to be extended to all alike.
3. Eight hours to be a legal maximum working day in all occupations.
4. A Workshops and Factories Act, to provide for the prohibition of the sweating system; the supervision of land boilers and machinery; and the appointment of representative working men as inspectors.
5. Amendment of the Mining Act, to provide for all applications for mineral leases being summarily dealt with by the local warden; the strict enforcement of labour conditions on such leases; abolition of the leasing system on all new goldfields; the right to mine on private property; greater protection to persons engaged in the mining industry; and Inspectors to hold certificates of competency.
6. Extension to seamen of the benefits of the Employers' Liability Act.
7. Repeal of the Masters and Servants Act and the Agreements Validating Act.
8. Amendment of the Masters and Apprentices Act and Trades Union Act.
9. Establishment of a Department of Labour, a national bank, and a national system of water conservation and irrigation.

10. Elective magistrates.
11. Local government and decentralisation; extension of principle of the Government as an employer, through the medium of local self-governing bodies; and the abolition of our present unjust and injurious method of raising municipal revenue by the taxation of improvements effected by labour.
12. The Federation of the Australasian Colonies upon a national, as opposed to an imperialistic, basis; the abolition of our present Defence force and the establishment of our military system upon a purely voluntary basis.
13. Recognition in our legislative enactments of the natural and inalienable rights of the whole community to the land—upon which all must live and from which by labour all wealth is produced—by the taxation of that value which accrues to land by the presence and needs of the community, irrespective of improvements effected by human exertions; and the absolute and indefeasible right of property on the part of all Crown tenants in improvements effected on their holdings.
14. All Government contracts to be executed in the colony.
15. Stamping of Chinese-made furniture.
16. Any measure that will secure the wage-earner a fair and equitable return for his or her labour.

The *Herald* was both satirical and a little fearful. 'The leaders of Labour', it commented,

seem to have set themselves a large task. They are preparing for more systematic and more completely organised action in the political world, and by way of preparation they are showing forth in a political sense the whole duty of men.

The newspaper doubted that 'men of intelligence and honesty' would pledge themselves 'to this fearful and wonderful programme', argued that the new type of pledge went far beyond acceptable limits and forecast a bleak future for any members of the Legislative Assembly so handicapped.[20]

Late in February as the TLC's parliamentary plans were moving to a successful climax George Reid took it upon himself to address his East Sydney constituents. In 1891 Reid turned forty-six, Sir Henry Parkes became seventy-six, and in May Sir John Robertson died at the same age. In the late 1880s Reid had emerged as 'the favourite' of Sydney, and the obvious successor to the two ageing knights as the chief standard-bearer of the deeply rooted values of colonial free trade-liberalism; his billowing waistline, monocled eye in a face beaming more and more like a bulbous moon as its hairline eroded, and dolefully drooping walrus moustache complemented a bubbling sense of fun, a witty, if sometimes unrefined turn of phrase, delivered in high-pitched colonial tones, and an incomparable conviviality: a gift for brilliant cartoonists. A barrister who had been an MLA since 1880, Reid was an astute and serious politician and a percipient observer of New South Wales society. He saw himself as the flowering of a long line of liberalism that went back to the

W. C. Wentworth of the late 1820s. He sensed the danger of the political disintegration of the colony apparent from 1887 and determined to do what he could to avert it.

Reid's East Sydney speech was orated in his inimitable style. He spoke for over two hours against a tumultuous background that exceeded the level of rowdyism acceptable in a colony where a public meeting was regarded as one of the nicest ways to spend an evening, especially when Reid was there. A general increase in disorder, reflecting the political and social malaise, had accompanied the expansion of the fiscal debate and had been accelerated in 1889 when Federation entered the field and various radical elements began to intervene. But Reid outmatched the interjectors and his main message came through loud and clear in the Protestant Hall on 25 February: Parliament was running down and had to be rejuvenated.[21] Parkes was his main target because, Reid claimed, he had not used his power to modernise the colony. 'You ought to endeavour to put down the present system of political jobbery between Governments and members of Parliament' he told his audience, and went on to condemn a political system that limited success in country seats to those who were adept 'in milking the State cow'; and to appeal for a 'statute book worthy of a free and enlightened community'. The *Herald* was stirred by Reid's analysis of 'the degeneracy of Parliament', a subject on which the newspaper had been vocal itself for several years, and agreed that 'what the people of New South Wales want to see above all things . . . is progress, and especially in the form of progressive legislation', and contrasted 'the pomp and ceremony . . . cost . . . labour [and] loud-resounding oratory [of the legislative machine]' with the 'practical outcome of it all'.[22] The *Herald* could perhaps be suspected of crying wolf, but not Reid: he had exposed the need for legislative and parliamentary reform in a way that could not be ignored. And he was patently correct in his diagnosis and sincerely concerned that a cure be found. His masterpiece of social criticism was augmented rather than diminished by his clear ambition to take over the free traders from Parkes, and his wary approach to national Federation. The reverberations of Reid's onslaught were felt around the colony and in due course reached out to help to make him a modernising and successful premier, in partnership with the Labor Party, in 1894–9.

Possibly unknown to Reid, although reported in the *Herald*, the TLC was in the final stages of its tenacious attempt to give a practical form to his vision of a reformed parliament. Indeed, what the Council was doing was what even Reid could not do in 1891, found a modern political party: and that was necessary for a new 'legislative machine'. On the other hand the vibrant communal quality of Reid's great meeting in the Protestant Hall, and its deep social impact revealed yet again, but without the direct attention of the TLC, that the Labor movement belonged firmly to New South Wales society. Reid was a great Australian. Not only Labor in the mother colony but all groups in the whole continent would have to take account of what he would do in the 1890s. He, in turn, would have to adjust to a new phenomenon, the Labor Party.

The parliamentary committee of the TLC met on 25 March[23] the day after final Council approval was given to the rules and platform of the Labor Electoral League (LEL). Among its other duties the committee now functioned as the central executive committee of the LEL. W. H. Sharp was elected chairman and became the first president of the LEL, Houghton became the first secretary and J. T. Gannon was made minute secretary. Some important decisions were taken. A by-election was to be held at East Sydney on 14 April and the Protection and Political Reform League wanted joint action with the LEL: the central committee 'agreed that the letter be not entertained, and that the same course be followed in regard to all communications emanating from political bodies' and decided to recommend to the Council that no action be taken at East Sydney 'owing to the immature state of the . . . schemes regarding the formation of labour electoral leagues'. A letter from George S. Beeby (1869–1942), a single taxer, sought help in starting a league at Newtown, but the executive decided it would do it itself as part of a decision to hold 'public meetings for the formation of branches of the LEL . . . in all city and suburban electorates'. The executive met again the next night and decided to recommend the TLC to send Fitzgerald to Newcastle to try to sort out disagreements that had arisen there between the embryonic league and the Miners' Union over the seat vacant because of the death of James Fletcher, MLA; 'some apathy' was reported from the coalfields 'because a general elections were thought to be close'.[24] The next general election was normally due about February 1892, but there were indications now that the Parkes ministry was tottering. This news galvanised the LEL executive and J. G. Gannon, a TLC delegate, wrote to the *Herald* to stress the fact that the LEL had sunk the fiscal issue and to appeal to 'one and all [to] buckle on the armour of trade unionism, sink our little differences and go to the ballot-box as one man'.[25]

The TLC's prestige was again acknowledged when C. C. Kingston, attorney-general of South Australia, addressed it on 26 March. Kingston was in Sydney for the Federation Convention. He delivered a long and cordial speech in which he pointed out, with a copy of the LEL platform in his hand, that South Australia had abolished plural voting forty years previously and had no need to abolish money deposits for candidates at elections because that colony had never had it. South Australia, he said, had had land and income taxation since 1884.[26] Parkes scented the strong gusts of reform and at Campbelltown, two days later, said, 'Let no one suppose that he . . . did not take a fervid interest in the endeavours of men who had nothing in the world except what they earned with their stout arms'.[27] Concurrently, in declining to run for the East Sydney by-election as a free trade candidate, B. R. Wise complimented the LEL for adopting a land tax plank, implied that fiscalism was outmoded and stressed that on the 'labour question' the 'labour party is more right in its principal contentions than the capitalist party'.[28]

Against this encouraging background the LEL executive revelled in its organising work. On 3 April it had ready a copy of a circular asking bush unions to form Labor leagues, and decided that no action would be taken to establish rural branches until replies were received from the unions.[29] By 1891 many bush unions were represented on the TLC, mostly branches of the Shearers' Union, but also including mining and other unions in the Broken Hill, Newcastle, Lithgow and Wollongong districts as well as, at times, small dispersed teamsters', labourers', drovers' and railwaymen's unions: nearly always these unions appointed delegates who lived in Sydney. In addition the TLC had helped in the 1880s to establish country trades and labor councils, notably at Newcastle, Broken Hill and Young. James Morton Toomey (1862–1920), secretary of the Young branch of the Shearers', was also the secretary of the local district council; he was the most vital of an extraordinarily active and intelligent group of Shearers' Union leaders who made the south-west area of the colony from Goulburn to Wagga Wagga a centre of potent radicalism. In 1891 they and all the shearers' leaders and most of the country working class, including many farmers, were agitated by a lengthy and bitter shearing strike in Queensland and New South Wales. Arthur Rae (1860–1943) and W. W. Head (1861–1939) were two of Toomey's associates. Bourke and Coonamble, in the north-west and Scone in the Hunter River district were other centres of zealous shearing unionism. None of the fiscal groups, or the single taxers or socialists had a framework of rural support to compare with the bush auxiliaries of the TLC. The times demanded that a viable political party should not only have a wide reform base but also properly organised colony-wide support. On 23 April T. Williams (1862–1953), secretary of the Scone branch of the Shearers' Union, told the Council that he was 'taking a tour through the Hunter electorate for the purpose of forming Labor Leagues'; the Northumberland Carriers' Union also promised its support 'in forming labor electoral leagues'.[30] Rae told the *Australian Workman* in May that he had formed leagues in Gundagai and Tumut and asked for organisers and pamphlets to help '[carry] our unionism into the political arena'.[31] In a circular sent to all Farmers' Unions throughout New South Wales, the Wagga Wagga branch of the Shearers' Union made a direct appeal to farmers to support Labor, arguing that 'the reforms sought . . . are as much interest to farmers as to wage-earners', and that the 'propriety' of political association of farmers and workers was indicated by 'the

Farmers' Alliance in the United States . . . [joining hands] with the order of the Knights of Labor'.[32]

With its whole administrative machinery at work the TLC contacted every union in New South Wales, and advertised in the press throughout the colony.[33] Within the Sydney metropolitan area the Council controlled firmly the establishment of leagues. The first one founded was at a public meeting at Balmain on 4 April when the Balmain Laborers' Union formed the nucleus of a large and enthusiastic branch.[34] Similar action by the North Sydney branch of the Amalgamated Navvies and General Laborers' Union produced the North Sydney league on 9 April.[35] Leagues were formed at East Sydney on 11 April, West Sydney on 14 April and South Sydney on 15 April.[36] Gradually the whole area was covered.[37] The radical ecumenism of Labor's appeal was shown when W. E. Johnson, a single taxer, became secretary of the Newtown League, S. A. Rosa, a journalist member of the Socialist League, secretary of East Sydney and J. C. Watson, a protectionist, but above all, a confirmed trade unionist, secretary of West Sydney. The foundations were being laid of the powerful role of the central executive committee as it dealt with a multitude of matters brought before it by the emerging leagues. Watson wanted to know if capitalists could join: he was told that individual leagues could determine their own membership in the light of the platform and rules.[38] The Goulburn league was told that no exceptions could be allowed to the rule that every member, including selected candidates, had to subscribe to every plank in the platform, and that any future changes in the platform would be made by the central executive committee.[39] Many letters from country centres sought advice on the formation and management of leagues. By 2 June delegates from six leagues had joined the committee,[40] beginning the process whereby, in due course, the branch delegates would outnumber the eleven members of the parliamentary committee.

The Federation Convention met in Sydney from 2 March to 9 April, with some of the leading public men of Australasia as its delegates, including Sir George Grey from New Zealand as well as C. C. Kingston. On 8 April the executive of the TLC, including Sharp, Fitzgerald and Houghton, together with W. G. Higgs and B. Backhouse interviewed Grey at the Hotel Metropole.[41] Grey was then aged seventy-nine; in 1841–5 he had been governor of South Australia and subsequently, in turn, governor of New Zealand, Cape Colony and, in 1861–8, New Zealand again. In 1877–9 he was premier of New Zealand and later acquired a reputation as a radical political reformer. By 1891 his prestige stood high as an elder statesman of the empire with strong liberal convictions and a persistent advocate of the principle of 'one man, one vote'. He told the Council leaders that of the Australian colonies only Western Australia, granted a constitution in 1890, was more backward electorally than New South Wales. 'Plural voting', he said, 'made elections rotten from top to bottom', and he was not confident of a democratic federal constitution emerging from the Sydney Convention. Fitzgerald asked him if the TLC should 'take some extreme action in the matter'; he replied that the people should be awakened to the problem, and he 'promised to do anything in his power to assist the council . . . [in] the greatest epoch in the history of Australia . . . nothing should be neglected to get a perfect Constitution'. The draft federal bill indirectly included plural voting in its provisions.

This incident was significant in the foundation of the Labor Party. Once again it showed how the TLC's influence extended: to the reception rooms of a top city hotel as well as the dingy meeting rooms of other types of hostelries: to a 'pro-consul of Empire' equally with a newspaper editor and a factory owner. The Council's public relations were superb, with Fitzgerald alert to every opportunity. The interview also showed how Labor was inescapably caught up in the large question of Federation: it could not opt out, no member of the TLC thought it should opt out. The spiralling complexity of the issue was almost desperately put by the *Herald,* partly in answer to Grey and the TLC,

> The work of establishing federal union is difficult enough without attempting to procure the assent of all the colonies to the dreams of impractical or revolutionary enthusiasts.[42]

This involvement automatically conditioned the development of the Labor Party as a reforming social element. The establishment of a sense of legislative purpose, in which the Labor Party was to play by far the most significant part in the 1890s, was a necessary pre-condition for the successful settlement of Federation in New South Wales.

As well, the *soirée* with Grey laid bare the durable essential core of Labor's reforming role. Labor instinctively upheld the constitution, the changes it fought for were not innovations that would disturb the basic freedoms taken for granted by every citizen: right of assembly, freedom of speech and of the press, the rule of law, including trial by jury. 'As secretary of the Trades and Labor Council', said T. J. Houghton,

> I believe I voice the opinion of every member of that important body and the opinion of every intelligent workingman in the country when I say that no greater calamity than the stifling of free speech could possibly befall the workers in this or any other land.[43]

Labor men knew enough history, especially nineteenth century European history, to realise the dangers of theories of social reconstruction that sought to improve the lot of the working man by promising freedom through the abolition of the social foundations and institutions that, to British peoples, made freedom possible. Labor was open to cosmopolitan schemes for improvement, but it fitted them into the acceptable democratic routine. Most Labor men had a deep-seated antagonism to capitalism, but it was not a mindless recoil, and was neither self-distorting nor self-destroying. Thus there was no incongruity in J. D. Fitzgerald playing a leading part in the pleasant conversation with Grey, though he was a protectionist and a member of the Socialist League, who claimed to be the founder of the first republican organisation in New South Wales. And the TLC executive was not condescending to a frail, white-bearded dotard, much less pandering to an imperial celebrity. Grey embodied the social advantages of the British system: the TLC wanted to retain and improve them. There was good as well as evil in the empire, but the balance was weighted on the side of universal human values: Labor's attachment to it was not a reflex tribal gesture. The executive's meeting with Grey was as natural as their attendance at Sydney's Royal Easter Show.

Sir Henry Parkes's physical deterioration symbolised the decadence of the New South Wales parliament. At North Sydney on 16 April he attempted to meet Reid's challenge and arrest the decline of his ministry as he submitted his program for the fourth session to open in May.[1] He spoke of his accident, a broken leg, in 1890 'which to me has been a terrible calamity . . . with indescribable suffering'. The meeting exhibited the customary colonial commotion, with the spectral harbour bridge appearing, the stuff of politics: 'That bridge—(laughter)—' said Parkes,

> that bridge, which is to cost many hundreds and thousands of pounds, is not to be erected by laughter. It is not to be erected in a month or a year.
> A Voice: 'Or five years'.
> Sir Henry Parkes: 'No, it may not be erected in 10 years, but the time is approaching—'
> A Voice: 'So is the millenium'.

Some of the old fire flared up when he recalled with passion that Reid had told

> the public that my life is a failure . . . what is his? I tell you what. When I look on his shining countenance and well-fed frame I think if he were only adorned with a fishwife's petticoat, and had a rotten broom in his hands, he would be a veritable representative of Dame Partington.

But only a tired smoulder flickered when he discussed his legislation plans: local government, civil service reform, electoral reform, including votes for women, and the draft Federation bill. The valedictory meeting ended aptly when the 'majority of the audience' cheered Queen Victoria, but 'a small section groaned very loudly'.

Parliament had been in recess since 20 December 1890. It re-opened on 19 May 1891. After a tribute had been paid to Sir John Robertson, who had died on 8 May, Reid revealed that his ten years' comparative parliamentary inertia was over and a new chapter was opening in New South Wales political history. He moved an amendment to the address in reply to the Governor's speech, claiming that the draft Federation bill was unfair, defective and undemocratic.[2] On 21 May the amendment lost 35 to 67, but the debate had disclosed that the fissures among the parliamentary free traders were widening. The Parkes ministry elected in 1887, and again in 1889, had not redeemed its promises to restore complete free trade, but had, on the contrary, perpetuated the 'mongrel tariff' and ignored direct taxation.[3] On 28 May Dibbs, nominal leader of the protectionists, moved a general motion of censure; it resulted in a tied vote, 63 to 63;[4] the speaker voted for the government, but Parkes regarded it as a defeat and resigned. Fiscalism had shown that it could not sustain parliament. The house elected in 1887 had lasted less than two years, that elected in 1889 just over two years. Since October 1885 there had been three general elections and six different ministries. In due course the 1891 elections were fixed for 17 June to 3 July.

The last session of the 1889–91 parliament, the fourteenth since responsible government in 1856, lasted nine days, had six sittings and produced no legislation. The previous session had extended from 20 April to 20 December 1891, in it ninety-nine public bills were introduced of which only thirty-three were passed; eighteen out of thirty-two private bills were passed. The *Herald* remarked that this session 'was chiefly remarkable for its length and for the scenes of disorder which character- ised it'.[5] Clearly it was also notable for its inability to process legislation, but it shared this deficiency with every session of every parliament since 1856. The disorder of the fourteenth parliament was similar to that which had marked all the parliaments since 1885; on at least two occasions it approached chaos. The era was ebbing quickly to its close in which the passage of a single outstanding piece of legislation, such as Robertson's Land Acts of 1861, Parkes's Education Acts of 1866 and 1880, J. S. Farnell's Land Law Amendment of 1884 and Parkes's Railways Act of 1888, each achieved after great political turmoil, could be rapturously acclaimed to camouflage parliament's inability to produce modern legislation consistently. In commenting on the East Sydney by-election of April 1891, the *Herald* said that the fiscal question

> has of late lost vitality, and has almost faded out of our public life . . . [with the effect] that the electors go to the polls not as orderly armies but as dis- organised crowds rather dubious what banner they are fighting under, and what principle will gain by their victory.[6]

That acute observation also correctly assessed the general position reached by the development of responsible government in New South Wales before the general elections of 1891. The classless approach to politics had reached its nadir.

The LEL, if not perfectly organised, was well prepared to play its vital part in rationalising the political system. On 4 June W. H. Sharp announced that the various leagues would soon accept nominations and where necessary local ballots would be held to select the official candi- dates; he indicated the successful Labor men would sit on the cross benches and force the introduction of 'measures in the interest of labour'.[7] The central executive committee now began to function as the chief

CC 5

electoral organising agency, setting general guidelines and giving advice on particular points raised by local leagues.[8] The platform and rules were comprehensive, but adjustments and new techniques had to be worked out to fit them into the dynamics of a general election. The Balmain league adopted a postal system to select its candidates: a special meeting was held on 5 June at which it was decided to run four men; nominations were called for, and received from nineteen members; one, D. H. Easton, had to pull out because he 'could not fulfil the . . . require-ment of withdrawing from the contest if he were not [s]elected'; each aspirant present addressed the meeting; and it was agreed to post ballot papers with the candidates names on them to all members of the league.[9] A correspondent to the *Herald* considered this a better system than 'the old manner of selection by committees'.[10] A problem arose at Redfern where selections were made at a league meeting and two of the six candidates for selection, W. F. Schey and J. P. Howe, were strong pro-tectionists also endorsed by local fiscal bodies. They signed the necessary pledge to adhere to the platform and resign if called upon by two-thirds of the electors, but refused to sign the pledge not to run if unsuccessful in the selection ballot. James Sinclair Taylor McGowen (1855–1922) a boilermaker, also a candidate,

> considered that as the labor party should be a distinct power in the House the committee had no right to retain the names of Messrs. Howe and Schey in opposition to the former decision of the league that all candidates should sign the declaration.[11]

Despite this protest at a disorderly gathering, Schey and Howe were declared selected with Sharp and McGowen. Further complications arose when the Redfern Protection Union endorsed Sharp but he soon clarified the position by writing to the Union's secretary, 'As my name is on your posters etc., without my authority, I demand its removal at once', and as president of the LEL he facilitated the recognition of himself and McGowen as the only official Labor candidates for Redfern.[12]

Similar procedures were followed in the country despite special diffi-culties conditioned by distance and poor communications. As with the metropolitan leagues, the country branches had to be approved by the central executive committee; and had to conform to the approved developing routine of selection, i.e., each candidate had to be a member of the league and had to sign a pledge agreeing to the platform, to with-draw from the election and help the successful candidate(s) if not selected, to sit on the cross benches if elected to parliament and to resign if called upon by two-thirds of his electors. Provided these con-ditions were met the successful candidate(s) were automatically endorsed by the central committee. The basic solidarity of trade unionism was being transferred to the LEL. However, this quality was not perfect even in the unions, and hence it suffered further in being grafted on to the

Labor Party; but it remained powerful enough to become a decisive and enduring factor in the development of the Party.

The process could be observed in events surrounding the establishment of a league in Bourke, a north-western outpost servicing an extensive and important pastoral area. The Shearers' Union branch was strong and there were also some small unions of other rural workers in the town. They formed a Labor league, but were dissatisfied with the platform and drew up one of their own, substantially based on the LEL program but containing several drafting changes and three new planks.[13] On 1 June the league selected H. Langwell (1860–1933), a protectionist, as its candidate; he said 'with him it was labor first and labor last'.[14] The *Western Herald* commented it was 'curious' that the Bourke Labor league should link up with the protectionists when elsewhere they 'either stood aside from existing combinations or else exhibited a strong tendency towards free trade'.[15] The central committee of the LEL settled the issue on 26 June by resolving not to recognise Langwell as an official Labor candidate.[16] This decision was a salutary exercise of authority; but the episode, considered with the Redfern incident, showed that fiscalism's rhetoric and ritual remained, despite the fact that it had lost whatever political validity it may have had.

In Labor's election campaign every grievance of the past, including the maritime strike defeat, was used to spark infectious hope for the future. The operations gave a fresh sweep to colonial politics, made more effective by the contemptuous disregard of older political groups, whose miscalculations arose from their failure to see that only the organised leagues were new, whereas Labor's influence had matured. 'One man, one vote' summed up the essence of urgent electoral reform, with stress on the need to abolish an archaic system that was an affront to all thinking democrats, and to inaugurate a new era in which voters could enrol themselves and in which people would not have to share political rights with property.[17] Sir George Grey gave practical help on this vital issue. On 26 May, as part of its general organisation of Labor leagues, and as the parliamentary crisis moved to its climax, the TLC held 'a monster meeting' at which Grey was the star speaker. The great event took place in the Centennial Hall and had a tremendous impact on Sydney; and its effects were felt even further afield. It was a notable influence on the chain of events that conditioned the substantial support given to Labor at the elections. Fitzgerald recalled the occasion almost with rapture,

> I shall never forget the scene . . . an immense audience . . . spread away into the remotest corridors and out into the adjacent streets . . . [Sir George's] voice could not be heard further than a few yards from the platform; they stood watching with rapt attention . . . knowing that Grey was advocating the fundamental principle of Australian democracy . . . During the election that followed the name of Grey was constantly invoked, and received always with enthusiastic cheers.[18]

Grey also invited Houghton to accompany him to Newcastle 'in order to prevent the possibility of political capital being made out of his visit'.[19] But Labor made capital out of it, for Houghton reported that Grey had addressed large meetings at Newcastle and Wallsend. Houghton took advantage of the trip to spur on the local Labor league, though he was unsuccessful in an attempt to persuade an opposition body, the Protectionist and Labor League, to disband and join the official branch.[20] When Grey left Sydney on 4 June the TLC adjourned their meeting 'at 9 o'clock and proceed[ed] in a body to accord a fitting [farewell] to the veteran statesman'.[21]

The TLC overseered the organising of the elections. On 28 May the Council appointed speakers for meetings in Botany and East Sydney, and on 11 June for St George's Hall, East Sydney and Redfern. The country was not overlooked: on 9 June E. Duggan was deputed to represent Council at a demonstration organised by Toomey's Young branch of the Shearers' Union.[22] The relationship between the Council and its subsidiary committee was being subtly transformed, but the full implications of the change were not realised during the electoral campaign. Houghton remained secretary of the TLC, but eased himself out of the secretaryship of the parliamentary committee when he was selected as the candidate of Glebe Labor league on 9 June. He was replaced by J. T. Gannon, who on 10 June was sent to the Illawarra to support Labor candidates and generally organise the district. Houghton reported that 'numerous telegrams were continuously being received . . . from all parts of the country in reference to the nominations of . . . candidates . . . [and] strenuous efforts are being made to secure the return of at least 25'.[23] The Council lent Sharp £40 for his nomination deposit and the Coal Lumpers' Union lent the West Sydney league £40 for a similar purpose.[24] However, all was not fragrant fraternalism; on 11 June Council had a sour discussion on

> the central committee of the Labor League not being in attendance . . . [to] supply any information to those requiring it, and also failing to see the necessity for . . . sending their secretary away to stump the country.[25]

The central committee decided on blue and white ribbons as Labor's 'distinguishing badge'.[26]

The local leagues and the individual candidates campaigned strongly. At West Sydney on 15 June the four Labor men, A. J. Kelly, J. D. Fitzgerald, G. Black and T. M. Davis, addressed an enthusiastic gathering of about 700. All based their speeches on the Labor platform.[27] Kelly said Sir George Grey's name 'would be . . . handed down to posterity'; he advocated a national bank and claimed Labor would uplift humanity through its reforms. Fitzgerald appealed for a vote against that spurious 'respectability' of which the 'tall hat' was the emblem, and wanted Federation 'on democratic lines' and said Labor would wait and work for it. Davis stressed a vital part of the novelty of Labor's approach to politics, 'Nobody else had signed such a pledge as they had and . . . none [except Labor men] were prepared to occupy their true position in Parliament, the cross-benches'. Black reinforced this point, 'they intended to form a compact third party and sit in judgment on the Government and Opposition'. W. Grantham told a meeting on 12 June that he 'stood before them as the selected candidate of the East Sydney Labour Electoral League' and proceeded to analyse the platform, with emphasis on 'one man, one vote' and education.[28] The main themes of numerous speeches by Labor candidates were abstracted from the platform; they all brought out the reforming role of the new party and its determination to act as a disciplined force to achieve its aims.[29]

In contrast the fiscalists were in disarray. Both groups had leadership problems. Parkes was visibly weakening and Reid flexing his muscles: Dibbs was uncertain of his following; a blusterer, courageous but not notably intelligent, who played politics by ear, his position was threatened by the intervention of Edmund Barton, who resigned from the Legislative Council to contest East Sydney, putting Federation before protection. Probably most protectionists, especially in the country, thought of their creed as a bulwark against inter-colonial competition; probably most free traders, especially in the city, thought that their dogmas guaranteed that the port of Sydney would always be full of overseas ships. But the belief was gaining ground that Federation would mean free trade between the Australian colonies and some kind of protection against the rest of the world. Hence Federation was helping to undermine fiscalism, and producing strange re-shuffling and blurring of political linkages.[30] Moreover the tariff excitement of 1885–9 was subsiding, even if the slogans remained powerful. Some cynicism and sceptical awareness had accompanied recognition that Parkes had not introduced the direct taxation that would have made complete free trade possible. Dibbs's actions in 1889 when he had headed a short-lived ministry, and his whole political style and record, did not instil confidence that he would, or could, design and implement a rational protective tariff. In fact the whole fiscal debate, in part a triumph of Parkes's remarkable political intuition, had camouflaged the real problem of devising modern methods to finance a colony that had reached a new stage in its development. That real problem was entering public consciousness in 1891 and had to be related to Federation.

Both the free trade and protectionist members, without cohesion in parliament, made efforts to rouse up activity in the electorates; but they had no permanent framework of support, let alone an integrated and disciplined party organisation. Neither Parkes nor Dibbs presented a policy to the electors, based on a set of political principles. Parkes made some effort to explain what he had done since 1889 and to use Feder-

ation as a prop for future political action, but he enveloped his speeches
in rhetorical clichés that had no relevance to the new colonial era.[31] He
did not campaign as a leader striving to get a party elected; indeed, as
became an old-style politician, he loftily disavowed interest in individual
seats, and submitted his own personal views to his St Leonards electors.[32]
Dibbs, on the other hand, admitted he had no policy, which implied that
he had no party; but his candour was related to his confusion about the
new political situation rather than his political honesty. The *Herald,* in
a muddle about the changing meaning of 'policy', commented that 'Mr.
Dibbs tells the colony that "he has no policy to disclose". What the other
side says is that it has none to conceal'.[33] Barton was scathing, 'Mr. Dibbs
is a daily conundrum. What can we do but give him up?'[34]

Without a policy and bereft of direction, the free trade and protectionist candidates were subject to every political cross-wind that blew,
some from the wastelands of colonial sub-cultures inhabited by both
disaffected Irish Catholics and Irish Protestants who looked longingly to
mother Ireland for sustenance rather than mother New South Wales, let
alone Australia. And exhilarating turbulence was emitted from the
temperance fans, to whom 'freetrade, protection or any other political
issues are as nought compared with the triumph of their own particular-
ism'. And 'the great and ever-present influence of local interest', reduced
Federation and other momentous matters to minute proportions 'compared to . . . [need] for a new road or bridge, a courthouse or a
post-office'.[35] These groups and others, many ephemeral, had been
hatched over the years as colonial responsible government had laboured
to find itself; randomly resurrected at election time, some of them
subdivided, overlapped; some were mutually antagonistic, some mutually
attractive. They were all called parties: 'liberal parties', 'denominational
parties', 'cocktail parties', 'wheat and corn parties', 'calico parties', 'liquor
parties', 'social purity parties', 'country parties', 'wild cat parties': any
vagrant pressure cell could be called a party.[36] Attempting to moderate
the 1891 medley, with the help of Parkes, Dibbs, Reid and Barton were
the 'free trade' and 'protection parties'. Reid, at least, knew something
about it all. Barton might have, but his eyes were unsteadily fixed on the
'Federation party'. The fiscal parties' candidates were confused.

The electors were not so confused, although on 17 June, the day of the
first elections (all twelve city and suburban, and nine country electorates)
the *Herald* said that questions of no ordinary character 'have to be faced';
New South Wales had to decide on whether 'Australia is to become a
great united nation' and

> whether the principles of Parliamentary government as we have hitherto
> known them are to be superseded by a system of representation of class
> interests, the ultimate effect of which would be to degrade Parliament into a
> nominee chamber of the Trade and Labour Council.[37]

Next day the newspaper classified the first results: twenty-seven free traders, seven protectionists and nineteen independents, of whom seventeen were members of the Labor party.[38]

In the three city electorates, each with four seats, the LEL nominated four candidates at West Sydney and won the four seats, two candidates at South Sydney and one candidate at East Sydney: a total success of four seats out of twelve with seven candidates. In the nine suburban electorates, returning thirty members, the LEL nominated fifteen candidates and won eleven seats.[39] A closer look at these figures showed that Labor's metropolitan strength was almost exclusively confined to a south-west segment of a circle centred on the General Post Office with a radius of three to four miles. Balmain, where all four seats had been won, Redfern, where two out of the four seats had been won with two candidates, and Glebe, where one out of the two seats had been won with one candidate, were by 1891 becoming hard to distinguish from the city as residential areas of the working class. Eleven of the sixteen metropolitan Labor seats (counting Clark at St Leonards) therefore were all virtually in the inner urban area.

Balmain was an interesting example of the fundamental social and political changes at work in the elections. Settlement began there in the eighteenth century and, with its natural beauty as a harbour peninsula, it developed in the nineteenth century as a high class residential area; but its proximity to Sydney Cove (Circular Quay) and its advantageous waterfront conditioned substantial growth in the maritime industry, including shipbuilding and ship maintenance. Mort's Dock was located there, one of the largest engineering works in Sydney. The shipowners, ships' officers and other middle class people who lived on the upper ridge had common economic interests with the working class who lived beneath them. Balmain was one of the strongest free trade centres in New South Wales. Jacob Garrard had won five elections there since his original success in 1880 and, in becoming 'a free-trader of the free-traders', had left his work as an engineer to be an estate agent and emerged as an ideal representative of the district, acceptable to both its middle and its working class voters. But Garrard and his free trade confreres were swamped by the Labor quartet in 1891, W. A. Murphy, a ship's officer, J. Johnston, a boilermaker, E. Darnley, a plasterer and G. D. Clark, a journalist who excelled as a temperance organiser as, to a degree, did Garrard. Balmain also had a strong wowser element. The outstanding Labor success there was a pointer to the metropolitan collective wisdom of New South Wales deciding for a change in the balance of forces on which the political system functioned: so that the ministry would become more of a firm controller of reform legislation and less of an inefficient administrative agency, and parliament would become less of a

disorderly legislative machine and more of a stable part of a new
approach to legislation and administration.

The unexpected Labor wins in Canterbury also reflected this new
opinion. This electorate covered a large south-west suburban area,
sparsely settled on its perimeter, with many of the middle class and some
working class nearer the city. Labor nominated three candidates including T. Bavister, a bricklayer and energetic liberal free trader, and C. J.
Danahey, a cosmopolitan engine-fitter, born in Detroit, USA, of Irish
parents, and they won half of the four seats. Likewise, the intriguing
situation in St Leonards showed how the Labor campaign, with its new
style of politics, had struck an eager social response. This constituency
covered a huge North Shore area stretching from Manly to Broken Bay
on the coast and roughly from upper Lane Cove to the Hawkesbury
River on the west, semi-rural for a large part. Parkes had held a seat
there from 1885, indicating its free trade, middle class majority, but in
the North Sydney area, just across the harbour from Circular Quay,
many of the working class lived and worked. They formed an active
Labor league, but, although at one stage G. Waite appeared likely to
run, they could not get a suitable candidate.[40] An independent free
trader, E. M. Clark, manager of a brick company, sized up the position,
and in his campaign said that he would support the platform of the LEL,
would press for eight hours legislation, and sit on the cross benches.[41] He
was elected, joined the Labor Party and was admitted to its first caucus.

Of the twelve electorates in the metropolitan area, with forty-two
seats, the LEL nominated in ten and won fifteen seats with twenty-two
candidates. Including E. M. Clark, Labor ran in eleven electorates and
won sixteen out of forty-two seats. Only in the electorate of Parramatta
had Labor not been able to organise effectively. This was a remarkable
achievement for a party conducting its first campaign within three
months of its foundation. The very magnitude of its success in these
circumstances revealed the deep social need for what it represented: a
radically different parliamentary way to the identification and solution of
large and urgent problems.[42] And the success demonstrated the vital
social role of the Labor movement in New South Wales as it tapped a
vast reservoir of protest and will to reform.

New South Wales consisted of 310,372 square miles (British Isles
cover 120,717 square miles) and in 1891 its population was 1,153,170 of
whom 383,333 lived in the Sydney metropolitan area. Given the huge
and sparsely settled area with relatively poor communications, the LEL
had a similar electoral triumph in the country to that in the city. The
electorates of Sturt and Wilcannia had been established in the far west in
1888 to make a total of sixty-two country electorates, returning ninety-
nine members. It is not possible to ascertain the exact number of Labor
leagues established in these constituencies before the elections were held,

but it seems that it was approximately twenty-five. Probably twenty-four leagues nominated thirty-one candidates, of whom nineteen were elected in sixteen electorates.[43] The country candidates campaigned similarly to the metropolitan men, and after the great result of 17 June several of the elected LEL candidates went to the country to help in electioneering and thus consolidate the common Labor front: Sharp, McGowen, Bavister and Danahey were among them.[44] Effective work was done in pastoral electorates where branches of the Shearers' Union were strong, Goulburn, Young, Grenfell, the Murrumbidgee and Balranald in the south-west, and the Upper Hunter, the Bogan, Gunnedah and the Namoi in the north-west. A mid-western section from Orange through Molong to Forbes, mixed pastoral and agricultural electorates, was also energetically covered. Newcastle, Illawarra, Hartley (Lithgow district) and Sturt (Broken Hill district), all centres of powerful mining unions, were enthusiastically worked over. Large areas were practically untouched, the coast north of Newcastle and inland to New England, and the coast south of Illawarra, except for Kiama and Eden, and inland to Quean-beyan and Monaro. The central executive committee of the LEL and the TLC kept in touch with most of the electioneering, and to a great extent maintained the same kind of control as in Sydney, as the Langwell (Bourke) incident showed. But complete surveillance was impossible and there were three instances of LEL candidates being supported by protectionist groups, Forbes, Nepean, Young; and one by free trade, Orange. The results showed that the country appeal of Labor was if anything stronger than its metropolitan influence, and they also revealed that the links between electioneering and unionism were different in the country from those in the city. Labor had widened its power base, but it would have to pay greater attention to rural problems in the future. The relationship of unionism to politics had taken on a new and intricate dimension.

When the full results of the elections were known on 4 July there were various guesses, ranging from thirty to thirty-seven, as to the number of Labor men returned. D. C. P. Donnelly, Carcoar, promptly denied that he was an official member, and Langwell clearly was not one. The official list is shown in the Table.[45]

Of these thirty-five Labor members of the Legislative Assembly probably eighteen held protectionist views and seventeen free trade; twenty-one were trade unionists, nearly all of whom had held executive positions; seven had been delegates to the TLC. Ten were native-born, eleven counting Rae. Of the twenty-five born overseas, in effect all except Vaughn were from the British Isles, for Newman was born of English and Danahey of Irish parents. Seven of the overseas-born were under twenty when they arrived in Australia; if they are added to the native-born, a total of 17–18 may be argued to have been personally formed in

Name	Occupation	Electorate	Religion[a]	Date of birth	Country of Birth	Arrival in Australia
T. Bavister	Bricklayer[bd]	Canterbury	M	18.6.1850	England	1883
G. Black	Journalist[b]	West Sydney	P	5.2.1854	Scotland	1873
J. H. Cann	Miner[ed]	Sturt	C	1860	England	1887
E. M. Clark	Manager, brickworks[b]	St Leonards	CE	12.4.1855	Tasmania	Native
G. D. Clark	Temperance journalist[b]	Balmain	M	30.7.1848	England	1871
J. Cook	Miner[bd]	Hartley	M	1860	England	1886
F. Cotton	Journalist[bd]	Newtown	M	1858	South Aust	Native
C. J. Danahey	Engine-fitter[bd]	Canterbury	—	10.1856	USA	1873
E. Darnley	Plasterer[bd]	Balmain	CE	29.1.1859	England	1885
T. M. Davis	Seaman[bd]	West Sydney	CE	21.1.1856	England	1876
A. Edden	Miner[ed]	Northumberland	CE	1850	England	1879
J. L. Fegan	Miner[bd]	Newcastle	M	1862	England	1886
J. D. Fitzgerald	Printer[ed]	West Sydney	RC	11.6.1862	NSW	Native
A. Gardiner	Carpenter[b]	Forbes	CE	1867	NSW	Native
J. G. Gough	Ironmonger[e]	Young	P	1848	Victoria	Native
J. Hindle	Commercial traveller[b]	Newtown	CC	6.4.1857	England	1871
L. T. Hollis	Medico[b]	Goulburn	CE	1865	NSW	Native
T. J. Houghton	Printer[ed]	Glebe	CE	1862	England	1866
G. F. Hutchinson	Saddler[e]	Forbes	RC	1844	NSW	Native
J. Johnston	Boilermaker[ed]	Balmain	P	1854	England	1857
A. J. Kelly	Wharflabourer[ed]	West Sydney	RC	1854	Ireland	1881
J. Kirkpatrick	Storekeeper[b]	Gunnedah	P	1840	Scotland	1871
J. A. Mackinnon	Stock and station agent[e]	Young	P	1841	Victoria	Native
S. T. McGowen	Boilermaker[ed]	Redfern	CE	16.8.1855	Victoria	Native
J. Morgan	Printer, miner[e]	The Bogan	RC	1853	Tasmania	Native
W. A. Murphy	Ship's officer[bd]	Balmain	CE	3.1858	England	1879
W. H. Newman	Clerk, miner, investor[b]	Orange	CE	1839	France	1841
J. Newton	Saddler, carrier[ed]	Balranald	RC	1850	England	1857
J. B. Nicholson	Miner[ed]	Illawarra	CE	1849	England	1882
A. Rae	Shearer[bd]	Murrumbidgee	CE	1860	England	1888
D. Scott	Ironmoulder[ed]	Newcastle	M	26.10.1844	New Zealand	1874
W. H. Sharp	Printer[ed]	Redfern	C	1848	England	1887
J. Sheldon	Clerk[e]	Namoi	CE	1847	England	1882
R. M. Vaughn	Builder[e]	Grenfell	CE	1835	USA	1854
T. H. Williams	Shearer[ed]	Upper Hunter	CE	2.5.1862	England	1870

[a] C Congregationalist   CE Church of England   P Presbyterian   [b] Free trader
CC Church of Christ   M Methodist   RC Roman Catholic   [c] Protectionist
[d] Unionist

the colonies. In 1891 about two-thirds of the New South Wales population were native-born.[46] But the fact that the Labor members comprised
a lower proportion of native-born than the colonial average is of minimal
historical significance. Practically all of the members had been well
assimilated by the colonial Labor/radical movement. W. H. Sharp for
example, after only three years in New South Wales had fitted in so well
that he had become president of the TLC in 1891. Similarly J. H. Cann,
after four years, was a representative Broken Hill mining union leader.
Black, after eighteen years in New South Wales was eminently a colonial
radical and Kelly, after ten years, a gregarious colonial union leader.

The ages of the members are of some importance. Just as Angus
Cameron at the age of twenty-seven had epitomised the fresh appeal of
Labor representation in the 1870s, so did a majority of the Labor members in the 1890s. Twenty-one of them were under forty, six in their
twenties. Ten were in their forties and only four in their fifties, of whom
two, Mackinnon (first elected 1882) and Vaughn (first elected 1880)
were really old-style politicians, seeking a new lease of parliamentary life.
The youngest man was Gardiner, aged twenty-four. The oldest was
Vaughn, aged fifty-six; only he and Mackinnon of the Labor members
had been in parliament before. The exuberant youth of the Labor Party
matched its reforming mission, but their inexperience would bring great
problems.

Looking back in 1893, 'One of Them' summed up the occupations of
the Labor members of 1891:

> we were a band of unhappy amateurs . . . made up somewhat as follows:
> several miners, three or four printers, a boilermaker, three sailors, a plasterer,
> a journalist, a draper, a suburban mayor, two engineers, a carrier, a few
> shearers, a tailor, and—with bated breath—a mineowner, a squatter and an
> M.D.[47]

Most lists of occupations are inaccurate and incomplete, and hence can
be very often misleading; their historical significance needs to be judged
with great care. 'One of Them's' summary illustrates the problem: W. H.
Newman, a man of many parts, was a mineowner of sorts; J. A. Mackinnon did have some pastoral investments and could be described as a
squatter; J. Kirkpatrick had been a tailor and sold drapery, among the
many wonderful commodities rounded up in a country store. E. M. Clark
had been mayor of East St Leonards, but A. Edden was mayor of
Adamstown and G. F. Hutchinson had been mayor of Forbes. Even so,
'One of Them's' impressions convey the obvious essence of the importance
of the occupational range of the pioneer Labor parliamentarians: it fitted
naturally into colonial society. Only about three or four had been
educated beyond primary school, and only one, L. T. Hollis, had been
to a university. Three, G. D. Clark, Fegan and Gardiner, were confirmed
teetotallers; E. M. Clark was reputed to be one. Among the thirty-four

whose religion is known probably the Methodists were somewhat over-represented and the Roman Catholics somewhat under-represented. But as a group the Labor men, even with their youthful bias, were typical colonists. They had no plan to restructure parliament in one session, let alone in one day. They collectively represented a colonial urge to improve the political system, and that made most of them determined reformers; but, if their ultimate objective was clear enough, their methods were embryonic and unco-ordinated. They had to grope their way in a strange landscape.

A notable feature of the occupations reflected the different texture of unionism as between city and country. The city with its differentiated economy had some 90–100 separate unions. The country had about fifteen, including mining and associated groups, and the bush unions of dispersed small groups of rural workers waiting uneasily to link up with the Shearers' Union. The consolidated structure of city unionism facilitated a close relationship between unionists and LEL candidates. Of the sixteen metropolitan members twelve were unionists, and Black was closely connected to unionism and G. D. Clark and Hindle somewhat less so; only E. M. Clark was a definite non-unionist. The TLC's attempts over the years to define a 'Labor candidate' as a unionist seeking to enter parliament had some relevance in 1891 in the city. But in the country only nine of the nineteen Labor members were unionists; there the LEL rule that a candidate merely had to be a member of a league had a portentous reality. The fact that six of the nine country unionist members of the Legislative Assembly were miners starkly revealed the difficulty of discovering suitable Labor candidates in many of the rural electorates, where the combination of small unions, travelling workers and some social inertia limited the field. The 1891 country Labor men set the rural pattern for the future. Most of the non-unionists were radically minded and sympathetic to unionism, but their occupations were not covered by unions and set them somewhat apart from the rest, although all were similarly pledged. But the country men outnumbered the city men. The solidarity-separatism of Labor had entered on a new phase.

The *Sydney Morning Herald,* sage colonial weather-vane, early in July 1891 judged that

> The labour members have been placed in a position of power and we may add of responsibility, for which they could not have been fully prepared, and any plans laid down beforehand may well be subjected to reconsideration when they have to be adjusted to so much larger a set of circumstances than was originally contemplated,[1]

and went on to stress the disadvantages of the members being unknown to one another and being delegates of a class rather than representatives of the people. But the upholder of transplanted British virtues took solace,

> if we are struck by the novelty of [the appearance of the Labor Party] we should also recognize in them an illustration of the instincts of the race. The voyage across the seas has not changed the ideas of Englishmen who are here now, and those who came in earlier days handed down their tendencies and traditions to their sons.

What was exercising the *Herald* was the prospect of the Labor Party deciding whether Parkes or Dibbs would form a ministry. As usual after a nineteenth century election in New South Wales it was not clear how many followers each leader commanded. But a reliable contemporary source estimated that, apart from Labor, there were forty-nine members of the Legislative Assembly likely to support Parkes, fifty possibly for Dibbs and six or seven independents.[2] There was no doubt that Labor was in a powerful position.

The whole complex Labor pattern for parliamentary action had been worked out over a period of about twenty months. Now it was about to be put to the practical test. The Party did have plans for controlled work, some explicit in the platform and rules, others implicit. Already some development had taken place in the notion and forms of discipline as experience had been gained in the election campaign. While electioneering at Glebe on 15 June T. J. Houghton had said that any elected LEL men would submit 'any question affecting the workers . . . to a vote of the labor party and a vote would be recorded [in parliament] as the majority decided'.[3] After the great success on 17 June Houghton, surrounded by congratulatory telegrams, told the *Daily Telegraph,*

As a party we shall elect our own leader before Parliament meets. We shall sit together on the cross-benches. On all questions embodied in the labor platform, we will vote in accordance with the decision of the majority of our party. On the fiscal question we will vote according to conviction untrammelled by the league.[4]

These statements reflected the persistence of attempts to transfer naturally trade union customs to the political wing of the Labor movement. The implied Party caucus and caucus pledge were associated with the authority of the central executive committee of the LEL when the secretary, J. T. Gannon, was instructed to invite to a meeting those Labor members who had 'subscribed to the . . . platform and who . . . agreed to sit on the cross-benches'.[5]

Before the caucus met much dissatisfaction was expressed with Houghton's assertion that Labor members were free on the fiscal issue.[6] In fact his view contradicted one of the basic principles of many election speeches to the effect that the question would be 'sunk', a necessary implication of sitting on the cross benches. At a meeting on 1 July, Houghton modified his statement by saying that 'the best thing to be done . . . would be to adopt the referendum' to solve the problem.[7] W. H. Sharp at the same meeting said that if Parkes submitted a legislative program in keeping with the Labor platform, the Party would support him. The flare-up of fiscalism showed what could never be denied, that Labor was not exempt from current social impulses. The TLC had erected barriers against them with some success. But the Council was an industrial body. The LEL as a political organisation was exposed on all sides to practically every opinion prevalent in New South Wales. And now the parliamentary Labor Party was about to be thrust into the arena where all the pressures met in concentrated form, and where seasoned and adept politicians had a fine disdain for raw reformers.

The first Labor caucus was held in the Temperance Hall on 4 July. It was chaired by Sharp, and Houghton was appointed secretary.[8] The natural feeling of jubilation on the part of the Labor members was tempered by the realisation that they were novices about to embark on a difficult and hazardous undertaking. The number of official Labor Legislative Assembly members was determined as thirty-five (omitting H. Langwell and D. C. J. Donnelly), although not all were present. No decision was reached as to whether Parkes or Dibbs should be supported, pending a statement of Parkes's intentions. Some hostility was expressed towards the premier and two of his ministers, W. McMillan and Bruce Smith, but Dibbs was likewise condemned. The matter of Party leadership came up, but was postponed after discussion of the possibility of a committee system being used until experience had been gained in parliamentary procedures and practices.

The history of New South Wales parliamentary 'parties' provided no sound guidelines for the new Party. Substantially it had to create its own methods of operation. To the old 'parties' a caucus meeting was a desultory and unimportant gathering that stressed rather than modified the independence of individual members; and, without a permanent or stable extra-parliamentary structure, the 'parties' had no serious system of pledging of selected candidates and no formula at all for parliamentarians. The Labor Party naturally fell back on the trade union tradition of firm acceptance of decisions freely made at union meetings and the similar practice of the TLC, all of which had conditioned both the form and content of the platform and rules of the LEL. The election campaign had drawn further out the notion of controlled solidarity and had forecast the next logical step of extending the pledge to elected Labor members. It was appropriate that the new pledge should be moved at the first caucus by Black, who represented the radicals absorbed by the LEL, and seconded by McGowen, who belonged firmly to the industrial wing of Labor:

(a) That in order to secure the solidarity of the Labor Party, only those will be allowed to assist at its private deliberations who are pledged to vote in the House as a majority of the party, sitting in caucus, has decided;

(b) therefore, we the undersigned, in proof of our determination to vote as a majority of the party may agree on all occasions considered of such importance as to necessitate party deliberation, have hereto affixed our names.[9]

The wording of the pledge made no reference to the Labor platform, but it clearly affirmed that the Party would hold caucus meetings when necessary and that decisions made at them would be binding on all members. At once eight members, Edden, Gough, Mackinnon, Nicholson, Scott, Sheldon, Williams and Vaughn stated they could not sign such a pledge, because of promises to favour protection they had given while campaigning.[10] Their action effectively placed them outside the Party though it was not clear at the time, for the substantial party edifice had to be adjusted on the basis of accepted principles as it evolved in relation to circumstances both inside and outside of parliament. Obviously the Labor Party was a completely novel phenomenon for parliament and society, but despite all the thought and energy devoted to its foundation over a long period, it could not be nor was it equipped to function perfectly in its first parliament. In a real sense this both proved the uniqueness of the Party and testified to its natural colonial formation.

In the event Houghton was able to get an important compromise accepted at the first caucus to the effect that no Labor members should propose any change of fiscal policy until the matter had been decided by the people at a referendum. This satisfied all but Mackinnon, who left the Party.[11] But the caucus proceedings suggested strongly that there was trouble ahead. The Labor men could not discard overnight the accumulated baggage of colonial involvement. And protectionist and free trade members of the Assembly would have noted the new Party's difficulties.

A second caucus was held on 13 July, the day before the new parliament opened, the fifteenth since 1856. The proceedings showed that neither Parkes nor Dibbs had made overtures to the Party, but that individual Labor members of the Assembly were very much concerned with the one or the other; 'indeed the fiscal question became exceedingly prominent during the discussion', which at times became acrimonious.[12] Instead of a leader, a committee of advice was set up, Sharp, McGowen, Fitzgerald, Gough and Houghton; Davis was made whip.[13] The consensus was that the right man would emerge naturally as the Party gained experience in parliamentary procedures and tactics, but the inability to decide on a leader immediately placed the Labor members at a great disadvantage. But the failure was inevitable and again emphasised the newness of the Party. The LEL had a rule that its office-holders had to resign if elected to parliament, but Sharp, who was the first president of the League, had no pre-emptive right to leadership of the parliamentary Party. In any case, neither he nor any other member was well enough known to make his accession certain. The Labor Party was indeed starting *ab initio*. The *Daily Telegraph* commented correctly, 'As the labor party are placed . . . they are without any means of determining who is the fittest man to lead them'.[14]

Henry Parkes had mixed feelings about the Labor Party as he reviewed its performance in the 1891 elections for the *Contemporary Review*.[15] Like some other observers he affected to believe that the Party's connections with the working class were tenuous and that they had displaced some 'truer representatives' of the workers. The normal member of parliament, he argued, was one who had won a seat as 'the prize of useful activity and honourable ambition', but this had not been so with the Labor members; they were unknown and had to be taken on trust. But as he studied them he noticed 'evidence of a self-restraint and close observation and a steadiness of purpose which old stagers in political warfare might emulate with much advantage to themselves'. He predicted that they were bound to 'lose something of their separate party character as time familiarizes them to the company into which they are thrown'. From the background of his incomparable experience of the old parliamentary system, Parkes forecast that parliamentary pressures would tend to divide the Labor men and he would not guess at their position at the end of parliament's term; but he presciently concluded that the electors would never unlearn the habit of voting for the Labor Party, '[its] strength will be renewed at the polls'.

With these thoughts in mind Parkes submitted a progressive program of legislation to parliament on 15 July:

1. Electoral reform; one man, one vote; extension of the franchise; self-registration; the abolition of candidates' deposits; single electorates

2. Federation to be brought forward without delay

3. Local government

4. Conciliation and arbitration

5. Regulation of coal mining

6. Amendment of the mining law to provide for mining on private property

7. Factories and workshops, with special reference to women and children

8. Water conservation and irrigation

9. Licensing reform; local option

10. Legal reforms; regulation of the medical profession; fisheries law.[16] This was a carefully designed program, not, by any means, entirely dictated by the need for Labor Party support. Parkes was prepared to accept the need for electoral reform; he, more than any other single Australian, had brought Federation to public attention; he had sought a reformed system of local government for years; and he favoured conciliation and arbitration as one of his reforms (and it was not specifically on the Labor platform). In many respects this was a typical old-style statement of a premier at the beginning of a parliament, shaped to appeal to as many members as possible, so that the governor's address might be carried and the ministry might sit back and await events. The debate on the address in reply was simply part of the formula by which the results of general elections were clarified. The statement of intentions did not indicate a firm and purposeful plan to prepare and press on with the legislation outlined. But even if the Labor members of the Assembly had adverted to this accepted tactic, there was nothing they could have done about it. Dibbs would have done the same thing as the premier. Parkes's program did include six Labor planks; and his first objective was virtually the same as Labor's. The Labor men decided to support the address in reply, which meant that they would keep the Parkes ministry in office.[17]

A necessary complement of the procedure was that a motion of censure be moved. This Dibbs did.[18] Immediately the Labor members were subjected to the cross fire of debate, a vital part of their assimilation to parliament. They were no longer simply elected members of Labor leagues, they were parliamentarians deciding the fate of a government. To ensure that they should clearly hear the whine of the bullets J. P. Garvan, probably the most capable of the protectionists, moved an amendment to the address which cleverly incorporated Labor's strong feelings that the Pastoralists' Union should meet with the Shearers' Union to settle the problem of 'freedom of contact', and insinuated the fiscal issue by seeking protective tariff changes and the execution of government contracts in the colony (a specific Labor plank).[19] If carried the amendment would have resulted in the Parkes ministry's resignation.

While the parliamentary debate was proceeding the city Labor leagues vigorously discussed the great issues confronting the Labor Party. Apart from the specific matters argued about, the fact that the leagues considered themselves qualified to review the role of the members of the Legislative Assembly illustrated the great significance of the extra-parliamentary structure of the Labor Party. Many of the city leagues were protectionist and the decision of the parliamentarians to support Parkes was far from popular. The controversies culminated in a general public meeting on 20 July. The audience was united in approval of Labor's power to make governments, but riven by mutual recrimination as to which type of government. They fought vocally among themselves and joined to drown the voices of the platform speakers. Even Cotton was silenced, and Fitzgerald was forced to raise his voice 'several tones higher'. Rae was somewhat more successful in a humorous vein. But 'at a quarter to ten' the tension snapped, and

> the platform was rushed . . . and a scene of utmost disorder and uproar ensued. A free fight was started on the platform . . . 'Old Brown' was pushed off . . . the gas was turned off . . . However . . . about two-thirds remained and illuminated the hall by continually striking matches. [A vote of 'perfect confidence' in the Labor Party] . . . was carried amidst cheering.

> Three hearty cheers were given for Sir George Grey, after which the chairman asked the meeting to leave the hall in peace and quietness, in order that it might not be said that they were a disreputable section of the country. (Cheers).[20]

After this unnerving example of participatory democracy the Labor members of the Assembly could have had little doubt that their actions were subject to scrutiny not only in parliament and the electorates but also in the Labor leagues. Two days later they had to vote on Dibbs's motion and Garvan's amendment. During the parliamentary debate Black had made Labor's keynote speech, lucidly summing up what had been made explicit during the election campaign: the independence of the Labor party and its associated policy of supporting ministries in return for implementation of its platform planks.[21] But the subtle pressure of the combined force exerted by the social aspects of the general parliamentary situation, the needling tactics of the 'old stagers' in the house, and the tenacity of the fiscal faiths shook the scaffolding of Labor solidarity. The caucus decision to withhold action on the tariff until a referendum had been taken should have guided the voting, but eight Labor protectionists (including Mackinnon) voted for Garvan's amendment and three abstained. It was somewhat better on Dibbs's censure (which lost 58/77); only five Labor protectionists voted for it, Kelly, Mackinnon, Morgan, Vaughn and Gough.[22] By the end of July, of the thirty-five original Labor members of the Assembly, twenty-four had adhered completely to caucus decisions.[23] In all the circumstances this was a satisfactory performance by the Party. The first weeks in parliament had been a general shaking-down period concerned with the fate of the Parkes ministry, and that question could be settled in the only way known to Legislative Assembly members at the time. There was no hope of the Labor Party forcing decisions on a class basis. Conservatives, liberals and radicals were sprinkled on both sides of the house. They were jammed in the vice of the old system and reflexly obeyed the fiscal siren. The Labor members could not avoid entirely the well-worn grooves of accepted behaviour.

But a new phase of the problem of coexistence arose in August when the ministry had some of its legislation ready. The law-making record of the New South Wales parliament was only a little less than appalling; now the Labor Party would have to face up to the bitter frustrations of entrenched legislative paralysis. The 'old stagers' had fused legislation so effectively with the game of 'ins-and-outs of ministries' that they were inured to the slaughter or disfigurement of bills, either in the Legislative Assembly or the Legislative Council. The Labor members of the Assembly were in parliament to change this shambles, but they had a lot to learn about it. On 5 August the ministry introduced eight bills, all of which were related to forecasts in the governor's speech; Labor was especially interested in the coal mines regulation bill, the representation of the people bill, with its associated bill, seats redistribution, and the trades disputes conciliation and arbitration bill. By the end of August practically no progress had been made in any of the legislation, except the Crown Lands Act amendment bill. To a degree the stalling was a result of the great complexity of much of the legislation, but, above all, it followed naturally from the in-built procedures of delay, illustrated by the ministry's failure to control the house effectively, the disruptive independence of individual members and the very forms of the house. The protectionist opposition naturally took advantage of the situation on 1 September when H. Copeland, a senior member of the group, moved that protective duties be imposed on imports that competed with local manufactures and on agricultural imports from other colonies that discriminated against New South Wales exports.[24] Barton reflected the new magnitude of intricacy added by Federation to parliamentary proceedings by moving an amendment to Copeland's resolution to the effect that, because Federation would bring a uniform tariff to Australia, the financial needs of New South Wales should govern the methods of raising revenue, 'rather than the rigid doctrines of any system of political economy'.[25]

Again a great squeeze was exerted on the Labor members. They deputed J. S. T. McGowen to make their main speech, explaining why

they considered that fiscalism menaced orderly legislation. Aged thirty-
six, McGowen had been well formed by colonial trade unionism; a
benign, bluff, stolid man with a black cascading moustache and black
hair, brushed back, he was heavily built and slow moving; far from
brilliant, he was close to being wise; he exuded a simple honesty that
complemented the high reputation he had gained as an Anglican Sunday
school teacher at St Paul's, Redfern. McGowen had an unshakeable
belief in, and a comprehensive understanding of Labor's reform mission
in Parliament. His effortless and painless integrity and developing skill
as a parliamentarian were clearly marking him out as Labor's natural
leader. Against some interjections he reviewed the history of the Labor
Party, stressing its class origin and role: 'A number of us', he said, 'were
taken from the workshops . . . [to represent] a peculiar class in the
community . . . which, hitherto, has been ignored in enactments . . . and
in their administration'. An interruption by J. See, a protectionist ship-
owner, enabled McGowen to state that as a protectionist himself he had
fought the free traders as See had done, but that the two of them 'have
never been fighting for the same class'. He emphasised how the Labor
Party had been conditioned by the trade unions, '[which] have taught us
to sink our individuality', and went on, 'When we formed the labour
party we clearly indicated that [to get working-class legislation] . . . it
would have to be by every one of us being prepared to sink our individuality for the good of the collective body'. The Party, he argued, had
sunk fiscalism in order to mould Labor free traders and Labor protectionists into Labor men. They wanted useful legislation 'and we care
not who gives it to us'; they did not want the honour of carrying
legislation, 'only [that] of getting it carried'. He acknowledged that
'Scores of men . . . have sent us here as a protest against party politics
as practised in this House for some time'. He contrasted Labor's action
on the Crown Lands Act amendment bill with that of the protectionists,
and asserted that free selectors would now see the advantage of his Party
and at the same time realise that the protectionists wanted office before
legislation. He stated an important principle when he maintained that
'more or less, the labour party are what they call "state socialists" ',
although he admitted that 'we may have broad definitions of our own
with regard to how far we go in socialism'. The object of the Party, he
concluded, was 'democratic legislation in the interests of the people. We
believe almost to a man in these lines of the English writer, Landor:
"Every government should provide for every subject the means of living
honestly and at ease" '.[26]

McGowen's important speech articulated some of the enduring features
of the Labor Party that could be restated after two months' experience
of parliament: its close relationship with unionism, its appeal to city and
country, its diffuse democratic socialism, its mandate to improve parlia-

ment, its basic adherence to the parliamentary system. The discourse also showed that solidarity was holding up; the Party was still compact and prepared to help Parkes with his legislation. Barton's amendment was carried 60 to 49, with twenty-three of the Labor men for it, and seven against; McMillan then successfully proposed another amendment, and finally the motion as amended was put, and lost 47 to 62; twenty-four Labor men voted with the ministry against it, and seven for it. Apart from the Labor Party there was much complicated cross voting in the divisions, all of which suggested the entanglement of parliament.[27]

Legislation remained the critical issue. By mid-October the ministry had brought down twelve bills and had achieved success with only one (assent was given to the Crown Lands Act Amendment Act on 15 October). Discussion had bogged down on several bills, but considerable progress was being made with the coal mines regulation bill, which was in its final committee stages on 13 October. The mining Labor members were particularly useful in the clause by clause analysis; clause 17 provided for the eight-hour day from Monday to Friday for employees aged between fourteen and seventeen; Cook moved for a general eight-hour day, for a six-hour Saturday and for certain improvements in methods of wage payments; the minister in charge, Sydney Smith, hinted at possible difficulties with the Legislative Council if the amendment were carried; Cook compromised with a simple change to a general eight-hour day, Monday to Friday, and it was agreed to without a division.[28] Edden's amendment was accepted, that the return air-ways should not be used as tunnelling roads. Clause 21 provided for 100 cubic feet of pure air per minute for ventilation for each miner. Cook moved for an increase to 150 cubic feet and his amendment was carried on a division by 29 to 10; as all the twenty Labor members present voted for it, it was virtually a Labor-controlled change in the bill. Amongst those opposed to it were Barton and Dibbs.[29] Before the committee stage was finished, A. J. Kelly also foresaw that the Legislative Council would be opposed to much of the bill.[30] But the bill was reported to the house and the report was adopted.

Two days later S. Smith moved the third reading of the bill and immediately W. McMillan, no longer in the cabinet, moved an amendment that it be recommitted for reconsideration of clauses 17 and 21.[31] Obviously McMillan, who admitted to his coal mines interests, had had discussions on the matter with Parkes; but the Labor Party, with a vital stake in the bill, was about to be put through the mangle provided by the old parliamentary system in case of emergencies. McMillan had not been present in the bill's committee stage; he was a private member seeking recommittal of a bill after it had reached the point where its final passage was a formality; and he was doing so with the support of the leader of the cabinet that had sponsored the bill through its secretary of mines. In his defence McMillan argued that it was not the same bill which had been prepared by the cabinet of which he was a member; and that the compulsory provision for eight hours constituted unprecedented class legislation.[32] Parkes supported him, and developed the crusted doctrinaire point that he 'distinguish[ed] very broadly between eight hours being sufficient for a man to labour and Parliament presuming to say how many hours he shall labour'; more logical than McMillan, he pointed out that he was absent because of a broken leg when the bill had first been drawn up in 1890, otherwise he would have objected to the original provision for a limited eight hours. Warming to his task, which was simply to torpedo his own ministry's bill, Parkes asked with geriatric grandiloquence 'I should like to know what Mr Herbert Spencer would say about this question', and provoked J. D. Fitzgerald to a brash retort, 'Smother [Spencer's] opinion. Is his opinion to influence this House? Are we intelligent men or are we to be insulted?' The premier tried to stop Fitzgerald with a rusty recollection of a conversation he had had with Thomas Carlyle thirty years before. What he was implicitly trying to do was to stem the onrushing tide that would change the parliamentary system to which he had contributed so much, but which by now had outlived its usefulness.

The debate had then gone past midnight and Barton moved its adjournment. Barton was not a follower of the government, but Parkes intimated that the ministry would not go on with the bill if the motion were not carried. The Labor Party was confronted with an exquisite dilemma. During the debate Fitzgerald had extracted a promise from S. Smith that if the discussion were postponed the minister would proceed with the bill in two days; Fitzgerald and other Labor men, with no time to hold a caucus, and no precedents to appeal to, had to decide on the spot how much Smith's promise was worth. Four of them concluded it was worth something: Cook, Cotton, Fitzgerald and Kirkpatrick. Twenty-three judged otherwise. Barton's motion lost 41 to 47. Parkes obtained the adjournment of the House, and on 19 October he announced his ministry's resignation.[33]

The composition of the Labor men who voted on the adjournment of the debate on the coal mines regulation bill revealed the predicament of the Party. Cook was a coalminer who knew only too well that the industry needed to be modernised as the bill proposed; he was also a confirmed free trader, as was Cotton, who was attached to Parkes. Both Fitzgerald and Kirkpatrick were protectionists with no love for the premier. On the other hand, among those who voted against the adjournment and indirectly brought down the government were three coalminers, Fegan, a free trader, Edden and Scott, both protectionists, and Cann a metalliferous miner and protectionist; of the rest, ten were protectionists, nine free traders. Fiscalism was irrelevant to the issue.

Those who voted for the motion wanted to salvage the bill, those against it sought to assert their right to have the bill read a third time and sent to the Legislative Council. Despite the clear passage of the bill to an advanced stage, neither group of Labor men had any chance of saving it once McMillan had prevailed on Parkes to agree to have it recommitted. The whole excruciating episode was a stark example of how the old parliamentary system resisted change in order to protect vested interests by inertia. Even if the bill had passed the Assembly there is little doubt that it would have been emasculated by the Legislative Council. The Labor Party seemed to have become lost in an impenetrable labyrinth of reaction. The position of power the Party apparently occupied on the cross benches was subject to all the subterranean shocks of parliament.

Parkes's resignation was remarkable even for him and, in a sense, even for the parliamentary system. It was explicable only in terms of his senescence and his obstinate, instinctive determination to preserve the old order by attempting to loosen the controls the Labor Party was forging so painfully. The opposition had not been formally involved in the proceedings: there was no censure of the government: Dibbs, who was absent from the final division, had no inkling of the possibility of a serious outcome to a minor motion on a government bill moved at a late hour by an independent private member. The disruption had come at the first sign that the Labor Party had manifested that it could influence decisively the details of legislation, and hence that it was a serious threat to the hegemony of the liberals who had ruled as long in New South Wales and whose chief representative was Parkes. Already the Party had also shown by its improvements to legislation in committee and its consistent attendance in the House by which, almost alone at times, it maintained quorums that it had begun to bring general order into parliament, a process that also menaced the established routine.[34] The government had no qualms about jettisoning its legislation; but, of course, it had done little about it. The parliament, so far, had been similar to all its predecessors; all but one of sixty-one public bills brought down had made no progress. The Labor members had shown their resolve to get on with legislation by introducing seven bills, none of which had any success.

The remaining old order leader, Dibbs, was commissioned and on 23 October formed a government that included Barton as attorney-general. The new ministry had no appearance whatever of reforming zeal, and there was a wry irony in the fact that Dibbs and Barton were in the same cabinet. But portents of great change came from the free traders, who, deserted by Parkes, elected not McMillan, or Bruce Smith, or even Wise, but George Reid as their leader. Reid immediately showed that he was prepared to increase the tempo of his efforts to reform the system from within. His first speech as the alternative premier contained some telling and accurate gibes at the ministry, 'A few years ago,' he said, all of them 'sat side by side with me as ardent free-traders', and went on to note the failure of the real protectionists to get into the cabinet, 'the proselytes have crowded out all the apostles', and to observe that the absence of E. W. O'Sullivan from the ministry showed that the 'Orange flavour has a distinct commercial value'.[35]

Dibbs's statement of the ministry's intentions included electoral reform, a new approach to financial problems, an amendment to the Railways Act and the establishment of courts of arbitration and conciliation.[36] The Labor Party, shaken and somewhat let down, faced another gruelling experience, for the intensifying difficulties of raising revenue would be solved in only one way by this government, increased indirect taxation by means of the tariff. See, the new colonial treasurer, at once made it clear in his financial statement on 1 December, 'We find that the country . . . has got to the end of its tether—that the money-lender will not let us have any more money at present for the construction of public works—and it is for [the legislature] . . . to say whether they will allow an increased amount of duties to be raised'. His proposed method was to impose 15 per cent *ad valorem* duties on certain imports, 10 per cent *ad valorem* on others and certain extra specific imposts. These additional taxes, he said, would stimulate both manufacturing and agriculture as they brought in an additional £836,000 per annum over the current tariff, which was, of course, not a complete free trade one.[37] Two days later Reid gave notice of censure on the government on the grounds that it was ignoring the need for urgent legislation by raising the fiscal issue, when the right thing to do was to have it settled by the people on the basis of one man, one vote:[38] artfully worded to bring the maximum of pressure on the Labor Party.

Reid moved his censure motion on 8 December. The Labor Party held a caucus and decided to stake its hopes of maintaining unity on an amendment to the effect that the fiscal issue should be submitted to a one man, one vote plebescite.[39] McGowen was appointed to make the opening speech. When he rose in the house on 10 December, not only was he attempting the impossible task of getting the amendment through parliament, he was also trying to alleviate the frustration of his colleagues, and that was virtually impossible. He was the Party's spokesman in an exercise that was essentially the re-affirmation of the caucus system: the Labor men were trying to avoid the fiscal issue, but of greater significance was their decision to fall back on an original caucus agreement designed to preserve unity. McGowen made a valiant speech, and in the long run it was one of the chief parliamentary reasons for the survival of the Labor Party and for his ultimate accession to its leadership. He again surveyed the history of the Party, the advice from press and community to seek parliamentary solutions for Labor's problems; in parliament already they had found they had often to choose the lesser of two evils; they had decided to support Parkes to get legislation for Labor and the people. The Party, he said, had sunk the fiscal issue and he, himself, a fervent protectionist, had been elected to parliament 'not . . . as a protectionist . . . but as what is called a labour man'. He exposed the near-despair of the Labor members of the Legislative Assembly when he made a strong case against party government because he argued, it was impossible to get legislation without the government's agreement, and if the Labor Party censured one government it would have to censure another. He moved Labor's amendment, but it was declared out of order.[40]

McGowen had in fact laid bare the perplexing position of the Labor Party. There seemed virtually no way out for it. Whatever it did, it would face difficulties that were practically insurmountable. Its very existence as a cohesive force was antipathetic to the institution it was pledged to reform. The fate of the amendment was the last straw. In these circumstances there was little wonder that the Labor men gave way to pessimism; in the early hours of the morning speaker after speaker analysed his own despondency rather than the censure motion.[41] With the loss of McGowen's amendment, the original caucus decision to leave the fiscal issue alone should have prevailed; but it was by no means crystal-clear just what this meant in terms of voting for or against Reid's censure motion. The caucus pledge had no reference to the fate of a government and there was no time for another meeting to decide the issue. On balance, the probable correct course was to vote for the motion (as Dibbs had raised the fiscal issue), and that is how McGowen interpreted it. But the Labor men did not reflect dispassionately on it. They voted as their fiscal faith guided them; except McGowen. Reid's motion lost 63 to 71. The Labor split was 17 for the motion (against the government), all free traders, except McGowen, and 16 against it (for the government), all protectionists.[42]

However, despite the great confusion, the split was not so serious as it seemed. McGowen's behaviour stood out like a beacon of unity; the working of the pledge and the operation of caucus hardly covered the particular situation; and the voting revealed that Reid had already attracted a large following, and he was a determined reformer who promised direct taxation and meant it. Disarrayed as the Labor Party may have been, there were significant signs that, subject to some curative treatment, it would have a vital future in parliament. Indeed the details surrounding the split of 1891 suggested that at last the Labor Party might be able to breach the old parliamentary system.

7   *The Leagues Take a Hand*

The Labor leagues had always insisted on playing their part as an integral section of the Labor Party. They were not entangled in the machinery of parliament. Now they resumed their active participation in the Party's growth. In December 1891 and January 1892 meeting after meeting was held in both city and country, concerned mainly with the voting of individual members on Reid's censure motion, and so, to a degree, duplicating the parliamentary disorder;[1] as with the meetings called after the July decision of the Legislative Assembly members to support Parkes, the underlying theme of the December–January gatherings was the implicit right of the leagues to discuss Party behaviour and the need for unity among the Labor parliamentarians, although no single and clear opinion emerged as to the solution of the troubles. Indeed the immediate result seemed to be increased confusion, as single taxers, free traders, protectionists and, to a lesser degree, socialists contended in the leagues, but the long-run result was to confirm the powerful position of the LEL. The central committee remained active; early in December it decided to hold the first annual conference on 26 January 1892.[2] But the TLC's formal position in the whole structure of the league remained as it had been at the foundation. Large and complex constitutional problems had to be solved by the LEL before any purposeful attempt could be made to restore unity in the parliamentary Labor Party.

On 17 September 1891 the TLC had recognised eighteen Leagues, fifteen city, three country.[3] It was well behind the action then, and continued to slip further back. The Council's parliamentary committee was officially the core of the LEL's central executive committee, but the specialised industrial work of the Council gradually took it away from the centre of political control; concurrently the leagues' representatives increased and by December outnumbered the eleven members of the Council on the central committee. Though the TLC had founded the LEL, there was nothing the Council could do about the position of the parliamentary Labor Party, described in December by the *Sydney Morning Herald,* 'after such a renunciation on the part of nearly one half . . . of the fundamental obligations on which the party was based, it is not to be supposed that the party practically any longer exists'.[4] The Labor experience of July–December 1891 had made it manifest that the LEL could not function as a mere appendage of the TLC. The inefficiency of the system had been revealed in October when it was proposed that Labor men be appointed to the Legislative Council. The central committee asked the TLC to handle it. The TLC commissioned its executive to approach Dibbs on the matter, and, of course, he refused.[5] In November Houghton sought an authoritative interpretation from the TLC of the eight-hour plank; the Council referred it to its parliamentary committee, in effect to the central committee of the LEL.[6]

The anomalous form of control was emphasised when the central committee discovered that the *en bloc* representation of the TLC's parliamentary committee meant that it was possible for one of its members not to be a member of a Labor league. This realisation set the spark to the determination of the central committee to bring the issue of control to the test. The annual conference of the LEL loomed as the ultimate source of power in the political wing of Labor. The central committee considered the position of J. Keegan and resolved on 23 December that the TLC be advised that the committee thought that he should not be one of its members. The Council's discussion of the matter revealed that most of its delegates still believed that they governed the LEL and ought to remain in charge, though G. Herbert said that 'as the Council wished to force [Keegan] there, the League intended to force the other way'.[7] The connection of doctrine to the dispute was touched on by Brennan when he claimed that 'if [Keegan] had been a single taxer he would have been received with open arms', but Watson, cleverly weighing up the constitutional problem in relation to new demands for orderly and effective authority, argued that trade unionists should join the leagues, 'if those leagues are in the hands of cliques it was because protectionist laborers would not do their work'.[8] The TLC could no longer as an industrial body represent unionists in the LEL. The Labor movement had begun a new era; it remained based on unionism, but the political super-structure was developing an identity of its own.

The confusion was not dissipated by a pre-conference discussion on 18 January between the central committee and twenty-two members of the parliamentary Labor party, under the chairmanship of J. Wilson, president of the TLC and of the LEL. This meeting was planned to restore unity in order to facilitate the work of the forthcoming conference. The *Herald* reported that 'The proceedings were of a disorderly character . . . The meeting . . . commenced at 8 o'clock, [and] continued until 11.45 when it was abruptly closed, the Chairman finding it impossible to conduct business'.[9] This evidence of continuing discord gave point to an observation a little earlier by the *Herald* to the effect that the public interest would be served by the disintegration of a party that had openly set before itself a politically immoral object—the sacrifice of the general interests to the claims of one class, and that had openly proposed the attainment of that object by a politically immoral method—the offer of its solid vote to the highest bidder.[10]

But the disappointing result of the unity meeting and the obvious persistence of reactionary objections to the Labor Party would have stiffened the determination of conference delegates to strive for the restoration of harmony.

The first conference of the LEL met on 26/27 January with W. G. Higgs as chairman and twenty-one delegates from branches. The main task of the meeting was to settle the urgent problem of jurisdiction. In the debate the fundamental importance of the industrial wing was clearly appreciated, but the general tenor of the discussion emphasised the disproportionate number of delegates the TLC had on the central committee. Higgs summed up the majority opinion: 'They should show the Council that the League did not in any way wish to slight [it] by reducing the number of delegates, but was merely of opinion that the present representation . . . was too large'.[11] The decision taken was to reconstitute the central executive committee with one delegate from each league and three delegates from the TLC. A sub-committee of three was appointed to go to the Council to explain the reasons for the decision.[12] Associated with these resolutions were important decisions relative to the central committee: all its members had to be financial members of some branch of the LEL, and it was redefined as 'the executive body of the Labor Electoral League and shall be the tribunal to which all disputes and all matters affecting the general welfare of the League shall be submitted for decision'.[13] The conference also approved the admission to the League 'of adult residents of the colony who have subscribed to the platform and paid their subscription (4/- per annum)', and made it possible for women to join.

Naturally, the disputes in the parliamentary Labor Party were also scrutinised. Conference assumed the responsibility to discipline the dissident Assembly members by resolving that 'members who voted in the House against the caucus decision should be called upon to resign'.[14] Although no direct results flowed immediately from this decision, it not only stamped conference's claim to plenary powers but also reinforced the significance of caucus. The meeting also confirmed caucus decisions to leave the fiscal issue alone until it had been settled by a plebiscite and ruled that the parliamentary Labor Party should form a distinct group and not 'merge into any other party'.[15] The conference went even further in modifying Labor's constitutional forms to remedy the defects exposed in the first half year of parliamentary representation; it combined and adjusted the pre-selection and parliamentary pledges to read:

Members nominated for selection as candidates shall, before a ballot is taken, given a written pledge (a) that they will not contest the seat in the event of their not being selected by the branch, and (b) also a written pledge to uphold the 'platform' of the league if elected to the Parliament of the colony, and to vote on all questions as the majority of the Parliamentary Labor Party in caucus may decide or resign their seats. All candidates to give a written pledge to resign on being called up to do so by a two-thirds majority of the financial members of the league.[16]

In effect the conference had staked a comprehensive claim to be the sovereign body of the entire Labor Party, exercising its power at annual meetings, with the executive interpreting and applying the rules between times. The decisions made were logically related to the whole development of Labor's political plans since they had been originated by the TLC in 1889, as modified by the events of 1891. The composition of the 1892 conference was irrelevant to its assertions of authority, though, of course, it was called in question. The usual spectrum of union and radical opinion was reflected at the conference, single taxers and the rest, including an anarcho-socialist, W. R. Winspear, who was opposed to trade unions; but they were all members of Labor leagues, and the changes they made to the platform were chiefly trade union demands. However, both the TLC and the parliamentary Party felt the powerful blast of assumed power and much negotiation was needed to reconcile them to it. The TLC was the first to confront conference.

On 28 January J. R. Talbot drew Council's attention to the pretensions of the conference. 'Many of [its members]', he said, 'were non-unionists', and he protested 'against such a body dictating to Council'.[17] A special meeting was held on 2 February to which the conference delegation came, but were turned away. The meeting was adjourned one week when the final resolution was to repudiate the conference's alterations to the platform and demand 'that the composition of the Central Committee shall remain as heretofore'.[18] The TLC was not going to give up its offspring without a fight. Again the Labor turmoil became a topic for public debate; the variation in the arguments associated with the form of the extra-parliamentary control made no fundamental difference to colonial society: it was accepting the novel political institution even as it developed. Partisans for and against the TLC used vocal chords and pens energetically. The Glebe league, strongly protectionist, forced their conference delegate J. Skelton, a single taxer, to resign and told the TLC that 'at least eighteen branches of the LEL . . . were not represented at the late Conference'.[19] Higgs sensibly pointed out that the issue was not the removal of the TLC from the central committee but rather a reduction in its representation, and said 'it would be a calamity for all concerned if the [TLC] . . . discarded the Leagues'.[20] From the Auckland Trades and Labor Council came a letter hoping 'that the difficulties would be satisfactorily settled'; and, not for the first time, the TLC was reminded of its primary duty when the Sydney United Laborers' and the Plasterers' Union wrote to protest 'against the manner in which trade union matters were being ignored by the Council'.[21]

The clash between the conference, with the central committee taking over on its behalf, and the TLC was not the extra-parliamentary counterpart of the struggle within the parliamentary Labor Party. The parliamentary conflict turned on the issue of Party discipline and unity related to the form of the pledge, the operation of caucus and the principle of solidarity: it was complicated by purely parliamentary factors including the guile of Dibbs, the reforming zeal of Reid and the inexperience of the Labor members. The outside contention for control was the key to the survival of Labor as a force in Australian politics: and it was by far the more intricate issue. Its settlement would automatically help to bring the members of the Legislative Assembly into line. It required for solution the arrangement of rival claims for control of the political wing, and the general acceptance of constitutional changes made by conference.

The parliamentary Labor Party did not disintegrate. In a sense it marked time pending the rapprochement of the TLC and the central committee. But it was divided into two. The seventeen 'solids' were joined by H. Langwell, all free traders, except Langwell and McGowen, who was their nominal leader, with T. Bavister secretary. The ten 'democrats', all protectionists, were keeping Dibbs in office; they had no distinct leader, though Fitzgerald and Houghton, who was secretary, were prominent.[22] Following the intervention of W. Trenwith, a Victorian MP, in February, a working truce had been formulated, by which McGowen arranged conferences between the two groups whenever important Labor issues cropped up, according to Roydhouse and Taperell 'The Party are practically united on all but fiscal questions'.[23]

In 1892 the economic depression that had already affected Victoria began to influence events in New South Wales. In 1891 the TLC had run into trouble with a libel suit against the *Australian Workman* and had to pay £700 damages and costs; otherwise the Council may have weathered the economic storm. Unions began to disaffiliate. In his half-yearly report of 30 June 1892 secretary J. Riddell wrote of increasing unemployment and hardships of unions.[24] The deteriorating financial position turned Council's delegates' thoughts to the Australasian Labor Federation (ALF), drawn up at the Ballarat Trade Union Congress in April 1891, as a way out. The Federation scheme involved political action and the Council's attention to it led to the re-opening of negotiations with the LEL central executive committee; on 29 June Wilson, Watson (now vice-president) and F. Flowers for the Council and S. J. Law, S. C. Parker and J. Skelton for the committee agreed on the following:

1. That the TLC president be *ex officio* chairman of the central committee

2. That the central committee consist of the chairman, plus six representatives of the TLC, plus one delegate from each Labor league

3. That one trustee of the LEL be elected by the TLC and one by the central committee

4. That the TLC have the right to veto any proposed alteration of the Labor platform

5. That the recent additions to the platform be approved by the TLC as in the interests of the workers.[25]

The agreement acknowledged the status of the TLC without allowing it to dominate the League executive: part 4 became a dead letter as the Council weakened. The Labor leagues achieved recognition as independent partners in the political wing and with the continued decline of the TLC in 1893–4 the leagues gained almost complete political power: when the Sydney District Council of the ALF was formed in July 1894, the infirmity of the scheme in conjunction with the depression, left the representative union body the junior partner in the Labor political organisation, although the Australian Workers' Union (AWU) made a powerful effort to fill the vacuum and did achieve a position of strength in respect of country areas.

Watson had become vice-president of the TLC in January 1892. Since his work in 1890 on the Council's newspaper sub-committee he had added to his experience and repute as he took an energetic and, at times, leading role in many of the momentous and stirring events that occupied the Council. At the age of twenty-five he already had been an executive of the Typographical Association and was the secretary of the West Sydney Labor league. Unlike some of the other youthful delegates of the TLC he had allowed his interest in doctrine neither to cloud his political insight nor to dampen his charitable understanding of people. In a sense he was fortunate that he had not been a candidate at the 1891 general elections, so that he had been able to observe objectively the painful experiences of the Labor members of the Assembly and to partake actively in efforts to adjust the constitutional framework of the LEL. From 1892 Watson was so placed in the Labor movement that he could analyse its dynamic problems from all the relevant angles. He had the intelligence, experience and stimulus to make accurate judgments on future policy, and the determination, energy and influence to make a strong effort to enforce them. Like F. B. Dixon and P. J. Brennan, Watson was an impressive example of the men produced by the Labor movement, educationally and financially under-privileged, who were nevertheless able to make fundamental contributions to social and political improvement. The terms of the settlement between the LEL's central committee and the TLC reflected his thinking. In August he became president of the Council and chairman of the LEL.

The restoration of unity in the extra-parliamentary section of the

Labor Party confirmed the power of both the conference and executive as defined at the January gathering. No one was left in any doubt that the LEL was determined to maintain the parliamentary Party in the form that was being so clearly set out. Unlike Cameron in 1874 the Labor members now were acquiring outside support and advice that was becoming more and more knowledgable about politics. Elements of conflict of course remained: the members of the Legislative Assembly were varyingly conscious of their parliamentary role and its often uneasy relations with their class and Party affiliations, and some of them did not welcome the strengthening of outside help. But both parliamentary and extra-parliamentary sections of the LEL were fused into a dramatic, if somewhat ambiguous, unity by the 1892 Broken Hill strike. The circumstances surrounding the strike were a salutary reminder of the continuation of the conditions that had, in 1889, forced the TLC to re-examine the need for political action. The reaction of the whole Labor movement to the strike showed that it, too, had no intention of relinquishing the political Party it had established with so much agitation and effort.

The strike gave Watson the opportunity to display his great organising ability. From his main power base on the TLC he effected full co-operation between it and the LEL, and exerted pressure on the Labor members. At the Council on 4 August it was reported that Labor leagues at Orange, Newcastle, Nymagee, Ashfield and Paddington were holding 'open air meetings' to support the strikers.[26] In parliament on 7 September J. H. Cann, MLA for Sturt, which included Broken Hill, urged an equitable and early settlement of the struggle and was joined by thirteen other Labor members.[27] At the time Dibbs was on his way back from an overseas trip, in which he had submerged his republican views to accept a knighthood from Queen Victoria, and George Reid had already planned to censure the government for its extravagance and legislative inactivity. Reid naturally took account of the growing excitement over the strike, although in his formal motion he made no mention of it. On 6 September he had given notice of his motion of censure.[28] Next week Dibbs returned to parliament; two days later, 15 September, news was received that the strikers' leaders had been arrested. Immediately Cann tried to get information about it from Attorney-General Barton, but failed. Reid's pending motion came straight on in simple, but shrewd terms 'That the present administration does not possess the confidence of this House or the country'.[29]

The TLC met the same night, and approved a strong executive recommendation condemning the government's handling of the strike and agreeing that the executive should interview the Labor members with a view to urgent retaliatory action in parliament. At once Watson, on horseback, led a deputation to parliament to interview the Assembly members and later reported back that they had had 'a thoroughly [satisfactory] discussion [with] about thirty'.[30]

Debate on the censure motion went on throughout the rest of the month. Again the Labor Party was faced with a complex parliamentary situation, not nearly so simple as the outside Party members, including Watson, thought. The Assembly members were virtually unanimous in their opinion that the government should be punished for the events at Broken Hill, but many of them wanted to ensure that, if the ministry were defeated, the new one under Reid should adopt a more enlightened and impartial policy towards the strike. Fiscal faith once more obtruded subtly. On 15 September Cotton moved an amendment to the effect that the House also disapproved of payment of £1000 towards Dibbs's travelling expenses without parliamentary authority.[31] On 20 September Cann concluded a strong speech by moving a second amendment that sought disapproval of 'the way in which the Government have administered the law at Broken Hill'.[32] As the discussion moved to its climax, with the votes to be taken on 29 September, the TLC carried another executive recommendation, 'That the Labor Party would be false to Cause . . . if they do not use every endeavour to oust the present government, after the latter's action in regard to the Broken Hill strike'. The decision meant that the centre of the protectionist strength in the Labor movement, the TLC, was backing the free trade majority that had more or less consistently adhered to solidarity in parliament. This was a significant event in the final exorcism of the fiscal demon from the Labor Party and in the consolidation of Labor unity. Watson again led the Council's executive to Parliament House and interviewed Houghton, Bavister and some others; he told Council that they 'now had some consolation in knowing that the defections in the Labor Party would be comparatively few'.[33]

Cotton's minor amendment was put first, and lost 52 to 82, with fourteen Labor members voting for it, all free traders except Williams, and nineteen against it, all protectionists except Black and Davis. Newman and Murphy did not vote. Cann's amendment was put next; if carried, it would probably have involved the ministry's defeat with the clear implication that the new government should adopt a more impartial policy at Broken Hill. This question was a real test for both the Labor members and Reid. The vote was on a fundamental Labor issue, an MLA could hardly vote against it and thereafter claim to be a Labor man. And Reid by his vote would show whether he wanted office with a Labor resolution poised above his head. The amendment lost 37 to 99, with twenty-seven Labor men for it and seven against: E. M. Clark and Hindle, the only free traders among them, but eminently 'law and order' men, and Mackinnon, Morgan, Newton, Sheldon and Vaughn. Newman did not vote. Reid by his vote against Cann exposed the basic difference between a Labor reformer and a liberal reformer. The vote on Reid's censure motion, however, was the one that would directly settle the fate of the Dibbs government in the only way possible in the parliament as then constituted; and it was this division that Watson, the TLC and the LEL regarded as the crucial test of solidarity. The motion lost 64 to 68, with twenty-three Labor men for it, sixteen free traders and seven protectionists, and eleven against it: Fitzgerald, Gough, Johnston, Kelly, Mackinnon, Morgan, Newton, Scott, Sharp, Sheldon and Vaughn, all protectionists. Newman did not vote.[34] Again there was some cross voting as between 'supporters' of Dibbs and Reid, but, so far as the Labor movement was concerned, only three extra Labor votes would have defeated the government that they regarded as having persecuted strikers at Broken Hill.

Of the eleven Labor Assembly members who voted for Dibbs only Fitzgerald, Kelly, Johnston and Sharp were still seriously regarded as members of the Party. The rest had consistently voted with the protectionists, and, indeed, some of them had publicly renounced the LEL. But the four renegades were all prominent city union leaders, especially Fitzgerald, Kelly and Sharp, who had been outstanding TLC delegates, Kelly and Sharp ex-presidents. Fitzgerald, of course, was one of the favoured sons of the Labor movement. In view of the pressure brought through the TLC and LEL by Watson on the Labor members, it could be argued convincingly that the four men had broken solidarity, despite their having voted for Cann's condemnatory amendment. This is how the movement saw it, unionists, fiscalists, single taxers, socialists of all varieties and, as they united in reprobation of the four, they drove the concepts of caucus, pledge and solidarity deeper into Labor consciousness. On 6 October the TLC responded to the avalanche of disapproval by resolving that 'this Council views with contempt the inexecrable conduct of Messrs Fitzgerald, Kelly, Sharp and Johnson . . . in the late political crisis'.[35] The novel fate of expulsion from the Labor Party awaited them.

Apart from being the hapless cause of a great resurgence of unity in the Labor ranks, the four members had indirectly helped the Party in another way. Parliament was obviously a slippery place for innocents. It was clear that Reid meant business in the reforming task he had set himself; but he had now shown he was a liberal rather than a radical reformer, and he was increasing his following. If he had gained office through his own censure motion, helped by a Labor Party consisting approximately of sixteen free traders and eleven protectionists, he would have made the preservation of solidarity even harder than it was. Kelly and the others had given him pause, and fashioned conditions for additional re-thinking by Labor of the problems of parliamentary activity. Kelly put his case in a letter to the *Star,* and, while he side-stepped the issue of solidarity as seen by Watson, he had some wise comments to make:

The real issue at stake in the vote of censure was the arrest of the . . . strike leaders and on that I voted to condemn the government. [Cann's amendment was not carried] *because the Opposition had not the moral courage to support it* . . . I deny that the Broken Hill matter was included in Mr. Reid's vote of censure.[36]

Known affectionately as 'plug-hat' Kelly, he was now finding his way around Parliament as nimbly as he had stepped around cargo on Sydney's wharves.

The crisis over the Broken Hill strike did not formally re-unite the Labor Party, but it showed that the structure of the LEL was capable of exerting sufficient influence to keep alive the basic principles that marked the Party off from existing groups. And it showed that the agreement between the League and the TLC, which had made possible Watson's decisive work, had created conditions favourable for inter-locking collaboration between the parliamentary and extra-parliamentary wings of the Party.[37] Further steps in the restoration of unified action and in the reinforcement of the constitutional bases of the Party were taken at the second LEL conference held on 26–7 January 1893. Watson was chairman and exhibited the masterly control of Labor gatherings that was to be a notable feature of his future career. J. McDonald Matthews was secretary, he was also secretary of the central executive committee of the LEL. Twenty-two delegates were present, including six representatives of the TLC.[38] As a token of its restorative mission the conference left the 1892 platform intact and ratified the terms of settlement reached by the central committee and the TLC in June.[39] The single taxers failed in an attempt to direct the Party to concentrate on land taxation to the exclusion of income taxation. Conference defined 'the sinking of the fiscal issue' to mean 'that labour members elected to Parliament shall support any Government that will give labour measures, and shall vote as a solid party until the fiscal question shall be settled by the people by the referendum',[40] which meant that the Party could continue to support the Dibbs ministry so long as it seemed likely to promote Labor legislation.

In addition, the meeting confirmed and added to the 1892 decisions on the principles of a distinct party and caucus discipline by directing the parliamentary Party to 'elect a chairman to preside over their meetings, the same to be the leader in the House', and 'to expel any of their members . . . who, do not abide by the rule of the majority in Caucus'.[41] Thus the great power assumed by conference in 1892 was carried on, and not questioned. It may have been possible to query the status of the first conference, although no grounds to ignore its decisions existed after June 1892. But the 1893 conference could not be challenged on constitutional grounds: it was acceptable to both the LEL and the TLC. By putting its imprimatur on the general authority of conference it left

no valid grounds for dissent thereafter, either by ordinary league members
or by Labor members of the Legislative Assembly. The January 1893
conference was an important milestone in the developing constitutional
forms of the Labor Party.

By 1893 the Labor members of the Assembly could reflect on their
position in the light of some stirring experiences. There had been some
irony in Fitzgerald's address to the League's central committee on 12
September 1892. He had just returned from his second trip to England
during which he had met Dibbs. Fitzgerald had brought down an
amending bill to the Trade Union Act, 1881, but it had lapsed and he
said he planned to re-introduce it. He spoke of the 'bedrock' need to
obtain electoral reform and how the upsurge of fiscalism had affected
the Labor members' attempts to 'sink the question'. He considered

> the first and most difficult part of a Labor member's career was the fear of
> his losing touch with the working classes. He would feel very sorry to think
> that he had, since entering Parliament, altered in any manner, and his sole
> idea was to help to make better laws.[42]

Soon afterwards the *Liberal,* a radical newspaper despite its name,
described the Labor men as 'amateurs' out-matched by 'professionals';
Parkes had played and dropped them, Dibbs would do the same and
then Reid 'will take them up'; the people outside the Labor movement
who had supported them 'expected intelligence, directness, cohesion,
energy; they have got blundering vacillation, [and] fratricidal animosities'.
What did the Labor men do during the Broken Hill strike, the *Liberal*
asked and replied that they were

> dining with Ministers, dangling free passes . . . occupying lounges at Parlia-
> ment House or assuring congenial gatherings that [members of parliament] are
> representatives of the whole country and not of any particular section.[43]

This kind of exaggerated criticism was an essential ingredient in the
process by which the Labor members were guarded against total absorption by parliament. But they defended themselves: Black envied the
freedom of other members from outside criticism; Labor men, he said,
were subjected to 'closer scrutiny' than even ministers were, and they
needed 'the wisdom of Solomon, the patience of Job, and, if possible, the
hide of a hippopotamus'. 'One of Them' not only surveyed the occupations of the Labor members, he also lamented the barrage of blame
and abuse hurled at them and concluded, 'We have discovered that the
political trade cannot be learnt in a few days'.[44]

Despite all vicissitudes the Labor members were learning their trade.
The 1893 conference had accepted the inevitable when it, in effect,
approved support of the Dibbs government. To a degree this regularised
the position of the four renegades and the other protectionists, and the
Party functioned more or less cohesively although no leader was elected.[45]

It had become clear early in 1893 that only a general election under a reformed law, in which the extra-parliamentary wing would assert its renewed authority, would finally clarify the parliamentary Party's position. Meanwhile, there was some improvement in legislation: in the period from its taking office, 23 October 1891, to the end of the first session, 1 April 1892, the Dibbs ministry brought down eighteen public bills (excluding finance bills) of which eight became law. The government carried the Trades Disputes Conciliation and Arbitration Act (1892); it sponsored bills on electoral reform (1891) and inspection of land boilers (1892), but neither was returned by the Legislative Council. The tempo of legislation increased in the second session, 30 August 1892 to 13 June 1893, when the ministry introduced twenty-six public bills (excluding finance bills) and ten became law; but the Legislative Council kept back five bills, three of which covered legislation urgently demanded by Labor, on the regulation of coal mines (1893), boiler inspection (1892) and mining on private property (1893). Electoral reform was at last completed in a complicated measure, the Parliamentary Electorates and Elections Act (1893) after protracted negotiations with the Legislative Council. The Council also showed its teeth ominously by retaining Treasurer See's income tax and income tax assessment bills (1893). The Council's actions were a grim reminder to the Labor Party that success in the Lower House would not guarantee the passage of legislation. And there were some signs that the Government was deviously prepared to push certain legislation in the knowledge that the Upper House would reject it. Labor had no members in the Legislative Council.

The parliamentary committee of the TLC in 1893 operated independently of the central committee of the LEL, confirming still further Watson's powerful role, for he was chairman of all three extra-parliamentary Labor agencies. The parliamentary committee reviewed all relevant legislation irrespective of who was introducing it;[46] even Fitzgerald's trade union bill. But the primacy of the central committee in Party affairs was formally acknowledged in March when the TLC referred to it the action of Labor members Bavister, G. D. Clark, Danahey, Darnley, Fegan and Hindle in voting for a measure contrary to the government contract plank in the Labor platform.[47] In April the deepening economic crisis precipitated bank failures and weakened further the straitened position of the TLC. Cheques of affiliated unions for sustentation and other purposes were being returned to the Council. In May it was suggested that combined union action should be taken 'to restore the monies locked up in the various banking institutions at present undergoing reconstruction'.[48]

8   *The Labor Conference*
Enforces Parliamentary Unity

In the depressed economic circumstances of 1893, politics took a back seat, but the approach of the second anniversary of 'the advent of the Labor Party to Parliament' provided the immediate occasion that stimulated firm moves for a definite settlement of the parliamentary division. The central committee invited Watson to preside over a celebration on 23 June. As all members of the parliamentary Party were to be invited, the point was taken on the TLC as to the position of the 'four traitors'. Watson replied that the Council would not be compromised by their presence, and said that 'In his opinion it was for the Council to consider if it would be wise to forget old sores and endeavour to bring the Party together again'.[1] Concurrently, there were moves in country areas to consider the implementation of the ALF scheme, already under examination by the TLC. J. M. Toomey had been pondering the scheme in relation to the organising of the Labor vote in the country and the continuing lack of unity in the parliamentary Party. At the Young district Trades and Labor Council on 21 July he moved that the TLC and the LEL central committee be approached to consider appointing organisers for 'all shearing sheds, mining districts and townships', and that, if they did not comply, the Young council would 'take immediate steps to organize a country political Labor League'.[2]

Toomey's proposal raised the vital issue of the relationship of city and country in the Labor Party. Alert and indefatigable, he was aware of the strength of the Labor vote in the country and of the fact that the control of the Party was in the city. Toomey was clear-sighted enough to see that Labor unity was essential for optimum progress, but he also knew that forceful methods were needed to achieve it. He carefully worked out modifications to the ALF scheme, and on 3 August sent to the TLC a comprehensive blueprint for the organising of each electorate in the colony. In reply the Council intimated that it no longer had the authority or the funds to sponsor such a scheme; but the hand of Watson was discernible in its expression of hope that the central committee of the LEL would co-operate with Toomey. The central committee did do that, and invited the Council's parliamentary committee to a 'conference of bush unions and Labor leagues' to be held in the Trades Hall on 16

August 'to get the co-operation of all workers to form one solid Labor vote at the next General Election'.[3] Watson chaired the conference, and Toomey's great contribution to it was acknowledged. Twenty-two delegates attended, including Langwell for the Bourke league, G. S. Beeby for Hillgrove league, and Higgs for South Sydney league. The country delegates stressed the advantages of the ALF scheme in enabling bush unions to resuscitate country leagues; Toomey returned to his strong demands for 'competent [Labor] lecturers' to work in the country; a letter from W. A. Holman advocated a conference of 'all reform societies'; J. Skelton, on behalf of Beeby, sought a 'conference representative of all Labor leagues, trade unions and democratic political organisations'. The union leaders present, including Watson and Head were wary of 'democratic political organisations', and eventually Toomey's amendment to exclude them was accepted. The conference was fixed for 9 November, with the central committee to make all arrangements on the basis of leagues and unions with up to 100 members to have one delegate, 100–500 members two delegates, 500–1000 members three, and over 1000 members four.[4]

Urgency was given to these moves by the deepening economic depression that indicated that the Dibbs government might have great difficulty in winning the next general election, which would be fought on a one man one vote franchise and single-member electorates. Unemployment was increasing. The need for a radically different approach to fundamental administrative problems had intensified, well illustrated by a deputation with 'an influential character' that interviewed Dibbs in April and recommended the building of railways on the co-operative principle. Watson and Brennan, as well as J. Creed, MLC, B. Backhouse and Canon Moreton, were on it.[5] A letter from E. D. Millen pointed to the pressure for the state to consider whether it should 'interpose to do that which it is necessary should be done, but which private enterprise is not doing'.[6] Dibbs and his ministers had neither the vision nor the energy to respond to the critical situation.

The central commmittee of the LEL was also in touch with the parliamentary Labor Party, which met on 10 October and agreed 'on the basis on which [they were] likely to become a strongly united party, [which] would contain over 22 members'. They at last responded to conference's direction that they appoint a leader and J. Cook was nominated by Black and L. T. Hollis. Next week 'at a largely attended meeting' Cook was elected unopposed.[7] He had been a useful but undistinguished MLA; his appointment over McGowen reflected the free trade majority of the 25–7 members who were still regarded as belonging to the Party. Both parliamentary and extra-parliamentary sections were now prepared for the great unity gathering, which was to meet on 9–10 November in the Seamen's Hall at Millers Point.

The central committee had interpreted its instructions liberally and
had arranged the representation of 'every organisation in any way
concerned in protecting the interests of Labor'.[8] About 200 delegates
were present, of whom, according to Black, sixty-nine were from trade
unions;[9] many more would have been unionists, including, of course,
Watson and the four TLC delegates.[10] Black also stated that the forty-
eight Labor league members of the central committee were delegates;
with the six members of the TLC parliamentary committee and Watson,
this would have given the central committee fifty-five votes, plus any
proxies held. The *Herald* detected four 'distinct parties' among the
delegates: Labor leaguers, trade unionists, single taxers and socialists,
with the unionists in the majority.[11] There would have been many
individuals who could have been classified in more than one of the
'parties'. Nine members of the Legislative Assembly were there: Cook,
Cotton, Rae, Langwell, Danahey, Edden, G. D. Clark, Bavister and
W. F. Schey, who was a member of the Redfern league as well as a
supporter of the Dibbs protectionist party, and represented the Wagga
Wagga shearers. The conference was by far the most representative of
the conferences held to that time; it was eminently fitted to speak
authoritatively on behalf of the whole Labor movement.

William Arthur Holman (1871–1934) was at the conference as the
delegate of the Leichhardt league on the central committee. A cabinet-
maker, his background had been typical of many of the young non-union
leader radicals; he had been a member of the Single Tax League and in
1893 he was still a member of the Socialist League; only his remarkable
intellectual gifts and superb elocution distinguished him from many
other members of radical associations. He was not in the centre of Labor
development, but he was a promising young Labor man, and his debating
prowess had obtained for him the task of presenting central committee
motions at the conference. He was to learn much about the Labor Party
from the experience. At this stage Holman's position in the Party was
not to be compared to that of Watson, who was chairman of the
conference.[12]

By November 1893 the time had arrived to regroup the Labor Party
and formally incorporate in the procedures of the parliamentary Party
the results of the hard lessons learnt in the conflicts of 1891 and 1892,
lessons that had conditioned substantial development in the constitution
and rules of the extra-parliamentary, governing section of the Party. The
moment of truth for the Labor Assembly members had arrived. Consequently the most important and spectacular part of the conference was
on the parliamentary pledge, though the work of the meeting was by no
means confined to it. Much of the undue significance attached to conference's deliberations on the subject arose out of the comparative failure
of all the old order parliamentarians, many of the Labor members of the

Assembly and nearly all contemporary political observers to judge correctly what had been done by the two LEL conferences already held, and their inattention to the way in which Watson had utilised the power that had accrued to him. Even after the first 1893 conference the *Bulletin* saw the Labor Party as 'practically broken asunder',[13] and this was also the opinion of the *Herald*. The ominous nature of the development of the parliamentary pledge had been overlooked, even by most of the Labor members, whereas it had actually been strenthened as part of the general constitutional consolidation.

The central committee had redrafted the pledge before the conference in a way that was acceptable to Watson. He had submitted it to the TLC and intimated that he thought the Councils' conference delegates should vote for it. Despite their president's suggestion, and the decision would not have surprised him, Council resolved 'That the matter . . . be left in the hands of the delegates'.[14] At the conference Holman moved the central committee's pledge:

(a) a Parliamentary Labour Party to be of any weight must give a solid vote in the House upon any question as it arises, and
(b) . . . accordingly every candidate who runs in the Labour interests should be required to pledge himself not only to the fighting platform and the labour platform, but also to vote on every occasion as the majority of the Parliamentary Labour Party may in caucus decide.[15]

The motion was not carried in this form. The vital significance of the concept of the pledge for an effective parliamentary party was apparent to most delegates; and there was a strong rank and file conviction, arising from the frustrations associated with failure of the Party to get 'democratic legislation' passed, that the reforming drive of Labor against 'monopoly' should be stressed. It was also considered that the proposed pledge was too general and did not cover parliamentary situations in which the fate of the government was in the balance. A long and lively debate ensued, finally ended by the closure amid great excitement.[16] The amended form of the pledge was then put as the motion and was carried in the following form:

(a) A Parliamentary Labour Party, to be of any weight, must give a solid vote in the House upon all questions affecting the Labour Platform, the fate of the Ministry, or calculated to establish a monopoly, or to confer further privilege on the already privileged classes, as they arise; and
(b) that accordingly every candidate who runs in the Labour interest should be required to pledge himself, not only to the Fighting Platform and the Labour Platform, but also to vote on every occasion specified in Clause (a) as the majority of the Parliamentary Labour Party may in caucus decide.[17]

The *Daily Telegraph* reported that the impracticability of the pledge was stressed,[18] probably by Cook and Edden, the only members of the Legislative Assembly to speak.

The central committee in its examination of Toomey's electoral organising proposals and in its own attention to the general election due in 1894, had planned to abstract from the general Labor platform a 'fighting platform' to be emphasised in electioneering. Holman submitted six motions to this effect and soon discovered that the committee's recommendations were subject to detailed review.[19] After considerable debate and amendment to his motions, the fighting platform became:

1. Land value taxation; cessation of alienation of crown lands; tenant right to crown leases
2. Mining on private property; no royalties to private owners, or compensation, except for damage
3. (a) Abolition of the Upper House
    (b) Introduction of the referendum
4. Local government on a democratic basis
5. Eight hours
6. Establishment of a national bank.[20]

The order of the planks reflected the clarity of the recognition of the importance of the country vote to the Labor Party.

Holman also put the executive's views on the need to obtain controlled conformity on the fiscal issue, and precipitated a fiery argument that lasted from 11 a.m. to 4 p.m. on 11 November, in which about fifty delegates spoke, including seven Assembly members, who opposed any direction to the parliamentary Party. The majority of delegates accurately diagnosed rampant fiscalism as a main cause of the vacillations of the parliamentarians and saw that its cure was essential for an improved Party. Of course the Assembly members did not agree with this opinion; the executive was prepared for what it considered a reasonable compromise, but the majority prevailed against the defeatist view that it was 'useless for neutral candidates to contest a general election'. The following amended motion was passed after a division:

> That, in the opinion of this conference, there can be no objection to any candidate who runs in the labour interest declaring to the caucus his personal convictions on the fiscal or any other question; but that no candidate who gives any pledge to the electors to vote on these questions in any way except according to the Parliamentary Labour Party in caucus should be recognised as a labour member.[21]

This was an unequivocal direction to the Labor members. The amendment substituted the word 'to the caucus' for Holman's 'where he deems it advisable', and forced fiscal adherents to divulge their faith only to their fellow members if they wanted to remain in the Labor Party. The conference was determined to protect them from the wiles of the 'old stagers' in parliament, and to ensure that the day of dual endorsements of candidates was over.

Finally the conference crowned their far-sighted use of sovereign power by expelling Fitzgerald, Kelly, Johnston and Sharp. The procedure and emotional language used symbolised the bedrock stress on unity that had permeated the whole proceedings. This was the first occasion in which a New South Wales political group had excommunicated a member. Indeed, no other group would have thought of doing it, and if they had, would have had no machinery to effect it. The initial move at the conference was conciliatory; R. Hollis sought 'the healing of the unhappy breach'. But 'a lengthy and heated discussion' broke out, in which the four men were labelled as traitors. An amended motion was carried by a large majority: 'that these deserters should be treated with undying hostility'.[22] According to Black this amendment was proposed by T. Dodd and W. J. Ferguson, and he states that Holman was 'an apostle of the vendetta'. Black correctly states that it was an amended motion that was accepted and gives its form as 'That they be regarded as traitors to the sacred cause they were elected to support, and treated with undying hostility'.[23] The expulsions had no reference to the protectionists who had kept Dibbs in office, but only to the four members whom the Labor movement had isolated as a result of their vote for Dibbs at the time of the Broken Hill strike in October 1892.[24] The actual decision was not so important as the principle of power involved. Fitzgerald and Kelly were subsequently re-admitted to the Party. But now the authority of conference was trumpeted loud and clear and in a way that most Labor members of the Legislative Assembly found obnoxious.

At the conclusion of the conference the essential base for the survival of the Labor Party was in sight: the final grafting on to it, with necessary modifications, of the form and substance of the Labor movement. Ultimate success awaited the decision of the people at a general election. The TLC had failed to control the Party. The Council's creation, the LEL, and specifically the League executive, took over with perfect legitimacy. For a time there was a danger that the executive would be swamped by diverse radical groups, chiefly single taxers and socialists, who had been invited into the Party, but who had to be kept in their place, fixed by their minority status, however useful their ideas. In the event, the TLC retained a powerful place on the LEL executive, consolidated by Watson, whose insight led him to encourage unionists to join the leagues, and to appreciate the vital importance of the country in the development of the Labor Party. Toomey, with whom Watson had formed a close friendship, helped him to comprehend that a Party confined to the city had no future at a time when survival for the TLC was becoming increasingly difficult and demands were being made for the implementation of the ALF scheme. And the way in which the November meeting had worked over the executive's proposals, together with its spontaneous expulsion of Fitzgerald, Kelly, Johnston and Sharp, showed unmistakably that final control rested with the rank and file exercised through the conference.

The Labor members of the Legislative Assembly were appalled at the exercise of power. In their reaction the great majority of them showed that they really had been swallowed by parliament, even as Angus Cameron. But, unlike Cameron, most of the Labor men of 1891 had made claims to be different from the old order parliamentarians, and had invoked the machinery of pledge and caucus, which, as restated by conference, they were now to condemn. The press attacked conference decisions, and the Labor members followed suit. The *Herald* immediately made a skilful, if conservative, analysis of the conference results; after contrasting the workers' stress on solidarity with the 'disintegration' apparent in the other parties, the newspaper congratulated Labor on making 'early preparations' for the next elections; it then reiterated the contemporary confusion over existing political 'parties' and revealed how the Labor party was revolutionising the very concept,

> The conference represents more than a political party inasmuch as it comprises men of different political opinions and belonging to various parties. It is something less than a political party inasmuch as such a party may be made up of members of all classes in the community, whilst the conference is professedly representative of but one.

Next, the *Herald* condemned the pledge as unnatural and immoral, and, in its summing up, attempted to separate the Labor members of the Assembly from the extra-parliamentary section of the Party: 'the course marked out is directly opposed to the principles of sound Parliamentary government, and could not be followed successfully without rendering the system corrupt and unworthy of trust'.[25]

The Labor members of the Legislative Assembly, with the probable exception of McGowen, Davis and Kirkpatrick, were united, if somewhat loosely, against conference.[26] Their general arguments were linked to the allegation that the reason for conference decisions was the plan of prominent members of the executive to get a seat in parliament in the confusion. G. D. Clark said so, and went on to assert that the new Labor system meant that a man would have to 'hand over to a caucus vote his religious convictions, his temperance principles, and his freedom of action on moral questions'.[27] Black had been understandably impressed by the great difficulties of obtaining quick action in parliament and he advised members of Labor leagues, 'admit that [Assembly members] may know a little more of what is possible in Parliament than you can, and do not trammel them with impracticable regulations'.[28] G. S. Beeby, Watson's deputy on the LEL executive, answered him,

> [Black] has entered on a crusade against the central committee . . . [who], in earnestly trying to carry out the wishes of the November conference, came into conflict with the consciences of certain [members of parliament] . . .

[and] have suddenly become the objects of childish and irrational abuse. The charge [of parliamentary ambitions] is easily dismissed. Out of an [executive] of over *sixty* men not more than *six* have been selected by leagues as candidates.[29]

Among the leagues, opinion very soon began to favour conference. This result was inevitable in view of the fact that each league was represented on the executive, which had not been rebuffed by conference, although it had failed to control it. Holman put the point of view that was already beginning to prevail in November, when he spoke at the Leichhardt league,

If any man would not bind himself conscientiously to solidarity in the way demanded, he would not be accepted as one of the labour party. If he thought free trade or temperance of superior importance . . . he must run as a temperance or free trade candidate.[30]

Two days after the conference had concluded, twenty-six country delegates had met, with Toomey as chairman, and agreed to recommend that all country leagues and unions co-operate with Toomey's Young district council of the ALF 'in completing the electoral organisation of all the country districts'.[31] Some results of this resolution were made known on 20 December by T. H. Hall, ex-secretary of the Bourke branch of the General Laborers' Union, when he told the TLC that conference decisions were generally accepted; but he made one important exception, 'the eight hours clause would do the country a lot of injury and act as a mill-stone around the necks of farmers if brought into operation'; nevertheless he concluded that 'no doubt in the course of time [country and city unions] would understand one another'.[32] Hall's presence at the TLC exemplified the basic unity of country and city workers, but it was not easy to combine them in one Labor political organisation. The Shearers and General Laborers' Unions conferences in 1892 had agreed to adopt the ALF scheme and in late 1893 and early 1894 branches were being formed in the country.[33] The Coonamble Labor league in February 1894 decided not to affiliate with the LEL, though it adopted a form of pledge in line with the resolutions of the November 1893 conference.[34] But again Toomey pointed the way to complete unity between city and country with a strong manifesto from Young, 'Working in conjunction with the Central Executive in Sydney'.[35]

The immediate problem, however, had to be solved in the city: the parliamentary Labor Party had to agree to accept the rulings of the November conference. The Assembly members argued that it was irregular;[36] and indeed it was an extraordinary conference, though constitutional. In the interests of unity the LEL executive stretched its patience to the limit, conceded the point that a normal conference was one comprising a single representative of each league and agreed to call one on that basis.[37] Against the background of the continuing economic depression and an imminent general election, the 1894 conference was held from 10 to 15 March in the Temperance Hall; it had seventy-four delegates, including seven from the TLC. Watson as chairman put the main issue clearly before the delegates: in view of the approaching elections should concessions be made to the Assembly members?[38] G. Downes, of the Goulburn league, moved that the pledge become simply, 'That the Parliamentary Labor Party to be of any weight, must give a solid vote in the House upon all questions affecting the Labor platform'. A welter of ten amendments followed and finally the amendment of J. Grant, Annandale league, was put as the motion, 'That the decision of the November Conference be adhered to', and was carried 47 to 25. A sub-committee of three, including Holman, was appointed to re-draft the pledge and it was accepted, 46 to 15, as follows:

> I, the undersigned candidate for selection by the .... branch of the Labour Electoral Leagues, hereby solemnly give my pledge that if not selected as a candidate for Parliament, I will not in any way oppose the candidature of the duly selected nominee of this or any other branch. And I also solemnly give my pledge that if selected by the branch I will, if elected to Parliament, vote upon all questions affecting the labour platform, the fate of a Ministry, the establishment of a monopoly, or the conferring of further privileges upon the already privileged classes, as the majority of the labour party may in caucus decide. I give this pledge upon the understanding that upon all minor questions I shall be left unbound.[39]

William Morris Hughes (1862–1952) had recently gained some experience in the country as one of the organisers appointed as a result of Toomey's efforts. He was active at the conference and had a motion carried that strengthened and extended the functions of the executive which was now,

> (a) to be the judge of the constitution and to interpret the rules,
> (b) to be satisfied of genuine publicity of initiatory meetings of branches, and
> (c) to have the power to declare a selection [of a candidate] void if the constitution is infringed, and to repudiate any league or branch not working in conformity with the platform and pledge where deemed advisable.[40]

Watson vacated the chair to ensure that the TLC remained represented on the executive '[to] guarantee [to] the unionists . . . that the leagues were being conducted in the interests of Labour';[41] the composition of the executive remained at one delegate from each league, six from the TLC plus 'one delegate for every ten [members] of the Parliamentary Party'.[42]

Hughes argued strongly that 'where practicable' be added to the eight-hour plank. 'The whole agricultural vote', he said, '. . . would be absolutely lost if the plank were retained as at present'. Watson again intervened to support the motion and helped to have it carried 50 to 20.[43] Country Labor people were being reassured that there was room for them in the Labor Party. Conference reflected the purposeful and invigorating growth of Labor political interest, sharpened by almost three years of hectic debate, by deciding to draw up a municipal platform and to run candidates for municipal elections;[44] and also amended the LEL objects to read

(a) To secure for the wealth producers of the colony such legislation as will enable them to retain in their own hands the full produce of their labour,
(b) to bring under one common banner all those electors who are in favour of such legislation, and to organize for concerted and effective action at all Parliamentary and Municipal elections,
(c) to secure the return of candidates pledged to the platform of the league.[45]

At last the decks were cleared for the final contest to determine if the new type of political organisation would endure. True, the country problem remained; but Watson's insight, Toomey's initiative and the general approval given in rural areas to conference decisions, suggested that a solution would be found once the executive could give full attention to the matter. The urgent objective still was to get the Labor members of the Legislative Assembly to conform or leave the Party in order to present official solidarity candidates at the general election, so that the electors might give the ultimate seal of approval or disapproval. The fate of party government in Australia was in the balance. Since 1891 the Labor Party had given notice that it was a 'distinct party', with a form and methods all of its own. The old parliamentary parties and most colonial observers, certainly all of the major city newspapers, had noticed the changes with some trepidation, much lessened, however, by the hope that the Labor Party would disintegrate and be digested by the old parliamentary system. Events in the House, manipulated often by Parkes, Dibbs and Reid, had indicated that the conservatives had probably correctly appraised the situation. Left to themselves the Labor members would almost certainly have disappeared in one parliament. But the parliamentary Labor Party was only a section of the Labor Party, and it was for the whole organisation that the people were about to be asked to vote. The extra-parliamentary section had resoundingly declared that the problems of the parliamentary section should not condition the growth of the whole Party.

The parliamentarians made a last-ditch stand on the pledge. Only McGowen, Davis and Kirkpatrick agreed with conference edicts. The rest gradually fell back on the argument that they would sign a pledge, but only one drawn up by themselves, which would have meant a plurality of pledges, and the end of the Labor Party. The *Herald* chimed in, as usual, 'Doubtless we need a reformed Parliament . . . [But] the presence of such [Labor] bondsmen in an Assembly . . . would be an illustration of the depths to which we had sunk below the ideals of past days'.[46] The Assembly members rejected the seats on the executive that

1 Beginnings of Bossism in NSW.
   Labour: 'Look here; if you start our candidate hampered by that rig, what show'll he have?'
   Labour Electoral-League Boss: 'Look here; who's bossing this show? That's the question.'   *The Bulletin*, 28 April 1894

conference had provided for them.[47] They held numerous disjointed meetings, variously attended, in March and April, rummaging for a way out. On 18 April Cook issued a manifesto on behalf of himself and eighteen others that showed how deeply they had been affected by the parliamentary environment: they spoke of the impossibility of mechanical rules achieving solidarity in a party: of how the pledge 'utterly destroys the representative character of the members'; and of their determination to have the issue submitted to the people to decide between themselves and 'the unrepresentative, proxy-packed, and largely self-selected conference'.[48] They still interpreted the ground swell of rank and file disapproval in terms of the ambitions of members of the LEL executive. The *Herald* gave them unqualified support: 'the split [has ceased] to be merely a matter of party discipline', it had taken on a grave constitutional complexion.[49]

The Labor leagues were prepared to analyse the conflict in any terms. A tumultuous meeting in the Domain on 22 April condemned the Assembly members and was animated by Hughes, who spoke of the propaganda vacuum they had left to be filled by himself and others, and ended in a fine farrago:

> They had picked these men up, breathed the breath of political life into their carcasses, and brought them into being. (Hear, Hear). They could as easily prick the bubble and these men would collapse into nothingness. (Cheers).[50]

But Watson carefully sifted the members' manifesto and demolished it point by point. In a long interview with a *Herald* reporter, his unrivalled experience and perception enabled him to draw an accurate picture of the external features and to explain the basic texture of the new Party. After two years at the centre of the action, pondering, directing, marshalling, regrouping, he not only comprehended the nature of the Labor Party, he also understood what it had to do to reform the New South Wales parliament. He surveyed the long and fruitless negotiations with the members of the Legislative Assembly, exposed their insincerity over the pledge, and stressed that unity was impossible in their terms. Despite the possibility of loss of seats, 'The workers outside', he said 'are determined that if they are to have another party it shall be at least a united and therefore effective one'. On the broad constitutional question, he made no bones about it, 'The League . . . insists that members shall be elected primarily as labour representatives . . . [because it was] formed for the purpose of carrying into effect certain well-defined reforms'. He stressed that the Labor executive was merely carrying out rank and file instructions and that it felt no ill-will towards the Assembly members.[51]

Watson had made it clear that, as well as seeking seats in parliament, the Labor Party was asking voters to make up their minds on the nature of a member of parliament: could he represent, partially or completely, a movement that was close to being a class, or must he be entirely a representative directly of his constituents and indirectly of all voters?[52]

As the Labor Party strove to find itself, the TLC prepared to go into hibernation. Affiliations and income had so fallen by April 1894 that the Council turned firmly to the ALF scheme as a means of escape. At a conference in February between the Shearers' Union and the General Laborers' Union, which led to the formation of the Australian Workers' Union (AWU), the TLC had been urged to form itself into the Sydney District Council of the ALF.[53] In April the Council organised a trade

2 *The Bulletin's* Straight Tip to the NSW Democratic Party.
The Bulletin, 9 June 1894

union conference to discuss the matter. Displaying his unfailing stamina and politeness Watson was in the chair. The negotiations went on until 28 June when the TLC voted its own dissolution and the Sydney District Council of the ALF emerged.[54] In the meantime the Council, with Brennan prominent, tried to maintain its influence in Labor Party affairs. On 26 April Brennan was appointed with two others to try to heal the breach between the Party executive and the Assembly members. The deputation soon became very busy, gravitating from the parliamentary Party to the executive, and back again, the while submitting progress reports to the TLC. There is no doubt that Watson guided the whole proceedings to the correct constitutional decision.

The Council's mediators drew up yet another pledge, known as the TLC pledge.[55] The members of the Legislative Assembly, grasping at straws, showed some interest in it. Brennan soon discovered that most of the members really wanted to be independent Labor members.[56] Watson was well aware by now that there was no chance of reconciliation with the parliamentarians as a group, but he was determined that the TLC should see it clearly, so that the dissentient Assembly members should be completely isolated from the Labor movement. At a LEL executive meeting on 16 May he influenced discussion to ensure that the TLC pledge would be submitted to the Labor leagues provided the parliamentarians 'give a written assurance [that] they accept [it]', and he was able to tell the TLC that this showed the good intentions of the executive.[57] Brennan persisted. On 23 May he brought a new pledge from Cook to the executive, but after another review of constitutional requirements it decided to take no further action.[58] Brennan pushed the TLC on to circularise twenty-seven Assembly members. Up to 7 June thirteen replies were received: only Black and Houghton agreed to sign the Council's pledge. Of the rest, Cook, Cotton, Darnley, Gardiner, Hindle and Nicholson agreed to sign Cook's pledge; Sharp refused to sign any pledge; Kelly said he had told his electors 'what he was prepared to do'; Fitzgerald acknowledged the letter; G. D. Clark thought any pledge unnecessary; Hollis, 'thought the country was being caucussed to death and therefore refused to sign'; Cook went further and said he 'regarded the Council's action as discreditable to the last degree'.[59]

Cook's words were a gratuitous insult to the well-meaning, if cumbersome and tedious efforts of the Council. But they helped Watson to close the affair with full honours to the solidarities. At the TLC on 7 June, Brennan proposed that the Labor leagues of Black and Houghton be told that they had Council's backing. Watson left the chair to get the motion defeated, and Council decided that the LEL executive be asked to look on Black, Houghton and Schey as 'genuine labor men . . . [and] friends who should not be opposed'.[60] With Council's feelings intact, Watson was able to administer the *coup de grâce* on the executive. At the TLC on 14 June the executive's last word on the matter was read, expressing 'every respect for the Council [but] fraternally urg[ing]' it to withdraw its support from Black, Houghton and Schey. After a rearguard action by Brennan, Council resolved 'to take no further action in the matter'.[61]

The great contention had ceased. The final note was that debate about the form of the pledge had to be subordinated to the constitutional requirement that conference had drawn it up and only conference could amend it; an appropriate ending to a prolonged probing of large issues concerned explicitly with the structure of the Labor Party, and implicitly with the nature of New South Wales politics, at a time when national Federation had developed as a topic for serious public discussion. It was patent now that the Labor Party had the task of making the major contribution to the reformation of politics so that a rational decision could be taken by the colony on Federation. More immediately, the separate identity of the Labor movement, so carefully defined and nurtured by the TLC, had been at last transferred to the Labor Party. The process had required extraordinary perception and dedication by many members of the Labor leagues in the face of obstacles that, on occasions, seemed to be insurmountable; it involved the re-structuring of the control of direct political action by Labor, at once delicate and massive, far removed in complexity from the Cameron experiment in 1874–5. In 1894 Labor Party control rested with its rank and file, all of whom supported the one comprehensively progressive platform, but all of whom were not necessarily trade unionists. The Labor Party, based on trade unionism, was not co-extensive with it; inevitably so, given the natural ambivalence felt by unions towards politics. In parliament Labor members could play their role only with extreme difficulty; indeed events had shown that reform solely from within, on the scale sought by Labor, was virtually impossible; Labor parliamentarians needed direct help from outside, a situation that underlined the basic adherence of all members of the Labor movement to colonial democracy: they soon organised the necessary assistance. It was appropriate that the final solution of the last phase of the Labor Party's intricate preliminary problems should have emerged from a confrontation between Brennan and Watson. Brennan, who had overcome many obstructions to initiate the action that had ended with the foundation of the new Party, retained an affection for it and an instinctive urge to maintain it in the form he thought best; but events had passed him by. Watson responded sensitively to the changed situation; with complete understanding of the significance of trade unions and with great forbearance he revealed to an uncomprehending Brennan that the political aims of Labor could only be obtained with the help of all sympathetic men and women; a 'Labor man' now was not simply one defined and backed by the TLC. Black, Houghton and Schey needed the seal of conference stamped by the Labor Party executive; to get it, more was needed than past services to the TLC. Watson, more than any other individual, had helped to mould the necessary conditions for the survival of the Labor Party; but he would have been the first to acknowledge the indispensable help in parliament of McGowen and the mass help of members of Labor leagues.

9   *Labor in Partnership*
with George Reid

There had been a short session of parliament, the third, from 26 September to 8 December 1893 in which the Dibbs ministry brought down fifteen public bills (excluding finance bills) three of which became law, including some important amendments to the Parliamentary Electorates and Elections Act; five bills were retained by the Legislative Council, again including coal mines regulation and mining on private property. Against a background of a familiar type of parliamentary scandal, involving Dibbs's two legal ministers, Barton and R. E. O'Connor, and in the face of mounting criticism of delays in having the new electoral rolls prepared,[1] the government arranged a fourth session, 17 January to 11 June 1894, in which they showed somewhat increased legislative activity by introducing thirty-one of the sixty-nine public bills brought down; sixteen government bills passed (excluding financial bills). But the Legislative Council was unrelenting so far as important Labor legislation was concerned; for the third time it stalled on legislation for both the regulation of coal mines and the inspection of land boilers. On the other hand, the Council at last agreed to a diluted mining on private property bill. At the dissolution of parliament on 25 June the only explicit achievements of the Labor Party appeared to have been electoral reform and some improvements to the law on gold mining; the Conciliation and Arbitration Act (1892) had proved a failure because of lack of compulsory provisions. But the new electoral law was basic to general reform, and the Party had been united on it. Of course other groups had also perceived that it was necessary, but the Labor Party from its beginnings had supplied the unremitting pressure, the purposeful drive, and finally the parliamentary influence that had made reform possible. Now the 1894 general elections would be held on one day, with single electorates returning 125 members on a single vote franchise.

Labor had had a subtle and powerful effect on parliament. Despite all its ups and downs the Party had been a field of force conditioning a new appreciation by all parliamentarians of their role. It had changed their attitudes towards attendance and other procedural matters. Writing in 1893 at the end of the second session,[2] George Black spoke factually of the Party's 'educational effect', and pointed out that in the session,

3 What Has the Democratic Dog to Say?
'Parkes will oppose Dibbs for any constituency in which Dibbs may offer himself'—Current Rumour.   *The Bulletin,* 20 January 1894

because of the application of Labor members, 'the House . . . never was counted out. An entirely new experience for the Parliament . . . whose sittings, under the old regime, often lapsed because there was not sufficient attendance'. Black also listed the considerable legislation introduced directly and indirectly by members of the Labor Party, and gave accurate details of their assiduous voting at divisions in comparison with the lackadaisical turn-out of non-Labor members. Black correctly argued that constant attendance at parliamentary duties was essential, 'inasmuch as the country's legislation is preceded by discussion and vote-taking'. Of greater, if complementary, significance was the fact that the Labor platform was a clear statement of progress, valid irrespective of free trade or protection. The Labor conflicts, complex as they were, could be reduced to arguments about the order and pace of reform, and most old order parliamentarians responded to them, and many were affected by them; thus George Reid discovered in the Labor Party a ready-made ally for his own plans to preserve free trade-liberalism by changes from within the existing system. Unable to effect reform on its own in the 1890s, the Party created conditions for Reid to play his strong hand.

Parliament was dissolved on 25 June; polling day was fixed for 17 July (Tuesday). For the whole of the first half of 1894 the Labor movement had been turned in on itself, making adjustments to the form of the political party it had begun nearly four years before. Where previously any candidate for parliament could say he favoured the 'labor party', and some of them were sincere about it, now two groups claimed to represent Labor: one group based its case on independence, more or less as defined by colonial political practice: the other strongly affirmed solidarity, as clarified by two conferences within the previous eight months and re-examined by extensive public debate. The issue was clearly before voters: did they want a united Labor Party, with a new approach to politics, or a loose fellowship of Labor candidates, virtually indistinguishable from the old order men? Only the official party had a large scale electoral organisation, and, inevitably, it had been seriously weakened by internal dissension. But the central control had actually been strengthened by the conflict. There was still no parliamentary leader; and Watson had been persuaded by Toomey to run for Young, while he contested the adjoining seat of Boorowa; there was no outstanding individual in charge, but the executive and other league members filled the gap.

Nevertheless the official Labor Party faced a daunting task. The impression that the whole Party had given the electorate was undoubtedly one of confused internecine strife. Perhaps a few attentive and discerning observers had detected the subtle transforming work of the Labor members of the Legislative Assembly and had calculated that solidarity would prevail, and they would have been joined by hopeful and loyal supporters to provide a party vote for Labor; but this backing would have been sapped by the remaining appeal of the independent Labor men. On the other hand the mass of voters would have decided to play it safe by avoiding Labor; and the reform vote that had helped Labor so much in 1891 now had a more traditional alternative in George Reid, who had revitalised the free traders. In fact Reid's reforming policy, while partly dependent on the new climate of opinion conditioned by the Labor Party, had a strength and validity of its own; although more limited and simple, it was adjusted more neatly and rooted more clearly than Labor's program in colonial political life; and it was presented by an incomparably efficient, experienced and popular leader. In 1894 Labor men could have no answer to Reid, and in a sense they needed him; he certainly needed them and, although an old electoral campaigner, he had learnt a few new tricks about political organisation from them. There was a high, hard mountain straight ahead of the Labor Party; its natural commitment to its society meant a slow and arduous climb. Colonial democracy had shaped conditions to ensure that all proposals for radical change would be well and truly tested before being implemented.

The general difficulties of the Party were starkly revealed by the problem of organising new leagues and reforming old ones, of selecting and endorsing candidates in the detailed constitutional way laid down for the 125 single-member seats set up by the new electoral law; eighty-five of the seats were in the country, including six in the Newcastle area, and forty in Sydney, made up of eleven city and twenty-nine suburban. In April the Party executive had circularised Labor leagues instructing them that no candidate would be endorsed who had not signed the pledge as drawn up by the March conference.[3] In May the executive went further and gave leagues twenty-one days to adhere to the constitution or 'be declared bogus'.[4] By early June of the eighty-four branches written to, seventy-two had conformed, four had refused and eight had not replied;[5] within two weeks five leagues, including Ashfield and Kahibah, had been disqualified.[6]

The executive's supervision of the legality of leagues was compounded by its oversight of pre-selection of candidates, including checking their credentials. While some of this work had begun early in the year, much of it was concentrated in the six weeks prior to the elections. Nevertheless the organising of the metropolitan area was excellent. Candidates were endorsed for ten of the eleven city seats, the odd seat was Sydney-Gipps, for which Black was running and he was a non-solidarity only on a technical objection to the form of the pledge: and twenty-five candidates were endorsed for the twenty-nine suburban seats; of the omissions, Schey had confused the issue in the inner electorate of Darlington. The work was much more difficult in the rural seats. The general city-country rivalry was reflected in the uneasy relations between the LEL executive in the city and the ALF district councils being formed by the AWU in the country. But there were promising signs of unity, concentrated mainly on Toomey's extraordinary grasp of the need for city-country co-operation to ensure the maximum appeal and success of Labor. In 1894 he had followed up his 1893 campaign by contacting many city and country leagues, seeking candidates for country areas, urging the formation and restoration of country branches in union with the executive, and arranging, where possible, organisers to traverse country areas.[7] With limited financial resources, he helped W. M. Hughes to organise in the south-west;[8] and the executive were encouraged to send Holman to Bowral[9] and other organisers to the north coast and the south coast.[10] Toomey's

Food for Reflection

4 Next Week's NSW General Election Democratically Considered.
The Bulletin, 14 July 1894

was a remarkable missionary effort and a main factor in the ultimate preservation of a colony-wide Labor Party, especially as his ideas and actions conflicted with the plans of W. G. Spence, the general secretary of the AWU to which Toomey belonged. To a great extent because of his work and inspiration, the LEL executive was able to endorse thirty-nine candidates for the eighty-five country seats. Altogether seventy-four solidarity men ran for the 125 seats. In all the testing circumstances it was a notable feat of political organising.

The LEL executive necessarily made the restoration and establishment of branches and the ratification of candidates its first priority. As Watson had argued, the executive decided that the presentation to voters of a reformed and united Labor Party was more important than winning seats. Of course they tried to win seats, but with the limited money, time and energy available, and without a leader, they could not mount a strong electoral campaign. Reid, on the other hand, fought with stirring elan and finesse, spurred on by his confident belief in his own reforming mandate. But Watson as president and T. Routley as secretary of the LEL issued a manifesto warning against 'bogus labor candidates' and listing some of the official ones.[11] Each of the metropolitan candidates worked assiduously and a well-planned operation was organised in the city, where the free trade opposition was at its strongest. On 30 June a conference of all the ten LEL city candidates and other league members decided, on Hughes's motion, to hold a 'monster demonstration' on the Saturday night before polling day; suburban leagues were included.[12] On the night of 14 July, after smaller public meetings at various city and suburban centres all the participants marched in tributary streams to the Queen's Statue where King Street joined Macquarie Street; illuminated 'drays and carts' displayed the names of Labor candidates; one placard exhorted 'Workers [to] rise, awake, or be forever fallen'; red lights, mounted marshals, brass bands commingled with thousands of enthusiastic people to dispel the wintry gloom. From this genial, if confused source, at a quarter to nine a massive procession, a half-mile long, flowed down King Street, into George Street and out to Prince Alfred Park, near the central railway station at Redfern, where several speakers held forth, including J. C. Watson, returned from an exhausting stint in the Young district.[13] This reaffirmation of Labor's social adherence, missionary, radical dedication and organising ability symbolised its durability and evidenced the public backing that would ensure its survival.

Toomey's great work in the country provided a basis for a settlement of basic constitutional problems; but so far as electioneering was concerned over vast distances, the general Labor tension combined with lack of time and finance to prevent the executive from getting a strong campaign off the ground. It was left to the individual candidates to do what they could. G. S. Beeby's efforts in Armidale gave an indication of the difficulties of a country official Labor candidate in 1894.[14] He was one of the several city men provided for country seats, because of the dearth of suitable candidates in certain areas; one of the Labor intellectuals, he had defected from the Single Tax League to the Socialist League, and became a useful deputy chairman for Watson on the LEL executive. Beeby was a very able young man indeed, but there was an aura of earnest stuffiness about him and a lack of fluency in his speechmaking that would have reduced his chances in what was a tough seat for

Labor to win in any case, if only because of the peculiar disadvantages inherent in a country three-member seat being reduced to a single-member one.[15] He got little support from the local league or from the press, but fought a long and active campaign based mainly on the Labor Party's 'fighting platform'. Reid's land tax proposals as a corollary of the 'new' free trade raised the general issue of the country being dominated by city importers and financiers, and Beeby became involved in it in a controversy with the free trade candidate E. Lonsdale; this made it somewhat easier for H. Copeland, a senior member of the protectionist group, to win the seat. In a 72 per cent turn out of voters Copeland got 820 votes, Lonsdale 684 and Beeby 632.

Despite the difficulties, however, Labor nominated in a range of country constituencies which suggested that, when the Party sorted out its control structure as between city and country, it would consolidate its powerful rural appeal. In 1891 in a total country electorate of sixty-two, Labor ran thirty-one candidates in sixteen constituencies. In 1894 in a total of eighty-five the Party ran thirty-nine in thirty-nine constituencies. Given the archaic and ponderously complex electoral system of multiple representation in 1891, with plural voting and 'plumping' (i.e. limiting one's vote to a fewer number of candidates than seats provided in a particular electorate), it is simply impossible to compare the voting figures as between the 1891 and 1894 general elections: the figures represent different types of aggregates. In 1891 the LEL had no more than twenty-five country leagues; in 1894 it had at least thirty-nine; in 1891 it won nineteen rural seats, in 1894 it won ten. In terms of seats won the Party had clearly suffered a reverse, and there is no doubt that there had been a fall off in voting support, even though it is impossible to calculate its extent. But just as certainly the Labor organisation in the country, despite wrangles that would have flattened a shallow-rooted party, had actually improved. The spread of seats contested in 1894 virtually covered the colony, with the exception of the south-eastern area in a line from Goulburn south through Yass, Tumut and the Hume and east to the coast; but there were at least rudimentary leagues in much of this area. The effectiveness of the north coast and north-west organising was reflected notably by the win of J. Willard in The Tweed,[16] the most northerly coastal seat, and nominations in Ballina, Hastings and Macleay, Tenterfield and Glen Innes as well as Armidale. Again seats were won in mining areas, A. Griffith (Waratah) and D. Watkins (Walls-end) in the Newcastle district, and J. H. Cann (Broken Hill), W. J. Ferguson (Sturt) and J. Thomas (Alma) in the Broken Hill district; and in pastoral seats in the far west, R. Sleath (Wilcannia), the north-west J. Kirkpatrick (Gunnedah) and H. Macdonald (Coonamble) and a mixed mining, pastoral and agricultural seat in the south-west, J. C.

Watson (Young). Toomey lost in Boorowa to probably the best political organiser the protectionists had, T. M. Slattery.[17]

To compare Labor's 1894 metropolitan vote with that of 1891 is even more fruitless than comparing the country votes, for in 1891 out of a total of twelve seats (three city, nine suburban) all but one (Paramatta) were multiple seats, eight with four members, two with three members, and one with two members; in 1894 a total of forty seats returned forty members. But, as in the country, the Labor Party suffered a definite loss of urban seats: in 1891 in three city constituencies (twelve seats) Labor won four seats with seven candidates; in 1894 in eleven constituencies it won two with ten candidates: in 1891 in nine suburban constituencies (thirty seats) Labor won eleven seats with fifteen candidates; in 1894 in twenty-nine constituencies it won three seats with twenty-five candidates, to make a total of five metropolitan seats. Overall, the Party's representation fell from thirty-five members of the Legislative Assembly to fifteen, from 24.8 per cent of a house of 141 to 12 per cent of a House of 125. But these percentage figures are misleading, too, for the thirty-five Labor men had not functioned as a unit and it is quite impossible to compute their effective cohesion; on the other hand, by electing McGowen as their leader the fifteen men of 1894 soon showed that they would be a united force in terms of their pledge.[18] Beneath the surface of a disappointing result for the Labor Party, there were powerful portents that suggested that the long-term results would make the Party's 1894 campaign, in all its aspects, a notable achievement.

The non-solidarity Labor men naturally eroded the appeal of the Labor Party during the general election. Probably sixty of them ran, including twenty-five of the thirty-five Labor Assembly members of 1891, some of whom were backed by Labor leagues repudiated by the Labor Party executive.[19] They won thirteen seats, all sitting members, except T. Brown, Condoblin, and W. H. Wood, Eden-Bombala.[20] This gave a total Labor representation of twenty-eight out of 125, 22.4 per cent; of course they were not a solid bloc, but it did indicate that radical reformers were still a force in a House that included fifty-one new members. Indeed, at least some notion of the persistence of the original Labor idea of reform may be had from the fact that the total percentage of Labor members had dropped from 24.8 in 1891 to 22.4 in 1894.

The official Labor Party consisted of fifteen, of whom ten represented country seats and five metropolitan seats. Only four of the original members were included, Cann, Davis, Kirkpatrick and McGowen. The newcomers are given in the Table following.

As in 1891, in Sydney Labor support was concentrated in the city and nearby suburban area, Sydney-Lang (Hughes), Sydney-Pyrmont (Davis), Redfern (McGowen) and Balmain South (Law); an interesting excep-

Name	Occupation	Electorate	Religion[a]	Date of birth	Country of birth	Arrival in Australia
W. J. Ferguson[b]	Engine-driver	Sturt	P	1859	South Australia	native
A. H. Griffith[b]	School-teacher	Waratah	CE	1862	Ireland	1871
W. M. Hughes[b]	Teacher-locksmith	Sydney-Lang	CE	1862	England	1884
S. J. Law	Auctioneer	Balmain South	CE	1857	NSW	native
H. Macdonald[b]	Shearer-journalist	Coonamble	P	1847	Scotland	1886
R. Sleath[b]	Shearer-miner	Wilcannia	CE	1863	Scotland	1882
G. W. Smailes	Clergyman	Granville	M	1862	England	1882
J. Thomas[b]	Miner	Alma	M	1864	England	1891
D. Watkins[b]	Miner	Wallsend	M	1865	NSW	native
J. C. Watson[b]	Printer	Young	P	1867	Chile	1868 NZ 1886 NSW
J. Willard[bc]	Ironworker	The Tweed	—	1857	England	1863
M. J. Loughnane[d]	Farmer	Grenfell	RC	1867	NSW	native

[a] CE   Church of England
M   Methodist
P   Presbyterian
RC   Roman Catholic
[b] Unionist

[c] disqualified by Elections and Qualifications Committee 15 November 1894
[d] awarded seat by Elections and Qualification Committee 24 November 1894

tion was Granville, an outer western suburban seat won by G. W. Smailes, a Primitive Methodist clergyman, who had ministered at Lithgow and Granville, both strong Methodist areas. Only three Labor members were non-unionists, of whom Law (1857–1939) was typical of the group of social radicals drawn to the Labor Party; he was a teetotaller, had strong support from temperance organisations and attracted Balmain's wowser vote, as G. D. Clark had in 1891. Arthur Griffith (1862–1946) and Hughes were somewhat similar to Law except that they were not tee-totallers; neither had an extensive union background, but both, especially Hughes, had been active in the Party disputes of 1893–4, as had Law. All three were fluent speakers, intelligent and well-educated; Griffith had been a teacher at Sydney Grammar School. Law and Griffith lacked the demagogic touch possessed in abundance by Hughes, but they were sharp and effective debaters. Griffith had answered the call to run for a country seat; Law and Hughes were well-assimilated city men, but Hughes's country organising and his experience on the Darling Harbour waterfront had made him peculiarly responsive to all-round Labor feeling. The remainder of the Labor men, except for Kirkpatrick, Smailes and Willard, were all experienced unionists, most of them union leaders; Ferguson and Sleath had been imprisoned for their part in the 1892 Broken Hill strike. There were more Anglicans (six) than any other religious group among the fourteen men whose religion is known, but the Presbyterians (four) and Methodists (three) had a higher proportion than the 'national average', Roman Catholics had disap-peared, though Loughnane brought them back in November. There is no evidence to suggest that religion had played any part in the lively affairs of the Labor Party in 1889–94, though possibly many Roman Catholics felt that it was not for them because of its socialist tinge and the fact that they seemed to be accommodated, however uncomfortably, in the 'protectionist mansions', where Slattery, O'Sullivan and Garvan resided, and to where Fitzgerald, Hutchinson, Kelly, Morgan and Newton had moved. Catholics, at least as much as any other group, had helped to mould the old parliamentary system.

Under McGowen's leadership the Labor members were part of an Assembly with a clear mandate for change, mainly taxation reform. Although the free traders had not been united in the general election, Reid had fought a magnificent campaign on the basis of free trade and direct taxation, especially on land. They won fifty-eight seats, most of them Reid's supporters, including a virtual clean sweep of the metro-politan area, thirty-three of the forty seats; the protectionists won thirty-nine seats, all in the country. Reid formed his first ministry on 3 August 1894, and showed that he was determined to try to draw Labor's teeth by including Cook as his Postmaster General, a superb tactical move that immediately assured him of the support of the seven free traders of the thirteen non-solidarity Labor members and pleased the six protectionists among them. The *Herald* noted the appointment of the first cabinet member 'chosen directly from the ranks of Labour', remarked that it would 'strengthen the position of the Ministry' and observed that 'This is the chief ground on which Mr. Cook could be considered entitled to a ministerial position'.[21] But Reid misread the official Labor position. The solidarity members of the Assembly, who were those he could not manipulate without liability, showed their defiance by deciding to run against Cook in his ministerial re-election.[22] Their candidate, J. Thomson, failed, though the gesture of freedom of action succeeded; but the *Herald* misinterpreted it as a move to support the protectionist group and looked to 'Cook and the untrammelled labour members' to uphold the true traditions of the Labor movement.[23]

This initial brush with Reid suggested the delicate relationship that existed between him and the Labor Party. Though he had a majority in the House it was not well-defined enough for him to ignore or unduly antagonise the solidarity men, yet he had to try to dislocate, and, if possible, absorb them: for their part, the Labor members appreciated the progressive vision of Reid in contrast with the obscurantism of Dibbs, and they were prepared to back him in his basic taxation proposals, but they were suspicious and a little fearful of his political resourcefulness. The great difficulties of the Labor Party had influenced the election results, but it was clear that Reid had simply outclassed them and indeed the premier was beyond question now the dominant political figure in New South Wales. Parkes's decline had continued, Dibbs was an irreparable blunderbuss. But the Labor Party had some considerable strengths based chiefly on its unity, and a vital leaven of four experienced parliamentarians, including a capable leader, to complement the effervescing intelligence of youthful newcomers, notably Watson, Hughes and Griffith. They knew that Reid's basic electoral principle, land taxation, was also the first plank of their fighting platform; they were aware that they were the heirs to the high reputation of the TLC and that the Council's decline had reduced their chances at the general election; above all, they knew they could come to terms with Reid, if only in the short run. The Labor Party was not overwhelmed by the premier. And his legislative proposals, announced in the House on 28 August, reflected in part the *modus vivendi* between the great liberal reformer and the radical probationers:

1. Amendment to the land laws, 'to provide greater facilities for agricultural and homestead settlement in accordance with the growing requirements of the population'

2. Review of fiscal policy, 'in order that the burdens of taxation may be more equitably adjusted'; repeal of 1891 *ad valorem* and other duties; to be replaced by taxation on unimproved value of land and on income

3. Inquiry into the public service
4. Local government
5. Amendment to Mining on Private Property Act
6. Re-introduction of coal mines regulation bill
7. Amendment of Conciliation and Arbitration Act to bring in compulsory provisions
8. Factories and workshops; alteration to Marine Board; amendment of navigation laws; medical and pharmacy bills.[24]

Reid's program included three planks from Labor's fighting platform and four others from the general platform: incontestable evidence of the effects of the Party's outstanding role in the debate about colonial reform since 1889. The primacy given to amendment to the land laws indicated the enduring significance of what had been one of the great political and social questions since responsible government, and underlined the persistent recognition of the economic and human values of the country life. Already the Labor Party had begun to come to terms with this basic social fact; one of the new Assembly members, H. Macdonald, drove the point home when he intimated that, though he personally favoured Reid, country people as a whole regarded his ministry as 'a city government'; and Macdonald said his Coonamble Labor league included one-fifth of the electorate's nominal enrolment and one-third of its effective enrolment; and he was prepared to give the solidarity system a chance to prove itself.[25] Macdonald had expressed a view that the Labor Party could not ignore; in fact, the Party was prepared to allow it a significant influence in its constitutional structure.

By the end of 1894 the temporary eclipse of the TLC had revealed the hard fact that the economic depression had virtually stopped the growth of trade unionism. But trade unions still carried on, and occasionally even went on strike;[26] and in the country, while the AWU was also feeling the effects of the depression it was making some headway. There was no chance that the Labor Party would exist without the support of unions, but it was clear that the LEL would have to be adjusted to take account of the changed conditions. Watson had ensured that even in the city, where the TLC's demise had dramatised the weakness of unionism, that organised workers should still be the backbone of the LEL. But the inflow of non-union members, including women, had had an effect upon the appearance and character of the Party. Griffith summed up the position when he said that 'a conscientious democrat can find solid ground nowhere but in the labor platform';[27] inevitably, the 'conscientious democrats' influenced the nature of the Labor Party, nor was it possible to draw a strict line between them and trade unionists. So as fiscalism began to join single taxism in its drift into the museum of discarded doctrines, socialism, in all its supple diffuseness, emerged more than before as a main quarry of slogans and ideas for Labor people: a complex process, conditioned by the social formation of the conscientious democrats: the socialism they used was moulded by their life-styles and channelled, as McGowen had put it in 1891, into a groping for Landor's ideal of a government that would provide for honest and humane living in order to civilise capitalism: expressed in the first object of the LEL, legislation to ensure for 'wealth producers . . . the full produce of their labour'. Most of the conscientious democrats, socialists and social radicals alike, were prepared to strive to make the honest and humane life a function of rational distribution of production, and to come to terms with whatever definition the electorate would accept for 'wealth producers'. In the end, this struggle for reform through social adherence would naturally appal all types of lonely socialist purists, though it was meant to provide them with an alternative to frustration. But the Labor Party, whatever its slogans and ideas and whatever their sources, was already in 1894 a mass party, and, short of a revolution, it would not be uprooted. It was providing an essential safety valve to facilitate the development of a harmonious and tolerant society.

Griffith's exposition of the Labor platform provided a discerning state-ment of where the Party stood in relation to its members and its society in 1893–4.[28] Described as 'a dangerous heavy-weight boxer, a fair oar and a crack swimmer',[29] aged thirty-two in 1894, Griffith had come from Ireland to Victoria when nine and later travelled extensively in the Australian colonies. In 1884–92 he had taught at the Sydney Grammar School and had developed as an intelligent and responsive social observer with some panache and a sense of humour. He appreciated the Labor Party's determined attempts to curb capitalism and in return was prepared to help it by arguing that it was not restricted to manual workers who were trade unionists. In his pamphlet he stressed that 'the spread of education amongst the toilers . . . is producing an upheaval just as general and determined [as the great struggle to defeat feudalism] against the grinding tyranny of industrial monopoly'. He saw the Labor Party as the main force in 'the rejuvenation of their country', with its platform as 'the only firm foundation . . . amid a wilderness of shifting creeds and jarring factions'; against Labor's idealism he contrasted the cynical manipulation of the fiscal groups, 'Each [of whom] formulated a *revenue tariff* differing only in detail'. A land tax, nationalisation of mines and the abolition of the Legislative Council, a national bank and the universal eight-hour day were necessary for civilised progress; and Labor led enlightened opinion towards collectivism, 'a protest against the right of individuals to do *wrong* to his fellows, even under forms of law'. He ridiculed the 'old party hacks' who had fallen back on the shibboleth of Federation, when all else had failed; no doubt Federation was fine and inevitable but 'we have to set our own house in order first'; and Labor did not want Australia grafted on to an aggressive and 'decaying

monarchical system, but rather a democratic Australian Republic!' He
put his finger on one of the most challenging parts of Labor's role when
he asserted that only the Party could 'check the cancerous growth of
militarism which is to-day eating the vitality out of every country in the
world, and will, if not extirpated, do the same thing here'.

Griffith's pamphlet was an influential appeal from a professional man
to all intelligent reformers, especially to 'the literary and clerical classes',
to see in the Labor platform an articulated answer to their protests
against the abuses they saw around them; it showed them how they
could profitably apply their feelings and energy to effect basic change
without violence; it reasoned with them to leave the side of monopoly
and join the workers in the contest between 'humanity' and 'tyranny', a
world-wide issue in which Australia could play a leading part. He urged
all workers to be unionists and all unionists to be 'Labor Leaguers'; to
all the existing members of the Party he made an eloquent and cogent
plea to endorse unitedly the important program that they had so fervent-
ly produced. Now, in 1894–5, at the organisational level the Party had to
re-incorporate formally the country leagues into the administrative
structure that had fabricated the platform; a task that involved the
invocation of the ultimate range of checks and balances that adjusted the
whole Labor constitution and its interpretation to community standards
without changing the essentially radical character of the Party.

The Country and the Political Labor League

The election of Watson to parliament coincided with the replacement of the TLC by the Sydney District Council of the ALF.[1] The close links between the unions and the LEL were dissolved as there was no provision for district councils to be represented in the League at any level, and Watson automatically retired as chairman. A new period of re-adjustment lay ahead for the whole Labor Party, but a firm foundation had been laid and built on, as the solidarity parliamentarians were showing. Griffith's pamphlet reflected the increased influence of radicals, including socialists, in the LEL, a result in part of the disappearance of the TLC and the general malaise of trade unionism. But the ALF scheme was a ready-made plan to weld industrial to political action, and, while the city unions were not in a position to use it to gain power in the LEL, the AWU was. William Guthrie Spence, the general secretary of the AWU, seized his opportunity; and it went even wider than a chance to come into the LEL, it was useful in his campaign to build up the infant AWU in very difficult times. Spence had some strong cards to play: clearly the Labor Party had no future without the country vote, and Watson as a country member joined the AWU and at once threw his great prestige and knowledge into the move to work out an acceptable solution to the new constitutional problem. For a while Beeby carried on as chairman of the LEL, but by the end of 1894 Frederick Flowers (1864–1928), a painter, an experienced unionist and delegate of the TLC, had taken over. With Watson on the country side and Flowers on the city, there was no possibility that trade unions would withdraw entirely from the Labor Party.

The ALF scheme had its origins in discussions at the trade union congresses of the 1880s, and was put into a definitive form at the April 1891 Congress at Ballarat. It was an elaborate blueprint, covering the Australian colonies and New Zealand, based on local district councils to control industrial and political action in certain areas, with provincial councils for each colony; and, finally, a general council that represented all the colonies. Only Queensland showed any interest in the proposals before 1894. As New South Wales unions in 1891 had a strong representative body that had already planned determined political action, no steps were taken there towards the ALF; but in 1894 the position had changed and by September at least six district councils were operating, Sydney, Riverina, Bourke, Moree, Scone and Coonamble.[2] The country councils were virtual extensions of the AWU. A conference on 9 November decided to form a provincial council for New South Wales;[3] all the delegates, except the two from the Sydney District Council were members of the AWU; they included Watson for Young, who had taken over Toomey's mantle as the apostle for city-country co-operation, and in the event was to prove too strong for Spence, who favoured separatism.

In the city the country developments had been well noted. The LEL was by no means dismayed by the July general election results and was, in fact, in a position of authority and assurance reminiscent of the TLC in its heyday. There never was any chance that the League would be swamped by the ALF. During the negotiations on the TLC that had led up to the formation of the Sydney District Council of the ALF, the usual varying points of view had been put about the relationship between unions and political action. P. J. Brennan had said that the District Council would leave politics to the LEL and be satisfied with some form of representation on it;[4] A. Newland had put the case for strong control by the unions as 'they now found that nine out of every ten of the selected Labor candidates were non-unionists', and was supported by J. Hepher though he agreed that 'there were many good men in the Leagues who did not belong to unions'; while J. Woodcock argued that 'the deplorable condition of Labor to-day' was a result of unions interfering in politics.[5] The LEL executive finally took the initiative in August and sought a conference with the Sydney District Council to discuss 'control of the political movement'. The talks were inconclusive. They showed that while many unionists were unhappy about having to pay twice to belong to their union and the local Labor league, others recognised that many people were unable to join unions and that 'many unionists had not always supported a Labor candidate'.[6] As the 1895 LEL conference approached, the recently-founded *Daily Post*, giving Holman's view, said that the LEL 'has officially nothing to do with unionism' and argued that 'it is generally regarded as likely to alienate support from the political labor movement to make it avowedly a unionist one'.[7]

Twenty-nine delegates attended the annual conference on 25–9 January 1895. Flowers presided; Hughes and Griffith represented the Labor members of the Assembly, Watson represented the Provincial Council of the ALF; Holman was among the delegates. Two proposals came before conference on the proposed amalgamation of the ALF with the LEL. Watson put the ALF case, which would have involved the end of the League; but he argued strongly that Labor voting strength was in the country and that there should be 'no lingering doubts in the

minds of those coming from the country that they were being overruled
. . . or dictated to by the city', and agreed that a reasonable compromise
was possible. The LEL executive wanted the ALF to fill a similar position
in the League as that of the TLC; eventually it was agreed that the
Federation be asked to do this and

> all members of the ALF and [of] all New South Wales unions not included
> in the federation be admitted to full membership of the LEL, on production
> of their union cards, and that district councils of the ALF and governing
> committees of other unions be invited to pay capitation fees to each league
> on their membership in each electorate.[8]

This motion was a clear reminder to the AWU that many unions,
nearly all in the city, did not belong to the ALF. On the other hand, the
LEL recognised the futility of trying to set up a country organisation to
compete with the ALF. Watson's vision of 'a reasonable compromise' was
shared by many other Labor people.

On 30 March a preliminary conference was held between League and
Federation delegates to examine proposals to change the name of the
Labor Electoral League to the Political Labor Federation, to revise the
platform and modify the pledge. A tentative agreement was reached
that the League should control metropolitan electorates and the Federation organise country seats. But no resolution was submitted as the
League delegates had no approval to reach a settlement.[9] Further discussions by the LEL executive led to a special conference of the leagues
on 23 May with Flowers presiding and Hughes and Griffith representing
the parliamentarians; the meeting affirmed 'the advisability of the adoption of a scheme to unite the Labor Electoral League with the Australasian Labor Federation and other union bodies for political purposes'.[10]
The plan consisted of twenty-eight points drawn up by the LEL
executive; they were duly amended and adopted. The next day representatives of the Provincial Council attended, Watson, president, Rae, Spence,
Macdonald, J. P. Cochran and J. Gilbert, all AWU members except the
last two. The new convention met for two days and agreed on the
amalgamation of the LEL and the ALF for political action, under the
new title of the Political Labor League (PLL).[11]

The new rules reflected the enlightenment of radicals who perceived
that their own differences had to be reconciled, and at the same time
composed in such a way that would not estrange them from their society.
The rules were a model of tact, setting down a basis of proportionate
agreement on the respective strengths and weaknesses of overlapping city
and country groups, unionists and non-unionists, politicians and voters.
Though inevitably not free from drafting errors, and in parts difficult to
apply, the rules showed how a modern Australian political party would
have to set about drawing up its constitutional and administrative
machinery. Above all, they revealed the basic pioneering role of the

Labor Party in providing a catalyst for the formation of real political parties. The new form of the pledge indicated the influence of the parliamentarians and of those who thought that the previous stress on 'monopoly' and the 'privileged classes' was both crudely unnecessary and provocative:

> I hereby pledge myself not to oppose the selected candidate of this or any other branch of the Political Labor League. I also promise that, if returned to Parliament, on all occasions to do my utmost to ensure the carrying out of the principles embodied in the labour platform, and on all such occasions, and especially on questions affecting the fate of the Government, to vote as the majority of the labour party may decide at a duly-constituted meeting.[12]

Members of the PLL were to be members of unions affiliated with the ALF and other adults; special arrangements could be made by other unions to have their members enrolled. The subscription was 4/- yearly, with district assemblies to fix rates for unions. Branch leagues were to be established in each electorate and commissioned either by the local district assembly or the central executive. District assemblies could be formed from not fewer than three leagues, with the proviso that there would be only one assembly in the metropolitan area, and, where poss-ible, co-terminus with district councils of the ALF; they were to consist of one delegate of each local league and three from the local district council; and were to have control over all local matters, and meet at least every three months. The central executive committee was reduced from the unwieldly group that had resulted from representation of every league, a system that also made it very difficult for country leagues to play a consistent part on it; the executive was to consist of a president and general secretary, seven members elected by conference, plus two delegates from the Provincial Council of the ALF; its power was reduced, but was still significant; it could not veto selected candidates, selection was left to the local leagues, but it could make known the past record of candidates and intervene in the case of fraud; all executive members could attend conference, but had no vote unless otherwise a delegate. Conference was to be held each January in Sydney; each electorate could have one delegate, and a district assembly could have one with a vote for each electorate making up the assembly; no delegate could have more than four votes. Candidates for pre-selection had to have been a league member for the three months before selection; and to vote at pre-selection ballots a league member had to have an elector's right and to have been a member of the league for the preceding three months. Two months' notice had to be given of amendment to the rules, pledge or platform, which could only be effected through Conference and required 'a two thirds majority of the whole Conference'.[13]

The original executive of the PLL was Flowers, president, T. Routley, secretary, and Hughes, Macdonald, Watson, Rae, Spence and James

O. Moroney, with two delegates to be elected by the Eastern Provincial Council (NSW) of the ALF.[14] The amended pledge meant the temporary end of the attempt to get a united Labor vote on every issue that came before parliament. Black was delighted that his opinion had been vindicated, ' "the splendid moral effect", trumpeted by J. C. Watson and others, "of voting solidly on all questions" was unattainable'.[15] In fact it was not so simple; there certainly was more flexibility in the new pledge than in preceding ones, but it was essentially a powerful form of control, which, in conjunction with consistent use of the caucus, clearly differentiated the Labor Party from other parliamentary groups, though, by May, the great pressure exerted on the Legislative Assembly and the Legislative Council by Reid's campaign to implement his fiscal reforms had produced such a state of excitement that an extraordinarily high degree of unity had prevailed in the House, including the free traders who supported Reid.[16] In a real sense this situation had resulted, probably chiefly, from the example of the Labor Party as it strove for unity and reform in 1891–4, and achieved the one and renewed its efforts for the other in 1894–5. By June Reid had obtained an unconditional dissolution from the governor and elections were set for 24 July 1895, by which time not only Black but also Edden had rejoined the Labor Party, and T. Brown, independent Labor member for Condobolin, had come over to the solidarities.

Reid believed in free trade and the liberalism that accompanied it. Commercial freedom to him was a corollary of personal freedom. Steeped in the dominant New South Wales traditions, his experience as a member for East Sydney, the outstanding free trade electorate in the colony, had not only confirmed his principles but had also introduced him to human suffering, for the area also included some of the worst slums in Sydney. Work as a Treasury clerk and practice at the Bar, as well as his political activities, had given him the total background to evaluate the pressing need for fiscal reform, as the colony's income from land rents and land sales contracted in the 1880s. He had decided that free trade could only be preserved by direct taxation on property and incomes. And he concluded it was not only expedient but also just to tax wealth; he knew how protection had been manipulated not so much as to protect native industries against foreign trade, but rather to protect the rich against a diminution of their wealth and privileges. His vision of reform did not exclude Federation; on the contrary, he wanted to implement such a fiscal system in New South Wales that federal taxation might conform more to his ideas of efficiency and justice rather than to what he regarded as the crudely blunt system of protection adopted by other Australian colonies, notably Victoria. He had won the 1894 elections virtually on this policy. His legislative proposals in parliament on 28 August 1894 showed that he meant business.

Reid soon found that reform from within the old parliamentary system was hard indeed. As a result of the writhings of the Labor Party in 1891–4 and with the force of his own sincerity and ability he had a majority in a reforming Legislative Assembly. But he had only a handful of supporters in the Legislative Council, which in 1894 had sixty-two members, many over the age of sixty. Members of the Legislative Council were appointed for life, and the tradition had developed that only 'non-party' men should be nominated, a practice that was of little significance before 1891. But the position had changed fundamentally by 1894 when parties were becoming better defined as a result of the operation of the Labor Party, and Reid had helped ensure that his new type of party would make a determined attempt to see that wealth contributed a fair share to the running of a modern state. Naturally, members of the Legislative Council were, almost all of them, men of position and wealth; professional men, mainly medicos and lawyers, pastoralists and business men. Moreover, the nature of their appointment consolidated their sense of importance and detachment from mundane politics: they were recommended by the ministry of the day, but were appointed by the governor: and he was just as determined as they to maintain their independence from party ties as expressed in the Lower House, and so retain an important prerogative for himself: a form of British crown control stemming from the 1820s in New South Wales, still surviving in the 1890s. And in a subtle way the Council was related popularly to the mystique of the 'British Constitution', exemplified by the pomp and place of the governor. The Council was believed to be a bulwark against ill-considered change as it apparently immovably upheld the best of colonial traditions. It was not to be easily shifted.

Out of fifty-three ministerial bills introduced in the Legislative Assembly in the 1894/5 session, twenty became law: 106 public bills were brought down, of which twenty-five became law (excluding finance bills). The Legislative Council kept back eight of the forty-three public bills that were sent to it; practically all the bills it allowed through were amended, some severely, especially the important crown lands bill. Reid kept his promise about the ill-fated coal-mines regulation bill and introduced it on 5 September 1894; he asked the House to deal with it quickly because it had 'often been before us'; it was sent up to the Council on 12 September after Parkes had recorded his continued opposition to it and Dibbs had asserted that he endorsed 'every word [Parkes] has uttered', and went further to argue that 'The bill is an interference with liberty'.[17] The Council returned it on 7 December with 'no less than 171 amendments' of which sixty were substantial and 111 consequential.[18] The Assembly considered the amendments and sent the bill back to the Council, which appointed a select committee to inquire into the bill; and its long report was adopted on 13 June, including objection to the compulsory eight-hours clause and insistence that boys should work a ten-hour day.[19] The Council took no further action and the bill lapsed on prorogation of parliament. Members of the Council pleaded expert knowledge and the best of motives to improve legislation in the case of the coal mines bill; it did likewise with the amending bill to the Mining on Private Lands Act and the amending bill to bring compulsion into the Trades Disputes Conciliation and Arbitration Act (1892). What it was really doing, of course, was revealing its class reaction by stopping Reid's reforming program. Yet this was part of the old system and Reid could do little about it.

It was different with the land and income tax assessment bill. Reid had received a clear mandate from the electors for this legislation; he prepared it carefully and introduced it on 14 November 1894; after full debate it was sent to the Council on 21 March 1895. There had been some signs both during and after the 1894 general election that Reid's radical proposals were shaping a coalition of wealthy protectionists and free traders as some noted that direct taxation could bring more compelling doubts about the old fiscal faiths. Reid had received essentially a popular rather than a privileged vote. The *Herald* had reported significantly that while merchants were generally pleased with the free trade victory, 'the hope was expressed that the tariff would not be interfered with in a doctrinaire spirit or in such a manner as to injure any existing industry which had been established under it'.[20] These sentiments were effortlessly absorbed by the Council as the prospect of paying direct taxes sharpened members' insight. On 25 June Reid reported to the Assembly that the bill 'had been destroyed' in the Council by 41 to 4; in a restrained but effective speech he went on to say that the government could not agree that, contrary to all accepted constitutional practice, the Council had the right to amend taxation bills, and he appealed to all members of the Lower House to support him on those grounds; he also stated that the government was fed up with the Council's stalling on the coal mines bill because people with direct business interests in the industry 'have set their personal interests above the lives of thousands of our fellow countrymen'; and, as he revealed that the governor had agreed to dissolve the house, he astutely proposed to send up to the Council some vital bills for urgent public works and necessary democratic amendments to the Parliamentary Electorates and Elections Act:[21] the amendments included the extension of the polling hours from 5 p.m. to 8 p.m., the earlier hour had prevented many workers from voting in 1894, and the reduction of time to allow transfer from one electorate's roll to another from three to one month, the longer period had disfranchised many voters in 1894.[22] Reid was obviously preparing the ground well on which to ask the voters if they approved of the Council's claim to have the power to reverse a popular mandate.

Naturally the Legislative Council did nothing about the proposed electoral amendments, but that snub, too, was grist to Reid for the forthcoming general election.

The Labor Party was inevitably swept up in the great argument about the constitutional role of the Legislative Council. Indeed, in a sense, the Party had begun the contemporary debate when, in 1889, it had included 'An elective Upper House' in its first platform and continued it by including 'Abolition of the Upper House, and the substitution therefor of the principle of the referendum' in the 1892 platform. Criticism of the Council's work was not new; beginning with proposals for an elective body in the early 1850s, reformers, notably Parkes, had occasionally tried to curb its powers by bringing it closer to the voters, but without any success. The Council was too well entrenched as an essential part of the old parliamentary system to be moved by men who had been moulded by the system; and too much a part of the imperial connection to be affected by transient protests. Given the way in which legislation was processed in the colony, there was no doubt that at times the Council had performed valuable work in revising bills that had been either hastily considered or inexpertly drafted in the Assembly.[23] Moreover, on occasions, important legislation, including significant reform bills, had been originated in the Council.[24] The Council's view that it was co-equal with the Assembly in law making was practically accepted, except in the field of finance bills where, however, there were large polemical areas: supply, appropriation and loan bills were hardly even questioned, but taxation bills were frequently thrown out; in fact, as Reid had said, there had been a steady rejection of taxation bills since 1886.[25]

It is possible that Reid's notion of the need for thorough-going reform of the Council did not survive long his great annoyance of June 1895 and his great triumph over the Upper House the next month; for he was essentially a renovator of the parliamentary system, however determined, and his range of reforms was limited, however important. He had no comprehensive program that would outlast his own political career; nor indeed, did he have a party that had any but an insubstantial identity apart from himself. So the advantages of the Legislative Council were always likely to recur to him, especially when he had gained his fiscal point and had pondered the great practical difficulties of reform of the upper chamber. Yet it is undoubtedly true that Reid's assault on the Council made it more aware of mass democratic feeling and a little less of a bulwark for the privileged classes.

The Labor Party did not take Reid's philosophical view of the Council; Labor concentrated on its class aspects, which were transparent, and on its crown links, which were obvious enough; and could only conclude that it ought to be abolished. The parliamentary experience of 1891–5, especially of 1895, certainly influenced Labor thinking about the proposed upper house (Senate) in the federal constitution. But so far as the 1895 general election was concerned Labor had no chance of mounting a campaign for abolition of the Legislative Council, and only a very few Party members thought that it should do so. Reid had crystallised the issue: it was not whether the Council had the right to amend legislation sent up to it, even on financial matters, but rather whether the Council had the right to destroy legislation based on a clear mandate given by the voters at a general election. This was a question that perforce engaged every colonist's attention, including members of the Labor Party; and Reid's plans for limited Council reform by setting aside life appointments threw the basic issue into relief.

For the third successive time Labor found itself at a considerable disadvantage at a general election. Its constitutional problems had indeed been settled and the PLL was formally a united body; but it had the task of regrouping country leagues and linking them substantially with city branches in a united electoral campaign. As the *Herald* had said at the end of the convention that turned the LEL into the PLL, 'Organizing work will be steadily proceeded with, and by the time of the next general election the labour party expects to present a solid front in the election fight'.[26] That was on 26 May. The elections were on 24 July. Time, as well as the nature of a large constitutional issue and the vigour and skill of a consummate political leader, was working against the Labor Party. There were other forces, less obvious, impeding the Party which, given the political situation, were of no immediate significance in 1895, but which had an important long range influence. Those forces were concerned with the comprehensive electoral acceptance of a social democratic Party that contained within it elements both of rapid and moderately paced progress. The vacuum left by the TLC had enabled extra impetus to accrue to elements that favoured rapid change; their tone was variable and sometimes related to a more tolerant life-style as well as less liberal politics. But it had to be harmonised with the total appeal of the Party to what was essentially a cautious electorate.

Watson and McGowen had led the way in showing in a practical sense that the new Party had a vital and acceptable contribution to make to social and political development, even without the TLC; Griffith had fluently argued a theoretical case for it; and Black had helped sow the seed.[27] But time was needed to reap a bumper harvest; longer than was thought by the most pessimistic Party member. Holman had detected the signs of partial acceptance on trial associated with the critical attitude of the 'literary and clerical' classes who had their abode in the suburban electorate of Leichhardt; and he noticed that they combined a vision of social uplift with strong views on the consumption of liquor, which mixed ill with his mild socialism and civilised approach to living. His defeat there in 1894 was the beginning of his adjustment to the facts of political life, given his ambition and talent for a parliamentary career. He had also noticed Watson's triumph in the country and the general Labor success there, and was aware that he lacked the rumbustious style of Hughes and Black and the solid union background of Davis to have a reasonable chance in the city seats. By chance, the Grenfell seat was available for a new Labor candidate. Loughnane who, at the age of twenty-seven, had won the seat on a recount in 1894, had found Parliament far from congenial to his outgoing personality and sporting interests; temperamentally a Labor man, he was immune to caucus, local league, and even his electors' demands; he had spoken only thrice in the House, twice by proxy, when Watson had asked questions on his behalf, once in person after some of his constituents had found him and prevailed on him to move the adjournment to discuss the unsanitary condition of the township of Wyalong. Holman replaced Loughnane in the 1895 contest for Grenfell. J. Kirkpatrick, the oldest Labor MLA, fifty-five in 1895, did not run either.

The 1895 general election marked a further great and complex step towards the modernisation of New South Wales politics. The momentum of change had begun principally with Brennan's thrust for a Labor Party in 1889 and had received powerful impetus from the pressure Reid had put on Parkes from 1891. Both Labor and Reid were affected by proposals for Federation activated by Parkes in 1889; Reid far more overtly than Labor. It seems that Reid, like most observers of the Federation movement, was convinced that it would succeed sooner or later and he decided pragmatically to do his utmost to ensure that New South Wales would be so prepared for the event that the colony's influence on the new constitution would be proportionate to his opinion of its importance as the oldest, most populous and wealthiest Australian colony. He correctly described his policy of free trade for New South Wales as a message of peace and goodwill to all Australians.[28] On the other hand, Parkes was a spent political force after October 1891; he had done an imperishable service to the whole nation by awakening New South Wales to the significance of Federation, but he had neither the ideas nor the energy to help to push on the movement; Federation to him became a desperate last straw to maintain his political prestige as he entered on the final stages of his deterioration. The other obvious proponent of Federation in the colony was Barton, who had ideas and a subtle understanding of constitution making but little political prestige and hardly any ability to relate Federation to democratic politics; in his own languid way he was as elitist as the members of the Socialist League, and had received the kind of electoral rebuff they consistently got when he was resoundingly defeated in 1894 in Randwick by David Storey. Left to Parkes and Barton, Federation in New South Wales would have foundered in a morass of senility and dilettantism. Federation was also an issue at the

1895 general election, but substantially in the terms being outlined by Reid and the Labor Party.

The Labor Party and Reid provided the stiff backbone on which an acceptable Federation scheme could be fleshed out. The 1894/5 parliamentary session had seen them strongly at work; most of the legislation, much of it substantially inspired by Labor, that Reid had sent up to the Legislative Council was designed to provide necessary parts of the bases of reform required by the colony. Parkes's wayward reaction to it had caught up an improbable ally in Dibbs. Both relics of the old parliamentary system joined forces to bar the advent of a new order. On 16 May 1895 Parkes, with Dibbs's backing, moved a motion of censure on Reid because he was 'retard[ing] the progress of much-needed legislation and seriously prejudic[ing] the cause of Australian federation':[29] a cynical exercise in futility that devastated the protectionists. Reid ended his reply to Parkes with a sonorous call to all types of democrats, liberals, radicals and socialists:

> I am beset with enemies . . . [who plot] to stop the progress of much-needed reform. I know that every big influence in the country is arrayed against me. I know that all the monopolists, whether of land, or of any commodity, or of wealth, are arrayed against us . . . , it is for this House, the first House elected under . . . real manhood suffrage, to say on this motion whether the tide of justice and progress is to be stopped, and whether we are to go back to a time when we heard magnificent platitudes and do nothing.[30]

The motion lost 34 to 67.

Reid aggravated the fossilised condition of the protectionists by campaigning at the general election on free trade, land and income taxation and reform of the Upper House; some of them actually agreed with the last two points. He also made things difficult for the Labor Party, many members of which, especially in the leagues, agreed with Reid's substantial policy. The North Balmain branch, for example, decided unanimously not to oppose the sitting member, W. H. Wilks, a Reid free trader, because parliament had been dissolved on the first two planks of Labor's fighting platform.[31] This additional evidence of Labor's social adhesion did not mean that Reid had any chance of taking the Party over. During the debate on Parkes's censure motion Griffith had been brutally frank as he said that Reid's government was being supported by Labor only because it was 'less objectionable' than its alternative,[32] a declaration that represented the basic Party policy; but the North Balmain league's decision did suggest that, in conjunction with other immediate problems, the PLL could not hope to organise a strong colony-wide campaign, let alone make any spectacular advances in the election.

The *Daily Telegraph*, the strongest press supporter of the government, complained that while Reid free traders were not opposing sitting Labor

members, the PLL was contesting several free trade seats.[33] In reply
Flowers said that the Labor Party was a distinct party with no ties with
the government, and it would oppose Reid free traders as it thought fit;
he went on to state that the executive had made no decision to bind the
individual leagues and they would decide the matter themselves.[34] The
Sydney District Assembly of the PLL resolved that official Labor support
could only be given to selected League candidates; and the *Telegraph*
asserted that the PLL's decisions would help the conservatives and were
unfair to the government, because Labor would get the votes of free
traders in fifteen seats while the government would receive Labor votes
only in those seats the Party decided not to contest.[35] Despite the controversy, the Labor Party was helping Reid considerably and Flowers
judged him the 'grandest premier' the colony had ever had.[36] The Party
had little choice; it could not support the protectionists, and it was not
strong enough to challenge Reid on the ground of reform, nor was it
expedient to do so, for he was seeking the maximum possible change
that could be had in 1895 by democratic processes. On the other hand
the PLL could not afford to lose its identity to Reid, and it did not. The
executive denied that they had a pact with him; and the Sydney District
Assembly reiterated that the Labor Party had to be separate and independent, stressed that no Labor candidate could also be endorsed by a
fiscal group, and ordered the Waverley league to withdraw its official
support from the local Reid candidate, or be declared bogus.[37]

The PLL officially nominated five candidates for the eleven city and
thirteen for the twenty-nine suburban electorates. In the country twenty-
five candidates were run for the eighty-five seats, including four members
returned unopposed, Thomas (Alma), Cann (Broken Hill), Ferguson
(Sturt) and Sleath (Wilcannia), all far western seats, mining and
pastoral; nine other country candidates were from unofficial leagues.[38]
There was a general reduction in the number of all candidates compared
with the 1894 general election, from 527 to 310:[39] the official Labor
number fell from seventy-four to forty-three: from ten to five city, twenty-
five to thirteen suburban and thirty-nine to twenty-five country. Reid's
influence and the general political situation were more important for the
decrease in the metropolitan area than in the country; Toomey's withdrawal from political activity had left an unfilled gap, and sufficient time
had not elapsed for the new constitutional Party arrangement to cope
with the vast job of organising in rural seats. But again the contested
country seats ranged evenly throughout the colony with the exceptions
of the southern tablelands, south coast and some northern tablelands
electorates.

The Labor campaign was typically spirited, especially in the city,
where a large demonstration was held on Flagstaff Hill on 20 July with
McGowen the chief speaker.[40] With Flowers prominent, a similar

gathering was held at Newtown on 22 July, with the main emphasis on a demand for the abolition of the Legislative Council.[41] At both these meetings and many others Labor support for the government was made clear. Much capital was made of the Upper House's refusal to agree to amendments to the Electoral Act; as a result, it was claimed, 15,000–17,000 who had moved within the preceding three months were disfranchised,[42] and closing the polling booths at 5 p.m. instead of 8 p.m. would make it impossible for many workers to vote. McGowen and Hughes visited the Newcastle area to help Labor candidates, Sleath was helping R. Scobie in Wentworth, and Ferguson had put himself at the disposal of the executive.[43]

Both the free traders and the protectionists were split, though less than in 1894. The intense excitement of the elections was increased by Parkes's decision to oppose Reid in the city seat of Sydney-King which comprised much of old East Sydney. Backed by powerful conservative forces, Parkes repeated his parliamentary criticism of Reid. Labor did not run a candidate, but many local league members helped Reid.[44] During the campaign Parkes's wife died. The night of her burial McGowen spoke at Redfern and sympathised with the great old man, despite the fact that he recalled that Parkes regarded him as 'a dullard'; but McGowen gently argued that Parkes's style of government was outmoded and had done nothing to improve social conditions. The same night, Hughes, on the corner of King and Kent Streets, assailed Parkes for being on the side of 'the club loungers, the National Association [the chief conservative electoral agency] and the monopolists', which showed that his liberalism was a mask and his free trade a shibboleth.[45] Reid did not spare Parkes, though he relented temporarily on Lady Parkes's death. Parkes, himself, asked for no favours and gave none. Although he was soundly defeated, his departure from public life had a sad and massive dignity amid the confusion created by some of his reactionary supporters, and was in accord with his whole enigmatic political career in which he had espoused large causes and courageously confronted variegated and resourceful enemies, though not always effectively or prudently. He had been defeated by much lesser men than Reid in a parliamentary life that extended back to Wentworth's and Daniel Deniehy's day in 1854. Parkes's downfall at King in 1895 reverberated throughout Australia.

In Grenfell, Holman found out that to win a seat in parliament more was required than a glowing belief that it should be a reward for a persuasive tongue, a handsome face, a lithe figure, and a modern outlook on life and politics. In Tamworth Dibbs discovered that to lose a seat it was not necessary to leave one's own electorate and face a redoubtable opponent on a vital principle, although A. B. Piddington, who defeated him, was an able young barrister, similar to Holman,

5 The Devil and the Deep Sea.
Premier Reid: 'Yes, forty-three and nineteen make sixty-two.'
The Bulletin, 10 August 1895

except that he was less conscious of his own talents. Barton urged Parkes on in King. Wise and Copeland also ran and lost, although on 17 October Copeland won Sydney-Phillip, after R. D. Meagher (1866–1931) had resigned because of his indiscretions as defence lawyer of George Dean, who had been charged with the attempted murder of his wife.

The 1894 Assembly had been a reforming one, checked by a self-assured Legislative Council. The 1895 House was radical, confronted by a somewhat chastened Council, anxious to maintain its great prerogatives by giving way on a few pieces of legislation, including the land and income tax assessment bill. In 1894 Reid was not completely dependent on the Labor Party. In 1895 he was virtually dependent on it; his following was an unsure fifty-eight; the protectionists numbered forty-one; there were eight independent Labor members of the Assembly, Bavister, Cook, Fegan, Hollis and Newman, who finally gravitated to the free traders, Schey and Wood, who joined the protectionists, and Nicholson, who remained more or less an independent. These reallocations gave Reid a nominal sixty-three votes against a combined nominal vote of other groups and the Labor Party of sixty-two. In practice, however, Reid, discovered that, given dissension in his own ranks and persistent vestigial 'independence', he needed the eighteen votes of the Labor Party to survive.

In November 1894, through the Elections and Qualifications Committee, Labor had lost The Tweed (Willard) but had won Grenfell (Loughnane). These changes had left it with fifteen members in the 1894/5 parliament. In the 1895 elections, Grenfell and Gunnedah were lost, Botany (Dacey) and Newcastle West (J. Thomson) won; Black (Sydney-Gipps) and Edden (Kahibah), 1891 members, rejoined, and T. Brown (Condobolin), an 1894 independent Labor member, joined the Party to give it eighteen members in the 1895–8 parliament; nineteen after H. Ross won a by-election at Narrabri on 3 June 1898. The new members were:

Name	Occupation	Electorate	Religion[a]	Date of birth	Country of birth	Arrived in Australia
T. Brown	Farmer	Condobolin	P	1862	N.S.W.	Native
J. R. Dacey	Coach-builder	Botany	RC	1856	Ireland	1859
H. Ross	Farmer	Narrabri	M	1839	Ireland	1860
J. Thomson[b]	Miner	Newcastle West	P	1856	Scotland	1874

[a] M   Methodist   [b] Unionist
    P   Presbyterian
    RC Roman Catholic

John Rowland Dacey (1856–1912) was the most interesting and important of the new members. Born in Cork, Ireland, he came to Victoria as a young child, became an agricultural blacksmith, moved to Sydney in 1883 and founded a moderately prosperous coach-building and wheelwright business in Alexandria, just south-west of Redfern. Interested in politics, in 1886 he became an alderman of Alexandria council, and mayor in 1888; in the 1889 general election he was a returning officer at Redfern; as a small manufacturer and a Roman Catholic he became a member of a local protectionist group, but his social radicalism jarred with fiscalism and in 1891 he joined the Labor Party. That year in the Redfern league of about 500 members he was narrowly defeated in the pre-selection ballot. After the redistribution of seats in 1893 he ran for Botany in 1894, but lost; next year he won, to become the member for a large suburban seat that stretched south from Waterloo and Randwick to Botany Bay. Dacey was the only Labor candidate to defeat a Reid free trader (W. Stephen) and his win suggested that, with suitable candidates and sound campaigns, additional suburban seats might be won by Labor; his election speeches of 1893 and 1894 revealed views formed by his wide colonial experience, adjusted by way of Leo XIII's encyclical *Rerum Novarum* (1891) to the Labor platform. Dacey was the first significant Catholic politician in the Party; he showed that as a social democratic party it was not restricted to Anglicans, Protestants and Free-thinkers, and provided evidence that there was room in it for socially aware employers as well as manual workers and the 'clerical and literary classes'.[46] Dacey was sympathetic to unionism and eventually became the leader of the Wool and Basil Workers' Union. Wise and energetic, he was a natural politician who helped to ensure that Labor's 'socialism' would not lose its appeal even as it became harder to define.

The country members (twelve) still out-numbered metropolitan members (seven). Dacey's win made four suburban seats to three city seats, but Granville was the only real exception to the fact that Labor's main Sydney appeal was close to the city area, for the northern and most populous part of the Botany electorate was within four miles of the GPO and Dacey received solid support there.

Reid was naturally jubilant at his great win at the 1895 general election, but the Legislative Council was far from cowed. A. H. Jacob, its chairman of committees, admitted to the *Herald* that he was disappointed with the result of the elections, but insisted that the voters had not endorsed Reid's 'offensive language' against the Upper House and had accepted that it had done its duty in using its constitutional power. Jacob also considered that the electoral verdict applied only to the taxation bill and not to Reid's proposals to reform the Council. He pointed out that the election of members of the Legislative Council would involve paying them a salary, and stressed a variation of one of the basic principles generally accepted as applying to the Council when he argued that new appointments, even if for specific terms instead of for life, should be made by the governor himself or with advice from the chief justice and judiciary; otherwise, he said, the government would appoint partisans, and the Council had to be above political strife. Jacob agreed that, if the Upper House twice rejected a bill or twice amended it in a way unacceptable to the Assembly, the Lower House should have the power to call a conference of the two Houses with a final decision to rest with a majority of members present. He considered that the Council would now pass the taxation bill in a form agreeable to the government, but would do so, not because of Reid's threats, but because the wishes of the people had been made clear.[1]

These authoritative views underlined the strength of the Legislative Council and the complete inability of the overwhelming majority of its members to admit that its concept of non-partisanship really involved control by a single class. The Legislative Assembly was in the process of shedding its belief in the classlessness of representation, and was admitting tacitly that legislation should be influenced by members avowedly speaking for the 'lower classes': the development of this modern approach to law making had been confirmed by the 1895 election results. The Upper House in effect claimed to be immune from change; but, to conserve its powerful role, it was prepared to make minimal concessions while asserting that its basic principles should remain undisturbed; a situation that laid bare that Labor's reforming mission was strongly opposed by great class defences in depth, camouflaged by appeals to powerful social traditions, relevant to colonial conditions of 1820–50, but archaic in the 1890s. Even if Labor won a general election, and that seemed remote in 1895, it would not gain control of the full legislative machinery. Great as the strain had been on the Party up to 1895 at all levels, the future held little respite: but there was no chance of the experiment being dismantled. Nevertheless, there were some immediate cheerful signs: J. H. Carruthers, Reid's minister for lands, who was coming to the fore as an outstanding lieutenant for the great liberal leader, saw the combined numbers of the free traders and Labor Party as a 'solid force' for further reform:[2] and W. J. Lyne, who would replace Dibbs as leader of the protectionists, in ridiculing Reid's congratulations of himself on 'a glorious victory', foresaw that the premier's 'troubles with the labour party have yet to begin'.[3] But however a Labor member looked at politics in 1895 there was still arduous pioneering work ahead.

Before the new parliament met on 13 August, Reid exposed a major part of his dilemma over the Legislative Council by prevailing on the acting governor, Chief Justice Sir Frederick Darley, to appoint ten new men to it. The members were typical; all of them were wealthy, including John Hughes, a Roman Catholic lawyer with large city estate holdings; six of them had been members of the Lower House, and three of these had been the premier's candidates at the 1894 elections. They were too much part of the social and political fabric to prepare to destroy the Council from within; but their appointments suggested tangibly that Reid would expect that Jacob's prediction would prove accurate and the Council would pass his fiscal legislation. Reform was another matter: the Council had the constitutional power and duty to consider whatever reconstruction details the Lower House thought appropriate, and that review would inevitably be a long, drawn-out process in which second and later thoughts would recur to putative reformers in both Houses. The ten new Council members did not regard themselves as Reid's appointments, even if they were more or less in agreement with his politics; nor did he look on them in that light. All Reid had done was to activate the machinery that had made them members. In the event they helped the Council to do its duty on taxation with less pain than had seemed possible in 1894; but on Upper House reform, as the political excitement of 1895 faded, they became indistinguishable from their fellow members; and, indeed, so did Reid.

At the opening of the Legislative Assembly, however, Reid indicated that his general reforming zeal had been enlivened by the election results. His program naturally placed his fiscal proposals first; and he showed that he was in earnest about 'this great and patriotic movement [Federation]', by next foreshadowing a bill to give effect to the resolutions he had moved at a conference of colonial premiers at Hobart in

6 The NSW Political Situation.
   Labor Voter: 'Wot yer goin' to do in there, Bill?'
   Parliamentary Labor Party: 'Oh, a little repairin', that's all.'
   L.V.: 'But the pup, 'e don't seem inclined to follow?'
   P.L.P.: 'Oh, 'e's all right—I got 'im on the string!'
   The Bulletin, 7 September 1895

January to set up a constitutional convention, consisting of ten representatives from each colony to be chosen by the electors; then followed
reconstruction of the Legislative Council and amendments to the electoral system. The premier's vision of administrative reform as an aid to
economic reform had been sharpened by his first year of political power;
he planned to drive ahead with the building of light railway lines and
to reorganise the colony's public service, a necessary base for practically
all reforms. To let the Labor Party know that he was conscious that at
least some of its specific demands fitted into his total policy, he promised
to look at the problem of immigration of 'Asiatic and coloured labour'
and to set up a royal commission on coal mines.[4] McGowen took the

opportunity to let the House and the colony know that the Labor Party had now been clearly defined as the channel of the workers' will to civilise capitalism; he contrasted their humane but determined approach through parliament with methods used elsewhere; 'All over the world', he said, 'there is a spirit of unrest abroad which manifests itself by socialism and anarchy, and in America by armed "Pinkertons" '.[5] The Labor leader's personal benevolence was unfeigned; but he had acquired the parliamentary craft that now enabled him to remind Reid effortlessly that political pressure was a reciprocal process. McGowen was well aware that blind, destructive forces, of both a capitalistic and anarchical nature, existed in colonial Australia, even if in diluted form compared with American and European patterns: he had to make his point in a way that would encourage Reid to co-operate in a great social mission by helping the Labor Party to achieve its aims. The development of the Party up to 1895 had ensured that its parliamentary pressure was not only resolute but also permanent.

With the comparatively favourable conditions prevailing in the first session (13 August to 20 December) of the new parliament, the Reid government brought down twenty-six bills, including four formal finance bills; twenty of these bills became law, a success rate for legislation unparalleled in the colony's history. The bills included the land and income tax assessment bill which was passed after both Houses had appointed managers, and agreement had been reached on eleven resolutions that fixed £240 as the exemption amount for land tax and £200 for income tax: the Labor Party had convinced Reid of the need for exemptions. The Council was not overwhelmed in the negotiations, though the Assembly achieved its substantial objectives; the resilience of the Upper House was shown by R. E. O'Connor, its chief negotiator, when he explained to the Council, against bitter minority opposition, that unyielding recalcitrance would have probably resulted in some swamping that would have destroyed it as an independent factor in government.[6] Land tax and income tax bills associated with the assessment bill were also passed; other items were the Australasian federation enabling bill, which set up the machinery for election of delegates to a new constitutional convention; the public service bill, which virtually marked the end of a vital part of the old parliamentary system, patronage in 'government billets'; and the customs duties bills, which removed any suggestion of protection in the tariff schedules. On the other hand, the Council held up important legislation on relief for selectors and amendments to the gold and other metals mining laws; the Labor Party was vitally interested in both bills. Hughes gave notice of an inebriates bill, but did not bring it down; and Griffith had his Public Instruction Act amendment bill, which sought free primary schooling, taken to second reading. The fate of these Labor bills and other private members'

7 Similia Similibus Curantur—or, NSW
Premier Reid in his laughable character
as the Fat Man's Enemy.
The Bulletin, 2 November 1895

bills suggested that the ministry was at last beginning to take firm
control of legislation, a process, shaped and strengthened by the purposeful support given by Labor to the ministry, that was an essential stage
in the abolition of the old parliamentary system. The change applied
especially to Griffith's Education Act amendment, which was stopped
from going into committee by a debates timetable adopted at the beginning of the session.[7]

If the Labor parliamentarians felt a glow of pride in work well done and a feeling that at last the Party was making a powerful and permanent impact on the Assembly, they were disillusioned at the 1896 conference, held in Sydney on 26–7 January. Flowers presided over 'about thirty' delegates, including members of the Assembly. The executive's annual report was bitterly critical of the Labor members and emphasised that a seat in parliament was not 'a reward for past services [but] rather a widening of opportunity for future work'.[8] The report went on to argue that members should be more active in propaganda work, especially in the parliamentary recess, and to complain that despite insistent demands for vital additional electoral reforms and for the abolition of the Upper House, nothing had been done.[9] This kind of adverse comment was not simply cantankerous. The executive was the focal point of a mass political party that expressed a deeply rooted striving for comprehensive reform; while, to a degree, the executive was insensitive to the intricate nature of the problems of Labor parliamentarians, it could not allow itself to be engulfed by them; that way led to stagnation, and a primary objective of the Labor strife of 1891–4 was to avoid that. Nor could the executive afford to give the impression to league members that it would follow the pace set by Assembly members; the rank and file regarded it as their spokesman and the custodian of right Labor principles and practice. The executive had to assert some authority over the parliamentarians, both to placate ordinary members of the PLL and to ensure that Labor members of the Legislative Assembly should never rest on their oars with the feeling that the race was over. In fact the whole Party had started on a contest that would never be won. And part of the game was the difficulty of each section of a complex Party in recognising and appreciating the problems of other sections: this poser applied particularly to relations between those inside parliament and those outside, but it was also apparent, in the personal tension inherent in the bonds that linked in perpetual dynamism the institutional sections of the Party, executive, assemblies, branches and conference, as well as the trade unions.

The parliamentarians resented the strictures passed on them at the conference. There were several clashes between them and other delegates, especially between Hughes and E. Riley, with the result that the report was reconsidered and the adverse comments on Assembly members withdrawn, after further allegations that they were also failing to attend meetings of district assemblies.[10] These exchanges were an essential part of the normal strain generated as the whole Labor movement maintained equilibrium; they did not prevent the 1896 conference from renewing, with great insight, the Party platform.

With the parliamentary wing functioning as an efficient unit and the electoral organisation restored and adjusted, the stage had been reached

at which fresh concepts, some related to practical politics, some to reforming doctrine, could be formally inserted into Labor's program. The
Party had consolidated its role as the community's signpost for progress
and sounding board for new ideas. So 'womanhood suffrage' was added
as part of a detailed list of electoral reform, after Moroney had argued
that 'the average woman would not support democracy in politics' and
R. P. Thompson had asserted that 'not one per cent of females had
identified themselves with the labour movement';[11] 'State pensions for
the old-aged and infirm' was also included. Neither of these reforms
had originated solely within the Labor movement; but resolute, efficient
and permanent pressure was needed to implement them, as with many
other practical reforms; and only the Labor Party could supply this kind
of support. At the level of far-sighted developmental change associated
with increasing state and municipal activity, conference decided to strive
for local councils 'to be empowered to establish and to directly conduct
any industry or institution they may deem advisable'; for 'All iron
required for State use to be produced from State Mines'; and for the
'Nationalization of all Coal, Silver, Copper and Iron Mines'. The Party's
continuing interest in education, sharpened by Griffith's specialised
knowledge, led to the acceptance of a plank for all education 'to be
absolutely free'.[12]

Again the integral position of country affairs in the Party's deliberations was emphasised. By 1896 rural pressure on Labor could be seen
to have complex elements, both radical and conservative, with strong
populist overtones. Despite the changes that had occurred in their
structures and activities, neither of the other political groups could now
comfortably contain country demands. Before the advent of the Labor
Party this pressure, chiefly from farmer-selectors and workers, was
exerted, by way of individual Assembly members, mainly on the protectionists; and in the middle 1890s it still conditioned the mainstay of
protection electoral strength, seeking tariffs on imported grain from
Victoria and South Australia. But the realignment of political forces
shaped by the success of Labor Party radicalism and Reid's new liberalism produced a growing awareness among many country people that
their interests were far from identical with those of protectionist city
manufacturers; and they were suspicious of the coalition of city wealth
that opposed Reid's taxation policy. On the other hand, pastoralists,
especially those operating as large freeholders or leaseholders, were
traditionally supporters of free trade, because of their export trade; but
they were not pleased with Reid's direct taxes, and found themselves
comparatively in a friendless political minority, supported, however, by
their representatives in the Legislative Council.

From the time of the great debate about land settlement in the 1850s,
climaxed by John Robertson's Land Acts in 1861, there had always been

a strong conviction among New South Wales liberals that large sheep runs should be reduced in size and shared among more farmers; although not without great setbacks, the policy envolved from this belief had resulted almost in a fourfold increase in the area under wheat between 1881 and 1896, from 221,888 acres to 866,112 acres.[13] This growth reflected important social changes in country centres with a maturing community of interest between bush workers and farmers, especially in the many instances of farmers who were also shearers or whose sons were. Gold and other metal mining retained both its mystical appeal and employment opportunity into the 1890s; indeed, as city unemployment remained high, mining actually increased in popularity as a relatively widespread rural pursuit, and added to the forces that were altering the political texture of the countryside. Associated with the changes was a persistent and popular belief, current in city and country alike, that there were strong moral and social advantages in living close to the soil; by no means entirely a superstition, if only because of the primacy of wool in the New South Wales economy. Labor was involved in this situation through its connections with the bush unions, above all the AWU; and the Party strengthened its foothold by its policy of sinking the fiscal issue, which attracted more support as the 1890s unfolded and Federation, with a nation-wide tariff, became more of a reality. The free traders were not so advantageously placed, but their transformation through Reid, well backed up by Carruthers, enabled them, with Labor encouragement, to respond to the changed situation. Carruthers's Crown Lands Act, 1895 (58 Vic. No. 18), although amended by the Legislative Council, and passed only after a conference between delegates of both Houses, set up, amongst other changes, a system of homestead leasehold that rapidly began to settle more people on the land; and his conditional purchasers' [selectors] relief bill, 1895, although kept by the Council, provided further evidence that the new legislative flexibility embraced country as well as city reform needs. Nevertheless there were deep, lingering doubts among country people that even a reformed free trade party could consistently act independently of wealthy city interests.

The analysis of country problems by delegates at the 1896 PLL conference revealed not only their understanding of the specific issues but also their foresight about the long-range role of primary industry in the Australian economy. The debate reflected further the vital work of the party in the general elucidation of issues related to Federation. Admittedly, the conference delegates did not consciously aim at this effect; but their work supplemented the efforts of groups and organisations directly concerned with the Federation movement, for every plank on the Labor platform was potentially the basic concept of an act of the colonial parliament. The conference decided to seek

The encouragement of agriculture by—
(a) The establishment of State mills for sugar, grain and other produce.
(b) The establishment of a State export department.

It also reconsidered policy on the mining laws and in a plank of five clauses set out the basis of a modern form of control of the industry.

The question of non-European immigration was revived in the middle 1890s, and the 1896 Labor conference took it up. So far as New South Wales was concerned the problem seemed to have been settled by Parkes's Chinese Restriction and Regulation Act of 1888, but renewed interest had stemmed from the increasing attention given to the problems of Federation as Reid showed his support for it by his active role at the Hobart Conference in January 1895 and his consequent enabling Act. Immigration was obviously a field in which any federal government of the Australian colonies would have a vital interest, but it was by no means clear in 1895–6 just how the power would be shared with the constituent states. The Intercolonial Trade Union Congresses of 1879 and the 1880s had shown that the whole Labor movement was luke-warm to European immigration and opposed to non-European, mainly Chinese, immigration.[14] Despite opinions to the contrary in the 1970s, in 1870–1900 the Labor movement was not primarily motivated by what is now known as 'racism' in opposing non-European migrants. It is true that the times demanded the rhetorical language of exclusion whenever alien labour was discussed, just as a century later similar occasions would reflexly call forth expressions of brotherly love; and it is consequently possible to find nineteenth-century ideas, crudely expressed by members of the working class, that offend late twentieth-century moral sensibilities. But these seductive cliches should not be allowed to obscure the basic cause of the objection of the working class to Chinese migration: trade unionists, especially, and workers generally were finding it very difficult to achieve and maintain what they regarded as reasonable conditions of work and living, and Chinese and other alien workers were obviously a clear threat to those conditions. Employers who wanted Chinese to come to Australia did not want to protect trade union conditions, much less strike a blow for the brotherhood of man. It was impossible, given problems of language and pioneering pressures, for trade unionists to teach to co-operate with them men who had no sympathy with union industrial aspirations and no comprehension of union notions of political and social improvement; unionists were having difficulties enough with 'blacklegs' and 'sweated' women and children as suppliers of cheap labour. Nineteenth-century trade unions were many sided institutions, but they were not, nor could they be, social agencies for the assimilation of peoples whose whole way of life was in great contrast with that of Australian colonists. Clearly there were differences in colour and social habits between colonists and Chinese, but the important incompatibilities were in religion and law, politics and industrial practices, including, above all, the fact that the Chinese were prepared to work longer hours and for less pay than the colonists, at a time when no general rules of pay and hours applied: alien races were simply not prepared to take part in 'the upheaval . . . against the grinding tyranny of industrial monopoly', as Griffith had put the basic Labor problem of the late nineteenth century.

Many members of the Labor movement, and practically all its leaders, had a total vision of improvement, which in time could come to encompass all peoples, but they had no alternative in the nineteenth century but to focus on the foreground of reform; and there was no congenial room there for groups who would supply cheap labour. Before conditions could be created in Australia for the harmonious mingling of peoples with very different backgrounds, Australians had to complete their immense task of nation-building on the foundations they had chosen, and Chinese and other non-Europeans had to change their views on basic political issues and on the status of the working class: they also had to liberalise their own outlook on immigration, for it was impossible in the 1890s for white people to migrate to either China or Japan, and very difficult even to visit there. To illustrate the fact that 'racism', or colour phobia, was an inconsequential and expendable element in Labor's attitude to Chinese migration were the TLC's decision on 4 March 1890 to allow the affiliation of the Wagga Wagga branch of the Shearers' Union, although it had some Chinese members,[15] and Holman's evidence, suffused with tolerant understanding, to the 1891 Royal Commission into Chinese gambling and associated matters, in which he said,

> I do not think there is much bitterness of feeling between the respective races now, although it may have been necessary to deter them from coming in, owing to their keen cheap labour competition with the Europeans.[16]

Holman's statement reflected Labor's satisfaction with the position of non-European immigration in 1888–95. The question had not been raised in the discussions of the first platforms in 1890–1, or at any of the conferences in 1892–5, although the exposed position of the furniture trades had been acknowledged in 1891 by a plank seeking the 'stamping of Chinese-made furniture'. In the country, however, especially in the west and north-west, appreciable effects were noticeable on general working conditions and wage rates by the activities of Afghans who contracted to transport goods by camels, with the result that some of the bush unions strove to use the political movement to protect their special interests. The unofficial Bourke league in 1891 had planks in its platform seeking the 'Exclusion from the colonies of inferior races', and 'An Act to prohibit the use of camels as beasts of burden';[17] and in 1892 the latter plank was added to the LEL platform. Suggestion of continued country pressure was contained in the 1894 'Political Platform of the Riverina

District Council [of the ALF]' which sought 'Absolute exclusion of Chinese and all colored aliens as competitors in the Labor market'.[18] The Labor conferences of 1894 and 1895 were primarily concerned with major constitutional issues and did not materially alter the platform, but in 1896 the way was clear for the country influence on immigration to be felt, especially, of course, as there was no objection from the city unions or leagues.

The Labor process fitted nicely into a general colonial reassessment of non-European immigration that followed the request of the British government to consider the provisions of the 1894 Treaty of Commerce and Navigation with Japan.[19] This treaty, highlighted by Japan's success in its war with China, provided, amongst other things, for reciprocal rights of residence; and there was every possibility that the Australian colonies would be required to admit whatever Japanese chose to come, including workers whose wages were lower and whose weekly hours higher than those of Australia. Britain's 'far-eastern' policy, in a most sensitive area, raised the question of the independence of the Australian colonies at a critical time, when the Federation movement was gathering momentum. The existing problems associated with non-European immigration were considerably ramified. There is no doubt that these events sharpened Reid's interest in Federation as the highest expression of Australia's separate nationalism, and that they conditioned the somewhat surprising precedence he gave to the proposal to bring down fresh legislation on immigration when he announced his plans at the beginning of the new parliament in 1895. Reid's alertness also exposed the great complexity of the question of non-European immigration; virtually the whole of colonial society, not merely the Labor movement, had a vital interest in it. But Reid's speeches on the topic gave irrefutable evidence that Australian nationalism, at once delicate and intricate, like Labor policy, was not based on racism.[20]

The 1896 PLL conference extended the stamping of furniture plank to include 'other manufactures' and decided to press for the 'Total exclusion of undesirable alien races'. More directly on Federation, it responded to the 1895 Australasian Federation Enabling Act by resolving to run a full team of Labor candidates for the ten New South Wales delegates' seats at the Federal Convention at which a fresh constitution would be drawn up. This decision was part of a special sub-committee's report on Federation which emphasised not only Labor's great interest in the subject but also how its judgment of it had been moulded by the experience of the Labor parliamentarians: thus conference approved of a policy that sought 'a House of Representatives elected on a population basis for single-seated electorates'; an Upper House, the States Council, with a limitation on the power of its veto, 'elected directly by the people of each colony on a population basis, each colony to vote as one constituency'; the election of ministers to bring about non-party government; and 'Direct initiation of legislation by the people in conjunction with the referendum'.[21] No other parliamentary group had either the interest or the machinery to examine Federation in this way. With their bedrock stress on democratic features, Labor's proposals influenced Reid's thinking on the subject and played an essential part in the growing public discussion of the largest issue ever to confront New South Wales; especially, the decision to run a full slate of candidates invested the forthcoming convention with a kind of significance no other group could visualise; though, in the event, in 1897, Labor's policy, translated into a strong campaign, was to draw sufficient support from Reid to enable Barton to top the poll of delegates.

The *Herald* mocked the delegates' work on Federation but implicitly acknowledged the permanence and complexity of the Party by commenting that,

> The deliberations at the meetings indicate what an attraction is possessed in the eyes of delegates by theoretical constitutional reform . . . Equally noticeable . . . is the hostility between the labour party in Parliament and the labour party outside;[22]

whereas *Liberty,* the organ of the National Association, the chief conservative agency in the colony, fearful of Labor's durability, began the arduous task of sundering it from outside,

> [The PLL] has latterly become a sort of headquarters for all the elements of discontent in the community, and the Socialists have got such a hold of it that it might with propriety be called the 'Socialists' league. The majority appear to look at everything from a purely socialistic or communistic point of view.[23]

The *Liberty's* comment was probably the first attempt to link the Labor Party with socially disruptive forces, none the less real and fearsome to conservatives for being vague and indefinable: 'socialistic or communistic' could refer to a multitude of evils allegedly threatening the orderly growth of the community. In fact, the most obvious mark of the Labor Party had been its natural formation within colonial society, with the manifest commission to effect necessary reforms, or give impetus to existing tendencies towards desirable change. The whole history of the Party to 1896 exemplified this role, and notable preliminary headway had been made against very great odds. So far from threatening society, Labor was consolidating it by providing machinery for natural progress. But the Party was indeed the meeting place for all kinds of reformers, the *Liberty's* 'elements of discontent', Griffiths's 'conscientious democrats': they, as with all league members, were anchored to society by parliamentary action; and the institutional checks of pledge and caucus and the sovereign functions of conference were the visible signs of the determination of the Party to keep them in that condition, subject to the ultimate control of the people voting at elections. Some of these groups were apt to become embittered at what they regarded as the slow progress necessarily involved in parliamentary action, but the Party's structure was designed to cope with internal discontent by providing flexible opportunities for disgruntled individuals or factions to try to do better than those members they criticised; some of them would give up in despair, especially those of strong ideological motivation, but the majority would conform, perhaps with a shrug and acknowledgment of the universal problems of life. There were, of course, obvious political ingredients in the criticism of the *Liberty;* conservative groups shrewdly assessed the long-term threat to their interests posed by the Labor Party, in contrast with Reid's milder and transient challenge, and were prepared to do and say anything, no matter how unscrupulous, that would reduce its electoral support.

Nevertheless, the internal tension of the Labor Party did expose small minority groups, from time to time, who looked on it not as a mass social democratic party seeking a consensus for radical reform, but rather as a socialist phalanx probing for deep and rapid change. In the 1890s many of these people belonged to the 'literary and clerical classes', rather than to trade unions, though the groups overlapped and were not entirely moulded by the occupations or associations of their members. J. O. Moroney, a tobacco worker, who had been active in Labor Party affairs from 1891, was a sincere and active trade unionist with advanced and resolute socialist views; he had the betterment of mankind close to his heart, wanted to effect it as soon as possible and was prepared to allow the Labor Party to help him. Many of the men who were elected to the Party executive from 1893 were similar in general outlook to Moroney, although only a few, notably Flowers, had greater union experience, and the degree of socialist knowledge and fervour varied among them.[24] As with the bright young delegates on the TLC in the late 1880s these energetic and humane men helped to feed in advanced ideas into the PLL, where they were moulded into acceptable form and placed on the Labor platform. The socialists' role was vital to the healthy development of the Party, but it could not be over-played without risking popular support: the two governing factors were the minority status of the advanced thinkers and the parliamentary adherence of the Labor Party. Sooner or later some of the socialists would have to decide whether the Party really deserved the time and effort they were putting into it; while the rest, and the majority non-socialists in the leagues, would have to consider whether the minority were too much of an electoral embarrassment to be carried further, in view of the opportunities they gave to the newspapers for adverse and distorted criticism. The General Council of the ALF, meeting at Brisbane on 3 March 1896, provided a general comment that was relevant to the complex position of the PLL: 'The continued success and honesty of the political labor movement is dependent upon the maintenance of industrial organisation'.[25]

The Labor platform of 1896 represented the limit of progressive proposals that the electorate was prepared to accept in the 1890s, and it was erected at a time when the importance of the Party and its survival were clear to friend and foe alike. The new reforms were labelled both 'municipal socialism' and 'state socialism' and their momentum at once affected Reid, who had, much to the chagrin of Sydney exporters, already established an advisory Board of Exports.[1] In 1896 Reid's growing pre-occupation with Federation was both a reason for and a measure of the beginning of the decline of his zest for reform; and the ultimate gulf between him and the Labor Party loomed as their different views of the role of the modern state became clearer. Again the *Liberty* in its exaggerated way, reflected the kind of judgment that retarded Reid:

> New South Wales may be said to have fairly started on the downgrade of socialistic legislation . . . the latest move is that to provide a system of old-age pensions, and pensions for persons in delicate health . . . It is one of the most dangerous, because most insidious, attacks upon the quality of manly independence which has raised the British people to their proud ascendancy amongst the nations, and this colony at present to its strong position.[2]

But neither the conservatives' wrath, represented by this artless comment, nor the aspirations of discontented socialists could disturb the solid social foundation of the Labor Party.

In August 1896, C. M. Barlow, who had been elected minute secretary at the Labor conference, replaced Routley as secretary of the PLL. Barlow was a determined socialist, similar to Moroney in seeing the Labor Party as a means to achieve his brand of socialism in his time, and similar in his ambition to shape the Party in terms of enlightened leadership from above. The opening of the Labor Centre and Solidarity Club at the *Worker* office in October illustrated the problem that confronted any one of the varied groups that sought to control the Party now that its social integration was obvious; the occasion also showed how league members, even the diverse socialists, strove to unify the elements that constituted the Party in order to relate them to colonial society and change it in one way or another. Flowers presided over the ceremony;

there was an attendance of about 150 including Moroney, Barlow and other socialists, as well as Assembly members Smailes, Thomas and Watson, who represented the *Worker* trustees, and Spence and Benjamin Backhouse, MLC, a Reid liberal and noted community figure.

McGowen delivered the main speech and, after stressing that the club was a sign of the desire of league members to work in unity with the members of the Assembly, he took the opportunity to answer criticism of the parliamentarians. He said that, despite the fact that there were only eighteen of them, the speaker of the House had recognised them as a 'third party' and several Labor principles, including land taxation, were now on the statute book; at the administrative level, they had been able to begin the process of replacing the use of private contractors on public works with day labour employed directly by the government; in addition, the idea of the referendum and of a national bank had been projected into public discussion. McGowen admitted that Labor could not form a government, so they had the choice of keeping 'the better of two bad lots' in power, the free traders who favoured the overseas monopolists, or the protectionists who preferred the local monopolists; nevertheless, the Party was achieving much, and 'might be described as the propellor in the legislative machinery'.[3]

McGowen's justification of the Assembly members was accurate and fair. Since Black's review of its role in 1893, the Labor Party had continued as the dynamic reforming force in parliament, not only in influencing legislation and administration, but also in shaping new attitudes towards the whole range of activities of a parliamentarian. But the pace of reform seemed insufferably slow to many league members outside parliament, who either thought they could do much better than the members or were doubtful whether parliamentary action could ever achieve much for Labor. Holman belonged to the first group. After his defeat at Grenfell in 1895, through misfortune rather than dishonesty he had served a brief time in prison as a result of his association with the short-lived *Daily Post;* he began the slow and, to him at this stage, somewhat irksome task of building up his support in the country seat, but remained active in Labor circles in Sydney. In October 1896 he revealed his frustration by writing to Hughes 'If we potter along as we've been doing for the last two years *we're* done, *you're* done, the *cause* is done'. In reply Hughes listed some of the legislation Labor had helped to effect, surveyed the practical problems facing a third party and said: 'It seems to me when you sneer at Watson "putting in a clause here and amending a line there" you do him and us and yourself, not to speak of the country, a rank injustice'.[4]

The *Daily Telegraph* looked at the Party from another angle; politics, the newspaper argued, depended on two parties, though Labor had survived long enough to obtain as much recognition as a third party

8 Their Little Tin God.
'We are a God-fearing Ministry.'—NSW Education Minister Garrard.
The Bulletin, 12 October 1895

could earn; Labor's position meant that it had to attach itself to one or other of the existing parties, but because it asserted the ability to replace a ministry it had 'to be reckoned with both as an active and potential power'; any progressive party would endorse McGowen's view of the role of the Labor Party, because all liberals and an enlightened electorate sought legislation for the general good. The *Telegraph* acknowledged an important and beneficial result of Labor's work when it admitted that the Party had increased electors' interest in parliament, which they could now see had become a place where more than talking took place. But the newspaper denied that Reid had merely appropriated the clothes of

Labor, and went on to argue that the Party's independence was limited by its bargaining with Reid; therefore it concluded that outside Labor members should support their Assembly members because: 'The solidarity voter has to face a condition in which, since he manifestly cannot get all he asks for, he must accept the best and most a dominant party will give him'.[5] While the *Telegraph* tried to convince Labor voters to accept the inevitable, *Liberty* tried to remove 'the propellor in the legislative machinery' by exhorting the free traders and protectionists 'to settle their differences and make short work of the self-seeking unscrupulous and intriguing [Labor] faction'.[6]

Against this background of a community acceptance that included intemperate and even unprincipled criticism, the PLL prepared for its 1897 conference. The energy and expectations of the organised socialists had enabled them to reach a position in which they had a degree of administrative power in the structure of the League out of proportion with their minority status. While there had been a gradual mass acceptance of the increasing power of the state to meet modern conditions of economic growth and social improvement, there had been no concurrent approval of doctrinaire socialism. Indeed McGowen's speech in the Legislative Assembly in August 1895 in which he linked unrest with 'socialism' and 'anarchy' reflected deep-seated popular opinion that too much concentration on planning to introduce a system of socialism would produce a situation in which blood would flow and drown individual liberty. The Labor Party had checked the development of social options that were restricted to unrestrained capitalism and blueprinted socialism. In their place, at least temporarily, Labor had put, with some help from Reid, modernised liberalism and working class radicalism, both of which promised eclectic reform; the one leisurely and cautiously, the other rapidly and exploratively, with neither policy endangering approved basic beliefs in democracy and personal freedom. But the fact remained that in none of the three general elections fought by Labor had the Party tested voters' views on direct socialism; a result had been that the prudence of the parliamentarians was assessed by some league members as defeatist and the visions of the socialists as sound. The latter were moved to consolidate their influence and make the Labor Party an avowed vehicle for their organised creed.

A major problem affecting the socialists was their disunity and confusion; indeed, it seemed that the more they organised to achieve their aims the more befuddled and mutually antagonistic they became. Some of them did not approve of the Labor Party in any sense and contrasted their zeal and doctrinal purity with the time serving of those who would use it:

> We are not [they said] weak-kneed, spineless, contortionating opportunists, fired with the soul-inspiring ambition to place our bleeding hearts on the altar

of our perishing country—to become apathetic, to slumber calmly, while around us exist conditions that are almost on a par with Dante's description of the infernal regions. But enough! Comrades of autocracy! Our paths lie far apart. You have chosen the broad—we the narrow—and now farewell! A long farewell.[7]

But in 1896 this was a sectarian view within a restless minority of the Labor movement. Most socialists saw the Labor Party as an institution worthy to be taken over. They formed a zestful minority at a meeting of about 150 delegates of city Labor leagues held at the Labor Centre on 15 October; Flowers went over the agenda of the forthcoming 1897 conference and reminded the meeting that the 1896 conference had decided to run ten candidates for the Federal convention; therefore, he said, much propaganda work was necessary. The meeting agreed on an extensive publicity campaign.[8] At least some of this organising included the resuscitation of city leagues; according to the *Northern People,* a newspaper with the motto 'socialism in our time', the work resulted in the election of several delegates to the 1897 conference who favoured 'the Collectivist movement'.[9] The *Northern People* also reported a proposal for conference from the Leichhardt league to the effect that the first plank of the fighting platform should become the 'Nationalisation of the whole of the means of Production, Distribution and Exchange'; and proceeded to state that the fate of this suggestion would probably fix 'the future political course of action to be taken by the Socialists of N.S.W.'; if it were accepted, '[they] will continue as in the past to form the advanced wing of the Political Labor League', and capitalist fiscalists would be forced to leave the Party; moreover, 'It will remove the stigma . . . [of] the Labor Party . . . being the tail of the Free Trade party . . . [and] will make the issue of battle the question of socialism versus Competitive Capitalism'.[10]

The *Northern People's* analysis of the relationship of socialism and the Labor Party was in the realm of fantasy. In a general formative way socialism had certainly influenced Labor policy and would continue to do so, but the Party was too deeply rooted in colonial society and too widely based on the working class to become the pawn of a minority group, especially such a motley band as the organised socialists. By late 1896 the substantial character that the Labor Party had already attained as an essential part of the new parliamentary system of New South Wales was unalterable, short of a cataclysm; and that character, conditioned by the overwhelming majority of Labor members and Labor voters, dictated the form and content of Party policy. In a lecture late in the year Hughes, by implication emphasised this basic position. He claimed that the imposition of the land tax was a great victory for the Labor Party which had 'popularized it . . . introduced it to thousands who knew nothing of it before, and . . . made its [acceptance by parliament] imperative'; he scorned the wild conservatives who were using 'much time and expense . . . as they phrase it "to frustrating the diabolical efforts of the gang of socialists who rule this country" '; he argued that the alternative to the caucus was rule by one man, but the people would not have that, although it would produce a very efficient party; Labor's platform was known to all, in contrast with that of men of the Lyne stamp 'whose policy changes with each change of weather'. He brought out an important result of Labor's parliamentary role when he asserted that 'what we prevent is almost as important as what we do . . . It isn't safe to openly rob the people now'. He admitted that the Party could be improved, but it had 'inaugurated a new era [and] there can be no going back'. Watson supported Hughes. 'The Labor Party', he said,

> is the best the workers can get. The only way to reform it is to make the leagues strong . . . It can only be reformed from within. You can't revolutionize society in four or five years. If you let a little shortcoming dishearten you, you can't do it at all.[11]

These were the authentic voices of basic Labor opinion. Advanced minority opinion had to be adjusted to it.

At the 1897 PLL conference held at the Labor Centre on 26 January, the socialist motion was moved by T. Keniry and seconded by T. Symons, who had been secretary of the TLC in the 1880s. The original proposal was to place it on the fighting platform, which would have highlighted it among the primary planks on which elections had to be fought; but after a long discussion and several proposed amendments it was included in the general platform; in the debate Holman admitted the soundness of the idea as a statement of principle, but argued it would be out of place on the fighting platform, 'which should consist of clear and definite proposals'.[12] This kind of compromise was an integral part of the process by which Labor policy was articulated, a mixture of comradeship and partisanship; in an important way the socialist plank was complemented by a decision to demand that the people be given the right of direct legislation by means of the initiative. Another decision of conference was much more relevant to the reality of Labor participation in affairs of state: the ten candidates were selected to run for the Federal Convention, Black, Ferguson, Flowers, Griffith, Holman, Hughes, McGowen, Sleath, Spence and Watson, all members of the Legislative Assembly, except Flowers, Holman and Spence. This was the best team that Labor could have fielded at the time, although a letter writer, with the apt pseudonym of 'Doubtful', asserted that they were all 'pronounced socialists', except McGowen.[13] The persistence of interest in Federation was shown by the decision to rescind the 1896 approval for two Houses of parliament and replace it with a plank seeking a single House. A resolution that medicine be made a national service affirmed the continuance of the social amelioration strand of policy; the previous year's proposals for increased government activity in the economy were extended by planks for the establishment of state woollen mills and clothing factories, and for a national bank to have the sole rights to issue bank notes. Flowers was re-elected as president, Barlow as secretary; the new executive included Moroney, Holman and Spence; and it was decided that future conferences should be held in 'the largest centres . . . [as well as] Sydney'.[14]

Although this conference met only on one day, the emergence of obdurate procedural characteristics could be noted: the attraction of resolutions and speeches as ends in themselves, the appeal of rigid protocol that demanded elaborate rules. These tendencies were, of course, present at all of the previous gatherings, but now that conference was clearly a permanent institution its developing ritual was manifestly part of the formal role of the Labor Party, providing opportunities of self-expression for its members and confirming their social adherence. While most of the newspapers concentrated their attention on the conference by adverse comment either on the socialist plank or on the Federation policy,[15] the *Worker* acutely observed that,

> About the details of the platform the really earnest Labor leaguer does not trouble much. He knows that many of those are not worth the labor spent in discussing them. But they satisfy some who in time will learn better than to exhaust the patience of their fellows in discussion about words.[16]

Nevertheless, the Labor platform was a document demanding attention from both its supporters and opponents.

The socialist plank, which affected the future of the Labor Party, was adopted soon after the conclusion of a parliamentary session in which the Labor Assembly members consolidated their growing reputation as indefatigable and practical parliamentarians. The session had opened on 12 May 1896 with Reid indicating through the governor that the ministry remained determined to reform the Upper House, chiefly by reducing the number of its members and abolishing their life tenure. He responded to Labor's stress on the referendum by a proposal to bring down a bill to seek the decision of the electors on all the matters on which both Houses had failed to agree. As he claimed that fiscal strife had at last ceased, he said he would be able to proceed with non-party legislation that had long been postponed by successive governments and which affected 'the industrial welfare of the whole community'. He also planned to press for public health improvement, the suppression of dangerous nuisances, the treatment of infectious and contagious diseases, the enforcement of sanitary precautions, control of food processing and reform of the Board of Health. Among other matters, he would seek electoral reform, relief for selectors and amendments to the Navigation Act.[17] The Labor Party approved all of this program, indeed had initiated much of it, and helped to prepare the ground for some of it: a noteworthy exception was Reid's attention to public health reform, which Labor had not seriously considered, although the TLC had been concerned with it in the 1880s. The whole proposals continued the Reid-Labor momentum of preparing discerning legislation to help in the modernisation of New South Wales.

By the time the session had ended, 16 November, the government had introduced fifty-six out of ninety-seven public bills, including two finance bills; the fact that twenty-nine became law showed that the reconditioned legislative machinery was still working well, with the government strengthening its control. But the Council had by no means abdicated what it regarded as its responsibilities; it kept back eleven government bills and amended several others, including the coloured races restriction and regulation bill (which was reserved by the governor), the factories and shops bill, the land and income tax amendment bill, and the mining laws amendment bill. The Labor parliamentarians continued to prepare private members' public bills; Griffith was most active with seven bills, none of which became law, while Cann succeeded with his Standard Time Act amendment bill (Act No. 4, 1896). All of the Labor members took an active part in parliamentary work, especially McGowen, Cann, Hughes, Griffith and Watson. As a group, their attendance was the best in the House, fifteen of the eighteen Labor men were among the fifty-two out of a total of 125 Assembly members who had 100 or more attendances at various divisions in the session; and their participation in the whole range of debates and questions was impressive. Altogether, they excelled in an exhausting session that featured many all-night sittings.

The Assembly's vote in November on the Council's amendments to the coloured race restriction bill was an interesting example of the many parliamentary situations in which a Labor solidarity vote did not apply. The bill had been thoroughly discussed in the Lower House and equally so in the upper chamber, which on this occasion acted as a useful house of review, making several improvements in the bill. The substantial object, the extension of restriction of entry from Chinese to other coloured peoples, was not changed; and that had been the basis of caucus analysis of the bill. But the Council made several amendments, including provision for coloured missionaries to be admitted to the colony. Reid had learnt to accede to the Council's wishes whenever to do so did not involve the loss of the essential principle of legislation; much as he disliked the various compromises involved in this practice, they were part of the way in which the rate of successful law making was being stepped up. On the occasion of the race bill he was agreeable to accept the amendments so that the measure might quickly become law. But there were several Labor members who considered that the Council should be resisted, and the Party split 8 to 7 in a vote of 61 to 14 to agree to the amendments;[18] many of the members who voted for the agreement, including the Labor ones, were influenced by the fact that the session was drawing to its close and delay would have meant that the bill would probably have been lost. The incident illustrated the multiform complexity and range of parliamentary practice; many similar instances arose in detailed committee analysis of clauses of bills. Controlled abstentions had been arranged in June in a vote taken on a censure motion moved on the ministry by Lyne in connection with the Dean Royal Commission, when only nine Labor members remained to support Reid; Watson argued that the Party had to give a shock to the government and 'things would be livelier [now] than the ministers might like'.[19] The rules of caucus and solidarity voting continued to evolve under the impulse of circumstances in the 1890s.

The Party maintained pressure on the government. In June Hughes moved the adjournment to bring up the alleged evasion of taxes by Tooth & Co. Ltd, 'the largest brewers in Australia'. This incident illustrated the role of the Labor Party in exposing abuses and seeking parliamentary action to improve business morality. It was a complicated case and Reid successfully defended the public servants involved in it; the motion lost 24 to 61, and Watson later described the affair as 'the worst act of the Reid administration, but the Labor Party found themselves helpless in the face of the united forces of the other parties'.[20] Similar action by Hughes also failed in November when he bitingly criticised the government for giving free railway passes for delegates to the citizens' Federation convention at Bathurst. Hughes gave generous praise to Reid for bringing Federation 'practically within "coo-ee" [of realisation]', but rubbished the convention as being formed by 'the diligent scraping of parochial nobodies from all parts of the colonies'.[21] Reid in reply at first jocularly remarked that he was surprised that anyone should object to the government bestowing free travel, which was one of the most acceptable perquisites of the times; but then he took the opportunity to tell the House that he had 'always desired to encourage the people . . . to take a practical interest in [Federation] themselves'; that he did not want a movement activated from above and was therefore pleased that the convention had been organised; and that he had neither ridicule nor contempt for any group of people who discussed Federation.[22]

The debates and votes on the factories and shops bill in a sense summed up the great value of the Labor Party to the whole reforming process as it affected New South Wales in the 1890s, and showed the inexorable limits to what the Party could achieve. The colony lagged well behind all the Australasian colonies, except Queensland, in legislating to control working hours and conditions in factories. Without the general improvements in parliamentary practice and the changes in social outlook conditioned by Labor, it is difficult to see just how any factories bill could have emerged from the New South Wales parliament.

This was a field in which free trade and protectionist opinion coalesced, and the consensus indicated how it would be possible for them to form a general and permanent conservative combination once fiscalism had entirely evaporated as a political force. The reluctance of the free traders to move for control of factories stemmed from their doctrinaire belief in economic individualism, so well illustrated by Parkes's objections to eight hours legislation. The opposition of the protectionists was practical: the factories were owned by wealthy members of the group; they favoured state action when it would further their interests, but rejected it when it would restrict them. Labor's notion of state action was also self-interested to a degree because it would protect the working class; but, nourished by various humane opinions, ranging from Dacey's *Rerum Novarum* inspiration to Moroney's Marxian intuition, its policy was essentially public spirited and socially beneficial. The Party's support for factory legislation was unequivocal, it had been inscribed on the first platform in 1890 and remained there; Parkes had responded to it in his 1891 legislative proposals, but there was no real chance of a factory bill until Reid took over.

Reid's new liberalism incorporated limited state intervention in economic and industrial matters; it gathered up the muted strands in free trade opinion that favoured factory legislation, and, solidly backed by Labor, finally prepared a bill, which was presented to parliament for second reading on 16 July by Garrard, now Reid's minister for education and also the colony's first minister for labor and industry. Garrard's able speech surveyed attempts from 1876 to initiate some form of legislative control over employment in factories, especially of women and children, and stressed New South Wales's backwardness in the field.[23] McGowen welcomed the bill though he regarded it only as a first instalment of reform;[24] his speech provided the basis of determined Labor action in committee, seeking to get the maximum concessions, and gradually focusing on the need to eliminate 'sweating', the practice of employing women and children in their own dwellings at extortionate piece rates that made excessively long hours of work, up to 100 a week, necessary for a meagre sustenance. With its vision of economic freedom to the fore the Legislative Council amended the bill, though again some of the changes were improvements, given the pioneering aspect of the legislation. When the Council's amendments were considered in the Lower House, the position had once more been reached where the alternatives were to accept the proposed changes or lose the bill. The Labor Party kept up its fight to the bitter end for a better law; but, with the aid of liberal opinion, the Party had already achieved the best possible legislation that could have been had at the time. The final vote to accept the Council's changes, which left 'sweating' virtually untouched, was 52 to 18, with the thirteen Labor members present voting with the minority.[25]

By 1897 parliamentary activities of the PLL had been obviously the main way in which it had established itself as a permanent and vital part of the new political system operating in New South Wales. Perforce, the League had elected to contest the Federal Convention elections to be held on 4 March, a decision that stamped its social role, clarified even more by the fact that seven of its ten candidates were members of parliament, and the remaining three soon would be: Holman and Spence became members of the Legislative Assembly in 1898, Flowers a member of the Legislative Council in 1900, and he had already contested several elections. There was a uniformity in the public actions of the League, even if there seemed a certain unpredictability about its internal behaviour. The Moroneys and Barlows were clearly not regarded as suitable representatives of Labor for the big occasions, an opinion in which, evidently, they themselves would have shared. Now, as the Party prepared to adjust its parliamentary zeal to a unique election, it was entering on an undertaking that was to help it to make accurate judgments about what it was doing and where it was going. And the process was facilitated by the fact that Holman played an active part in it; already, although still chafing at his exclusion from the real action of the Party, he was beginning to agree with the parliamentarians that its total structure should reflect more decisively its basic role as a social democratic mass parliamentary party. This meant that the organised socialists had to be helped to reach the correct decision in their agonising over whether they should stay in the PLL or leave it, for, while they believed in the goodness and intelligence of people in the abstract, they had no firm faith in the working class as the basis of a radical mass party.

Although considerable educative work had been done by many individuals, chiefly Edmund Barton, and some groups, notably the Australasian Federation League, it was George Reid's decisive parliamentary patronage that by 1897 had produced a situation in which Federation was accepted in principle by the people of New South Wales. Reid was incontestably the outstanding man in the colony; an essential ingredient of his work had been his comprehensive reform policy which, consistently aided and at times regulated by the Labor Party, had gone a long way in transforming colonial society: politics were more rational, social groups better articulated and better related one to another. The Labor Party had provided an indispensable part of the means by which the colony had been prepared to make clear-headed judgments about Federation. Apart from its political co-operation with Reid, the Party had formally placed Federation in its 1891 platform, had kept it there and had evolved a clear policy about the subject: no other parliamentary group had analysed it on this scale.

In 1891 Labor had presciently linked Federation with the defence power in seeking 'Australasian' union 'upon a national as opposed to an imperialistic basis' and the replacement of the permanent defence force with a voluntary system. There were clear 1891 overtones in this plank; at the time New Zealand was thought of as a possible constituent state, and the vague idea of a British union based on England was still in the air, hence the words 'national as opposed to an imperialistic basis'. But there was more to the formulation: by 'national federation', Labor also meant an inward-looking, peaceful and self-reliant union as opposed to one outward-looking, aggressive and dependent on Britain: there were also some elements of anti-British crown sentiments in the phrase, though the stress was rather on the initiative and self-reliance of Australia than on reaction against the mother country. This view of Federation provided a useful corrective to the compliant and restricted expectations of most of the delegates at the 1891 Federation Convention. The plank was left in this form in 1892, except that 'Australasian' became 'Australian'. By 1896 the defence force link had been removed, and the plank was 'The Federation of the Australian colonies on a

National, as opposed to an Imperialistic basis'. The Labor Party had given clear notice that in supporting Federation, it was determined to make it as democratic and as Australian as possible. This policy was influential with Reid. He was battling strenuously against conservative forces in local politics and did not propose to allow them a free hand in Federation affairs. The Labor Party helped him in the national as well as the provincial area.

Labor's campaign for the election of Federation delegates exposed the Party's major electoral problem. It was an organised radical party, and its total impression was one of zestful and youthful drive as it attempted to change ingrained colonial attitudes to politics. It had had considerable success up to 1897. But basic difficulties remained, emphasised by Labor's attraction for the organised socialists. The electorate was cautious, anxious to take advantage of Labor's crusading spirit, but always trying to keep it within acceptable bounds. In a real sense the Party was still on probation, and a large number of the voters' hesitancies about it were based on direct opposition, compounded of reaction, fear and snobbery. Much of this resistance could be eroded in time, but by no means all of it. The Party had found the going hard enough at ordinary general elections when it could tap special sections of support in particular seats; now it had to campaign over the entire colony with the results being determined by the total vote. This was a situation in which Labor's progressive nature could prove only a handicap, especially as Federation, despite Reid's efforts to have it emerge from the people, was inevitably a movement in which the elite, in one form or another, predominated.

The Labor men were oblivious to these problems. It could not have been otherwise. When they worked out a policy that would exclude an Upper House in the federal system, they automatically placed themselves outside of serious consideration as contenders for convention seats. But their experience had revealed to them that an Upper House was the major political bulwark of privilege. They saw such a House as a danger to democracy, compounded in a federal system. Others saw it as democracy's preserver. When Labor countered with a plan for the members of the federal Upper House to be elected proportionately to each colony's population, the cry was raised that this would destroy the identity of the smaller colonies and they would never federate. There was no way out for Labor. The making of the federal constitution was a task for the educated middle class. Australian democracy needed the active participation of members of the working class, but was not mature enough in the 1890s to admit their representatives to the august work of drawing the blueprint to make one nation out of six colonies.

Cann was made the director of the Labor bunch's campaign. As well as a unicameral system of Federation, the Party sought one adult one vote, payment of members, elective ministries and the initiative and referendum:[1] basic democratic features, some of them approved by other groups, all of them having a powerful, if subtle, effect on the thinking of voters on the whole problem of Federation. But this election was concerned with a convention that would undertake the task of drawing up a constitution, free of any presuppositions, except the unstated ones that would bind it to the British crown, the inbuilt conservatism of both the legal profession and the mass of the middle class, and the provincialism of separate British colonies. The publicity media soon made it clear that the Labor approach was anathema. The decision to run ten candidates was regarded as dangerously deviant; Hughes's reply was incomprehensible to the conservatives and to the majority of voters who were prepared to be led by them; even Federation, he argued, was a matter for argument on principle, other parties may leave it to private judgment, but not the Labor Party.[2] Hughes berated the Victorian Labor movement for including members of other parties in its bunch, and said, 'We don't recognise that there is a political labor party in Victoria'.[3] The whole New South Wales campaign revived some of the obscurantist features of past elections in the colony that had seemed to have been put to rest in the Reid-Labor era: Cardinal Moran was a candidate, and inspired a Protestant backlash; the United Protestant Conference drew up its 'approved bunch' and included McGowen in it. The PLL executive protested in vain.[4] Reid and Barton strenuously stumped the country, emphasising the advantages of Federation as well as their own convention candidatures. The Labor Party likewise worked hard, but it soon became evident that the best known politicians were to be the winners.

On a great day for the colony, declared a public holiday by Reid, Barton topped the field of forty-nine with 105,000 votes, beating Reid into second place by some 15,000 votes; a notable achievement, helped above all by his great extramural work for Federation, but also by his position on the ballot paper, he was fifth and Reid thirty-eighth; by the premier's increasing loss of support among the middle class because of his coalition with Labor; and by Labor's campaign, which attracted a 'bunched' radical vote away from Reid. Six of the ten successful delegates were lawyers; nine of them were politicians, only Barton and Wise not in parliament. Fiscalism hardly counted, but Reid, Brunker and Carruthers were new liberal free traders and cabinet colleagues, McMillan an old-style free trader, and Lyne a protectionist. J. T. Walker, a banker, was the non-politician. All of them were fervent federationists, except Lyne. McGowen did best of the Labor bunch, coming in fifteenth with some 42,000 votes, about 15,000 below the last of the successful men, Wise; Ferguson was twentieth, Black twenty-second, Sleath twenty-fifth, Hughes twenty-sixth, Watson twenty-eighth, Spence thirtieth, Holman

thirty-second, Griffith thirty-fourth and Flowers thirty-fifth. The per-
formances were not so bad as they seemed at first sight. But in the light
of the Labor candidates' expectations they appeared disastrous. Soul-
searching began with the spontaneity that comes naturally to radicals
at times of rejection.

A post-mortem was held at the Labor Centre on 8 March. Moroney,
who presided, thought that sectarianism had been responsible for the
débâcle in conjunction with the anti-Labor combination of conservative
and reactionary forces; the Party had to become more aggressive. In
contrast, Holman based his analysis on modern electoral tactics: Labor
had to complement public meetings with house to house canvassing, and
to realise that 'their platform was advanced enough now to serve for the
next twenty years'; he regretted McGowen's significant absence from
the convention and astutely noted that the elected delegates were men
whom the community thought had a monopoly of intelligence and
education. Watson, ever practical, did not think that the vote was relevant to parliamentary elections; he was adamant that sectarianism
should be banned from the Party and considered that Cardinal Moran
had been the unwitting pawn of the conservatives to down Labor; but
he was not downcast and was confident that more seats could be won in
the country, though not in the city. Flowers judged that a strong
educational program was needed because even workers, many of them,
associated the Labor Party with anarchy. In a letter, Griffith, irked at his
low vote in his own seat, pointed out that many other candidates had
suffered the same indignity; he concluded that most Labor voters gave
their candidates little chance and 'gave a solid vote for the Protestant
bunch to keep out the Cardinal'.[5]

A fortnight later Black in an article in the *Daily Telegraph* summed
up the reasons for Labor's defeat. He, too, stressed sectarianism and
lambasted the style of the Labor campaign, 'Our crude, ill-considered,
bumptious manifesto, and the vague flabby vapourings published later in
support undoubtedly did us harm'; but he followed Holman's lead and
stressed what he judged to be the main cause of the rebuff, and the
typical Blackian hyperbole did not conceal what was coming to be
accepted as the basic truth:

> So far every . . . Labour . . . Conference has done harm. The wirepullers
> have controlled them by the aid of bogus Leagues, and Leagues hurriedly
> organized for the occasion . . . the opinions of most of us are many years
> ahead of our time . . . and as it is the mass we hope to benefit by reform, we
> can gain nothing by having them far in the rear . . . political striving for the
> unattainable, often rendering moderate reforms impossible, will be suspended
> in order that the moderate, when accomplished, may be used as stepping-
> stones to bring things otherwise impossible.[6]

Labor's defeat had been a traumatic experience, making it impossible
for Party members to comprehend that Federation was not a political

issue and that their decision to fight on a specific policy had placed them outside the arena. Electors had been conditioned to believe that the making of a constitution was an esoteric exercise suitable only for the right men, 'the intellect of the colony'. Indeed, until the advent of the Labor Party, to a large degree this was also how parliamentary activity was regarded, but it was diffusely complex enough to allow the concept to be challenged and the Labor Party was in process of widening a breach in accepted political ideas and practice that they had made in 1891. Much of the Party's analysis of the convention election fiasco was wide of the mark and more relevant to the general uneasiness that the Legislative Assembly members were coming to feel about the kind of Labor people who were in virtual control of the extra-parliamentary wing of the Party. The parliamentarians were in fact worried about ordinary elections and their concern pre-dated the 1897 defeat and was intensified by it. What they did between March 1897 and January 1898 was to align, so far as they could, the outside structure with the facts of Labor's parliamentary mission as they saw it, so that Labor might continue its role as the main reforming force in New South Wales. At the same time they and their supporters fashioned a situation in which the organised socialists could decide their future political action.

In 1897 it was clear that the Labor Party could only survive as a powerful force if it adjusted its total activities to the requirements of the electorate: working class radicalism did not have to be abandoned, but it had either to shed formally its extreme minority element or to contain it in an acceptable way. McGowen's view of the role of the Labor Party as a moderate but decisive reforming institution and his vision of a Labor man as one who subordinated his own particular fads to the general consensus were about to be generally approved. His leadership was none the less effective for its benevolence. By 1895 he had won over the Labor Assembly members; by the middle of 1897 he had convinced Holman and Flowers. Holman's conversion was vital, for he represented the most active and intelligent of the young socialists outside parliament. His adherence meant that the Labor Party would not be cut off entirely from one of its essential sources of ideas, and that young radicals would still be encouraged to join the Party.

The centre of the Labor Party strength of the organised socialists was in the Sydney District Assembly of the PLL, with Moroney playing a leading part. District assemblies had significant powers under the League constitution, and to a degree rivalled the executive: e.g., assemblies approved the formation of branch leagues. The Sydney Assembly delegates saw the problem as one of reorganisation, in which moribund leagues would be revived and new branches formed, strong in socialist fervour. In April an Assembly motion to censure the parliamentarians failed only on the chairman's casting vote. But the executive was the base of the Party machine; with Flowers president and Holman, Spence and two representatives of the ALF, the parliamentarians' line had a solid core of support there, opposed by Barlow, Moroney and Keniry, with J. H. Thompson, E. Riley and A. M. Harper not firmly attached to either side. By July it was clear that supporters of moderate tactics had the numbers on the executive, when the Sydney District Assembly censured the executive for failing to publicise the 1897 platform.[7] By September Barlow, Moroney and Keniry had resigned from the executive,[8] and H. Lamond (1866–1947) became acting secretary of the PLL. Lamond was the editor of the *Worker,* and in 1902 became Spence's son-in-law. The way was now open to readjust the electoral image of the Labor Party. By the end of the year Lamond reported that at the request of the Labor members of the Assembly several meetings had been held between them and the executive with a view to amending the PLL constitution, and he submitted details of the proposals to the ALF 'prior to [their] being put upon the business paper for consideration at the next Conference of the PLL'.[9]

The events of March–September 1897 in the Labor Party should not be over-simplified as a purging of those socialists who were organised in various groups. They were confronted by a crisis just as the PLL was. It is difficult to generalise about them, as they were not a united band. But from its foundation the Labor Party had welcomed all progressive groups into its ranks; it had no rule disbarring any particular sect. Labor policy, while grounded in a generation of trade union practice and moulded by basic social forces, had been influenced by socialism in its broadest application, as, indeed, had the whole of western society. In this sense socialism was an integral part of the Labor Party and Mc-Gowen and many other others had acknowledged it. There was no dissimulation in this, only a recognition that any radical party had to absorb at least some elements of modern advanced social theory. The 1897 conflict in the Labor Party was essentially an argument about the place socialism should occupy in the Party's structure and about the nature of socialism's influence on policy: there was no question of banishing socialism. The organised socialists were within their rights in seeking to make the Labor Party an acknowledged socialist party. They saw the Party as a means to gain the mass support they could not otherwise attain; and most of them, above all Moroney, were sincere altruists, indefatigable workers for the betterment of mankind.

Unfortunately for these men, their very concentration on achieving a socialist society alienated them from their own milieu and linked them, however tenuously, with overseas revolutionaries who seemed to want to sacrifice some people in order to perfect others. So that the organised socialists in the PLL were an embarrassment to a Party that eschewed violence and sought improvement through democratic pressure and rational argument. The Labor Party was expressing itself through parliament, it had to gain more votes and win more seats to implement its policy fully. The Labor men in parliament saw the Party's problem in this way. Their view prevailed because it reflected the natural social absorption of Labor, and as a result they received majority support, both inside and outside the Party. But there was some understandable disappointment and genuine perplexity in the assessment of the *Australian Workman* as it reproached the Sydney Assembly:

> In taking our farewell of the Sydney District Assembly we . . . tell Labor men . . . our honest opinion that . . . it would be better to drop the existing PLL altogether and let the [labor] parties reconstruct themselves on separate lines. There is no reason why they should not work together harmoniously when they are not falling over each other's feet in a vain attempt to assimilate each other. Let [those] who want a State Socialist Party come straight out and form one, and let those who think it better to proceed with as radical a platform as they think attainable, to assist the workers in working out their own salvation by industrial combination and purifying the spirit of public institutions, do what they can independently.[10]

This view revealed that one of the big questions involved in the 1897 Labor dispute was the proportionate influence on Party platform and constitution that should be exercised by purely working class and trade union experience and by middle class theorising about the working class. The practical element prevailed, though the theoretical element was not destroyed. The socialists' position also exposed one of their major weaknesses, integral to their essential elitism: they had no comprehension of the part played in democratic politics and in the Labor Party by country people. This ignorance was in marked contrast with the insight of Watson and of Holman, whose conversion to McGowen's policy had been facilitated by his work since early 1896 in the Grenfell electorate.[11]

W. J. Ferguson, who represented the far western seat of Sturt, chiefly metalliferous mining with some pastoral activity, by 1897 had mellowed from the fiery leader he had been in the 1892 Broken Hill strike. Addressing a farewell gathering for Ben Tillett, the British Labor leader, who was leaving Sydney in October, Ferguson uncovered the iron that remained in his soul despite his solidarity with his parliamentary colleagues:

> It's not a bit of use you cheering a man like friend Tillett when he says he's an extremist. Actions speak louder than words. It's votes that count . . . Two-thirds of the Sydney workers are not prepared to go to the lengths of Trades Unionism, and Socialism is a step beyond [that] . . . The man who comes forward to fight the workers' battle will find his bitterest opponents among the men he's fighting for.[12]

Next month, for different immediate reasons, though probably arising from the same basic universal problem that ultimately confronts all dedicated radicals, Moroney also expressed his disillusion when he told the Sydney District Council of the ALF that 'as an honest individual he had decided to sever his connection with the Political Labor League and devote his leisure time to the study of Socialism'.[13] Moroney followed up his resignation with a long letter to the 1898 PLL conference, which virtually ignored it. The statement exposed the bitter disenchantment with the Labor Party of a worker whose radicalism was conditioned by his reflection on socialism rather than his trade union experience. There was no doubt about Moroney's sincerity; like many other young socialists he had grasped the Labor Party as a means to implement his principles on rational living. But he had romanticised his doctrine, misinterpreted the Party and misunderstood the people; and his bitterness reflected his failure. 'The position now is', he said, 'that the PLL has degenerated into a mere vote-catching machine, doing no educational work, and generally following a policy of compromise and supineness . . . defined as "Practical Politics".'[14]

From August to October 1897 a strike of gold-miners at Lucknow, near Orange, had provided some important background to the process of the Labor Party shedding the socialists. Although the strikers were not affiliated to the ALF, the Sydney District Council attempted to raise funds for them, but provided only minimal help as trade unionism remained in the doldrums.[15] The strike had been caused by dismissals following allegations of stealing and subsequent proposals by the proprietors to re-employ the men provided they would accept wage reductions and sign an agreement signifying that they did not object to being searched. The strikers also sought help from the Labor parliamentarians. McGowen, Watson, Ferguson, Sleath, Brown and Thomas visited them at various times, attempted to arrange a negotiated settlement, especially after many free labourers had been imported from Victoria, organised funds, provisions and clothing for them and publicised their plight. The parliamentarians failed in their immediate objective to end the dispute in the strikers' favour, but they showed by their determined efforts that practical aid and comfort could be given by Assembly members to the Labor movement, and in the long run their work helped to improve working conditions for miners and put a stop to degrading searches of workers. Their experience also strengthened the movement's growing conviction that amended industrial legislation was needed to provide for compulsory arbitration and awards.[16] This work of the Assembly members was far removed from abstract arguments about a 'socialist society' and the 'nationalisation of the means of production', and illustrated the great range of duties falling them under the heading of 'Practical Politics'.

The strike also brought out some of the parliamentary forms of 'Practical Politics'. Aware of the Labor Party's misgivings over certain aspects of the government's handling of the strike, on 2 November Lyne moved a censure motion alleging 'that the action of the Government with reference to the Lucknow strike amounts to a maladministration of justice'.[17] In a masterly speech McGowen avoided the trap Lyne had set, and pointed out that the Labor Party's complaint about the government was not that it had intervened too much, as Lyne had claimed, but rather that it had not gone far enough in its attempts to settle the dispute.[18] In contrast, Hughes vehemently attacked the protectionists for their failure to support the strikers, and exaggeratedly expressed a view widely held by the New South Wales Labor movement about free labourers from Victoria when he said, 'There has not been a strike . . . [in this colony] . . . but it has been defeated uniformly by people from that paradise—Victoria'; but like McGowen he refused 'to be "nobbled" ' by Lyne.[19] E. W. O'Sullivan tried in vain to divert criticism of the protectionists as 'representatives of monopoly' by asserting that Reid was duping the Labor Party; 'I want', he said, 'to show the utter falsity of trusting to a man who wears an eyeglass'.[20] The motion lost 33 to 65, with all seventeen of the Labor men present voting against it: had they changed sides the government would have lost 48 to 50.

The Lucknow strike committee had no doubt about the value of the Labor Party's help, it sent to McGowen its 'heartiest thanks for the brotherly and effective manner in which [your Party] worked on our behalf', and emphasised that 'we recognize how necessary it is in the interests of the workers that the . . . Party should be a part of our political life'. The *Worker* was pleased that Lyne's motion did not ensnare the Party.[21] The Lucknow incident graphically revealed the broad base of humanitarianism that helped to give the Party its real shape and strength and to substantiate the validity of its natural pragmatism. Doctrine had its essential place in the Labor Party; but warm relations with people owed nothing to theory; indeed, were potentially prejudiced by it.

With abundant rank and file backing the parliamentarians prepared to reassure the electorate that the Labor Party contained no hidden devices of destruction. The 1898 conference met on 26 and 27 January at the Cambrian Hall, Newcastle, the first one outside Sydney. Thirty delegates were present, including ten Assembly members, Black, Brown, Dacey, Griffith, Hughes, Law, Macdonald, McGowen, Watson and Sleath, and several of their strong supporters, including Spence, Lamond, and Donald Macdonell (1862–1911), a rising leader of the AWU. Both Lamond and Macdonell were already ably illustrating the revitalised interest of the AWU in the Labor Party, following the union's beginning of financial recovery; Macdonell, from Bourke, had taken an effective part in the previous year's debates about the nature of the Party, injecting a powerful plea on behalf of the country movement for concentration on organisation rather than policy.[22]

Although there is little doubt that the parliamentarians had prepared

plans to scrap the socialist plank adopted in 1897, the conference's handling of the proposal was a salutary reminder that its general style and
the rigidity of its methods posed difficulties for any group who planned
to control it completely. Just as the socialists had failed to place the
socialist plank on to the fighting platform in 1897, so did the parliamentarians fail to remove it from the general platform in 1898, though
presumably each group had the required numbers. The incident also
revealed that the Labor Party could retain a formal principle, provided
it had at least some remote connection with its aims, even though it had
lost its essential meaning: a reflection of the comradeship of the whole
Labor movement and, in a sense, a gesture of defiance to the society
that bound it.

The nullifying motion, moved by John Hepher (1851–1932) a socialist
friend of McGowen, was a badly drafted compromise, 'That the socialistic plank carried at the last conference be removed from the platform,
with a view to its insertion as a declaration of principle'. It immediately
brought out the way in which many conference debates had a life of
their own apart from their substance and any plans to stagemanage
them. J. Henderson, Illawarra league delegate, went right to the heart of
the matter:

> the failure of the Federal elections should teach them that their future policy
> must be based on political possibilities . . . If they told the people they would
> stand or fall on this one principle, then their fall would be a decided one.[23]

F. Butler, Narrabri delegate, revealed that at least some country league
members wanted socialism in the platform; but Macdonell argued that
hundreds of league members were not socialists, though they believed in
many of the socialistic planks, 'but to say that they were in favor of the
nationalization of the means of production and exchange would be wide
of the truth'; he moved an amendment to delete reference to 'the
declaration of principle', but Flowers disallowed it and his ruling was
upheld 13 to 11. Lamond said that the aim of the Party had always been
socialistic and a vote against the motion would not make socialism any
less important. McGowen asserted that the socialist plank was superfluous
and therefore unnecessary, likewise with the declaration of principle; the
Party was founded, he said, 'with the one object of extending the
principle of the State as an employer . . . and . . . a great mistake was
made . . . when they began to define what was meant by that extension'.
Dacey tried to wind up the debate by attempting to have the chairman
instructed to put the motion in two separate parts; Flowers ruled against
him, but dissent was carried 13 to 12, whereupon he put the motion,
'That the socialistic plank . . . be removed from the platform', declared
it lost 12 to 7, and adjourned for lunch. After the break, when four more
delegates had arrived, including Black, Brown and Hughes, Lamond
tried to have the debate reopened, but Flowers ruled him out of order.[24]

Obviously the parliamentarians did not have it all their own way by any means, and Flowers, for one, was prepared to assert his independence. The debate was only peripherally connected with the substance of the socialist plank, for a tacit consensus had been reached that, for many profound reasons, the Labor Party could not be a party that directly sought a socialist society; so that the plank did not really matter, though it would continue to have some vague stimulative qualities; and delegates believed, correctly in the event, that electors would see the plank as a symbol of the Party's will to radical reform, without the inhuman overtones that they instinctively feared. While delegates accepted that the proposals of the parliamentarians should prevail, and, after all, they comprised a third of the conference, delegates still saw that the parliamentary line should not be completely triumphant. The debate was really about the readjustment of the electoral organisation of the PLL and the associated recognition and equitable disposition of the different interests in the League; and those delegates who were not in parliament were giving notice that they would not be ignored. 'Wheeling and dealing' had become essential to a reform movement that covered a broad spectrum of doctrine and a wide range of sectional interests, and a necessary part of conference, camouflaging, often to the despair of the fastidious, methods that ensured that no one faction should dangerously dominate proceedings. And personal pride played its part. Flowers lacked fertile insight, but he was purposeful and capable, the kind of man who would grow in stature with the Party. All delegates had to pay attention to him.

The organised socialists were not deceived by the retention of the socialist plank. Their exodus had begun before the 1898 conference. Barlow wrote a long letter about it to the *Northern People*.[25] Illustrating the virtuous amnesia of all foiled manipulators of the Labor Party, he agreed with Black that allegations had been made that every Labor conference had been packed by one faction or another; but he argued that 'the charges . . . never [had] such force as against this one of '98'; he listed nine leagues, five country and four city, whose delegates included six Assembly members, and 'question[ed] strongly' whether any, with the possible exception of Waterloo, McGowen, was genuine. Barlow went on to allege that Sleath had two proxy votes, Macdonell three and 'the number Mr. Watson had up his sleeve is not known'; Watson and Sleath were the chief conspirators, he asserted, and they had egged on a somewhat unwilling McGowen; and the Party leader had disillusioned the Labor men: 'A number of us had endeavored to believe there was one fairly straight man in the party, but Mr. McGowen has . . . exploded that belief'. Barlow affected not to be surprised 'at the treatment [the socialist plank] received', but he revealed a deep faith in God's understanding of human affairs by calling on Him '[to] save Socialism from such socialists'.

Barlow scorned the new fighting platform, and mischievously asserted that it should be summed up as 'Reid and his platform', a jibe that would have surprised and amused the premier and added to the fear of the conservatives who were already having doubts about him; on the other hand the shaft would have struck home with those Labor men, including Holman and Dacey, who were becoming bored with the sneer that their Party was 'the tail of the free-traders'. Barlow noted that some delegates had proved not 'quite so pliable as was hoped for', but drew no conclusions from it; nevertheless, he claimed that the parliamentarians had taken over the Party, and added ominously that 'those who have had experience of Labor members and their practical politics know what [that] means'. He predicted that Assembly members would keep the organisation in existence until the next general election, due later in the year, and would then bury it.

The letter reflected the resentment of a young socialist who really was trying to organise a socialist society. It had elements of regret and spite so mixed as to blunt its author's political judgment. Above all, it betrayed a basic misunderstanding of the nature of the Labor Party. Barlow belonged to the variegated band of organised socialists who had, themselves, tried to take over the Party, and had found that it was too complex to swamp. He might have foreseen similar problems for the parliamentarians, if, indeed, they had succeeded where the organised socialists had failed. But the parliamentarians' objective was not the same as the socialists': the parliamentary line was to adjust the PLL's control and activity so that the League would operate competently as the machinery by which the Labor movement sent representatives into parliament. This was why the PLL (LEL) had been founded. It was what Labor politics was about. The parliamentarians' success was therefore not a takeover, but part of a reorganisation of the League, not a constitutional overhaul as in 1893–4, but an administrative reformation in which the organised socialists had to go; and they, themselves, knew it. The great problem of the future was not to maintain control, but to sustain efficiency.

Barlow's comments on stacking of the conference, and corrupt use of proxy votes was of a piece with similar judgments of Cook, Black and others in 1893–4. These were minor parts of the essential logrolling that made Labor conferences functional. Inevitably, any defeated group would righteously criticise the machinery that denied them victory and would regard the system as normal when they won. Undoubtedly there was some skullduggery at the conferences of the 1890s, and later; but, although it is impossible to compute its magnitude, it is clear enough that it did not affect the healthy growth of the Labor Party. Barlow's egregious error about McGowen's role reflects his basic inability to assess the total impact of the 1898 conference. He also failed to observe the importance of the work of Macdonell and Lamond, and of the success of Samuel Smith (1858–1916) who defeated Flowers for the presidency 16 to 14. These were strong indicators that unionism was at last beginning to emerge from the depressed state that had conditioned the dissolution of the TLC in 1894, and to make a significant return to the Labor Party. Smith was a leader of the Seamen's Union; in 1894 he had succeeded P. J. Brennan as president of the Sydney District Council of the ALF and remained as its head until the Sydney Labor Council replaced it in February 1900. In January 1898 he was aware that his Seamen's Union colleague, T. M. Davis MLA, was seriously ill and would not run again for the seat of Sydney-Pyrmont, and Smith was preparing to replace him. Flowers had been president of the PLL since it had replaced the LEL in 1895; he took his defeat with typical urbanity, remarking that he could not expect to have a monopoly on the position. George A. Jones (1867–1938), a printer, was elected secretary.[26]

If the parliamentarians did not achieve all they wanted, they nevertheless did get conference's approval for much of the reorganisation they had planned. McGowen's proposal, that the executive be reformed by the addition of all the Labor members of the Assembly, was amended, after the members present had decided not to vote on the issue, to include them all but with only five votes;[27] in this way country leagues were firmly represented on the executive. The executive replaced district assemblies as the authorising agent for the establishment of branch leagues, and was made the final court of appeal, subject to conference. It was decided that no league could be represented at conference or select a parliamentary candidate unless it had 'at least 25 *bona fide* financial members on the roll'. Sitting members were to be regarded as the selected candidates unless the local league should decide otherwise; candidates were to be selected at least three months before the election, and no selection was to 'hold good for more than twelve months'. The revised rules consisted of thirty-three clauses in place of twenty-nine; amongst other things they confirmed the power of the executive, ensured, as far as possible, that minority groups could not form spurious leagues, and attempted to safeguard the Assembly members in their seats. But the rules did not limit the autonomy of individual leagues. The Labor Party remained a grass-roots party, with the rights of the rank and file preserved, especially in Rule 18, which gave the executive power 'to recommend the District Assembly or Branch the withdrawal of any candidate whose past career proves him unworthy of confidence', but provided that 'The Executive shall have no power, to otherwise interfere in the selection of candidates except in cases of fraud'; and in Rule 33, which restricted changes in the 'Platform, Pledge or Constitution' to a

two-thirds conference majority or, if passed by a lesser majority, they
had to be submitted 'to the Branches for their final decision'.[28]

In keeping with Holman's view that the platform was advanced
enough 'to serve for the next twenty years, it was hardly touched; only
'The early closing of shops' was added, on the motion of Black, who
argued that it was necessary for campaigning in city seats, with Dacey
highlighting one of Labor's metropolitan electoral problems when he
asserted that not 'one per cent of shop workers were in a league', and
Griffith emphasising Labor's duty to 'support all reforms'.[29] With a
general election to be held in 1898 the fighting platform stressed four of
the planks:

1. (a) Abolition of the upper house
   (b) Introduction of the initiative and referendum;
2. Establishment of a national bank
3. State pensions for aged and infirm persons
4. Local government.[30]

The whole platform of twenty-five planks remained a signal program
for progress, unparalleled in its democratic and rational radicalism by
any other political organisation. It also threw into sharp relief the
continued failure of the free traders and protectionists to produce a
program that would have helped to give them some of the cohesion
required by a modern political party. Reid, with his exhausting work
for reform and Federation taking its toll, was beginning to run out of
ideas and drive at the same time as his radical liberalism had marked
him for the revenge of a powerful group of the free traders' conservative
backers. The protectionists, under the ponderous Lyne, had virtually no
ideas and little drive, but they had ambitions for office and the vestigial
ability of old-style politicians to smell out a political crisis and take
advantage of it. With a determined Labor Party, its extra-parliamentary
structure readjusted, relentless in its impulse for reform, with the
Federation movement reaching a crucial stage and some indications of
a relapse into the old 'ins-and-outs' unruliness in an election year, the
stage was set for a new phase of the Labor political experiment. The
Labor Party was well prepared for the new test.

Both the *Herald* and the *Telegraph* accurately evaluated the conference's work. The *Herald* was under the delusion that the socialist
plank had been jettisoned; as a result some of its heavy sarcasm back-
fired, but it correctly noted 'the most satisfactory aspect of the proceedings', the decision of the Labor Party to discard 'a large part of the more
extreme elements' in order 'to secure a Parliamentary majority . . . [by]
persuading other men who do not wholly share their views'.[31] The
Telegraph observed that only twenty-nine leagues were represented at the
conference, nineteen country, ten metropolitan, and that most of the
country branches had proxy delegates. This comment was meant to

stress that the Labor Party should keep its place, which the newspaper saw as that of Reid's inferior partner; but it overlooked both the general problems of reorganisation that had confronted the Party and the particular difficulties including financial, that delegates, most of them, had to face in travelling long distances to conferences, aggravated in 1898 by the decision to hold the meeting at Newcastle. But the *Telegraph* also saw that Labor had to gain votes from all kinds of electors, not only from trade unionists, and that because of this hard fact, the parliamentarians had accepted the necessity of gradualism.[32] By implication both the senior Sydney newspapers perceived the possibility of the Party widening the gap it had forced in 1891 in the middle class domination of parliament, and discerned the likelihood of the process being facilitated by the casting off of the Party's more extreme elements. The organised socialists formalised their break with the PLL at a conference of the Australian Socialists' Leagues in Sydney in April, when they decided on independent political action, and debarred their members from belonging to any other political organisation.[33] The single taxers, although no longer a force, also resolved to run their own candidates at elections.[34]

The reformation of the Labor Party was a prelude to a year of strenuous and exciting electoral and parliamentary work. The referendum to adopt or reject the Federal Convention Bill (the draft Commonwealth Constitution) was to be held on 3 June 1898, and the colony's general election would be held soon after: it was subsequently fixed for 27 July. Federation had at last reached a formally decisive stage in which it virtually swamped ordinary political questions, and put an intolerable strain on the already shaky cohesion of the free trade and protectionist groups.

Reid himself was vitally affected. He had taken a leading and exhausting part in the 1897 work of the convention that had drawn up the constitution now to be put to the vote of the people. From June to August 1897 he was in England for Queen Victoria's diamond jubilee celebrations and an important imperial conference. Domestically, the administration of his unprecedented taxation legislation had had preliminary problems that resulted in some legal challenges and validating legislation (the Land and Income Tax (Amendment) Act, 1897, No. 21), which had helped to incite the Legislative Council and crystallise the growing conservative opposition to the premier. The National Association looked forward to a group of 20–5 revenue tariffists in parliament who would abolish direct taxation, and it resented Reid's attempts to establish a Public Trustee who would take some of the business of the two existing trustee companies.[1] Reid's reform of the public service had reverberated in various directions; many parliamentarians were nettled by their loss of patronage, many public servants were piqued at what they regarded as harsh retrenchments and reclassifications of positions.[2] His relations with the Labor Party remained, on balance, warm. The Party was pleased with the government's growing substitution of day labour for contracts for public works, although this policy increased the anger of employers' groups. But Labor was concerned with Reid's loss of domestic reforming momentum, and were in no mood to relate it to his wider responsibilities. In 1897 a Labor resolution had been carried in parliament against the ministry seeking to reduce the working week of nurses and female hospital attendants from seventy-two to forty-eight

hours, but Reid had ignored it.[3] Reid had not been able to reform the
Legislative Council and it remained adamant on reform legislation.[4] On
the other hand, early in 1898 Griffith invited Reid to speak at Hamilton
and the premier argued that 'The freetrade party and the labor party
were at one in their belief in broad and liberal reform, and it was the
game of the latter to get the Government to go faster than they would
otherwise go'.[5]

For various reasons, not least of all Federation, the Labor Party's
'game' was growing more difficult in 1898. But the Party remained
inextricably involved in the big events that were shaping great changes
not only in New South Wales, but also the whole of the continent; and
Labor's work helped both to clarify the problems and provide solutions
for them. The ultimate form of national Federation was decided in New
South Wales in 1898. Part of the process was the revitalisation of the
PLL, in which the AWU, principally through Lamond's vigorous editorship of the *Worker*, played a powerful part. Lamond did not consider
that socialism was being evaded by Labor simply because the Party
had decided to seek it one step at a time,[6] a view that further reassured many radical reformers who had no wish to share in the
eccentricities of the organised socialists; and he restated the democratic
appeal of the Party and its traditional aim:

> The real object of the [PL] League is the rallying of the people who share in
> certain general ideas to discuss and formulate from time to time a working
> platform, and to organize for securing representation in Parliament by
> persons in sympathy with the ideas and who will accept the platform as
> general instructions from their constituencies, instead of going into the House
> to do as they darned well like.[7]

By publishing weekly reports of local leagues' activities, the *Worker* also
encouraged Party members to attend the regular meetings of their
branches.[8] In Sydney the Solidarity Club still met regularly at the
Worker building and continued its work as a centre for radical discussion
of current political, economic and social affairs.[9]

The Labor Party's policy on Federation was well known and in 1897-8
had significant repercussions on the formation of public opinion on the
constitution as set out in the convention bill. Labor's criticism could be
summed up as a strong assertion that the proposed constitution was
undemocratic. Since 1891 in New South Wales the Party had fought
relentlessly for 'one man, one vote', for the widest possible franchise, and
for the curbing of the power of the Legislative Council. Indeed, this
missionary work had given a general tone of democratic consistency to
the Labor parliamentarians, even in the embryonic confusion of 1891-4,
and had conditioned them to reject a federal constitution that gave
equal representation in the Senate to all of the constituent states irrespective of population, that gave the Senate equal powers with the Lower

House in money bills, and that provided for a three-fifths majority to resolve differences at joint meetings of the two Houses. There was nothing provincial about Labor's attitude: it was based soundly on democratic principles. And it was a view that received considerable popular backing, made none the less significant because some of the support was from people who thought that the interests of New South Wales were being unfairly sacrificed to the demands of the smaller states.

As the convention bill referendum loomed, Reid was in a troublesome predicament. He was a sincere federationist but, in his own liberal way, he had been moulded by the great democratic upsurge in New South Wales that followed the advent of the Labor Party; moreover, he was a radical free trader who found protection distasteful not only on political grounds but also on philosophical grounds. At the convention Reid was only one of fifty men (Queensland was not represented), the majority of whom were protectionists; and the thirty delegates of smaller states, South Australia, Tasmania and Western Australia, naturally were not so concerned about the formal requirements of democracy as about their rights, as they saw them, not to be swamped by the larger states. Federalism was not necessarily opposed to formal democracy or to free trade, but the majority of the convention behaved as if it were; and the constitution that emerged had noticeably undemocratic features, and it clearly envisaged a protective tariff for a federated Australia. While this was the only kind of constitution that such a convention could have produced, it was not acceptable to the New South Wales Labor Party; it seemed to confirm only too well the prognostications of Cardinal Moran and Bruce Smith that Federation was a way to keep Labor down.[10] The constitution was not acceptable, either, to many other colonists, some of them provincialists who thought that New South Wales should not federate, some of them concerned that their wealthy low-tax colony would have to increase its charges in order to subsidise the other colonies.

Reid, who had done so much to help create the conditions that had shaped all these opinions, could only be responsive to them. But as a member of the body that had drawn up the constitution he was also bound to it. He was indeed in the grip of a cruel dilemma. Barton, lacking not only the premier's great responsibilities and achievements but also his imaginative flair, had adjusted naturally to the conservative and protectionist tone of the convention and to its grandee style; Barton could not begin to understand Reid's position and could campaign strongly for the convention bill. Reid could not. He told a packed Town Hall on 28 March,

> And now I would say to you, having opened up my mind, having shown you the dark places as well as the light ones of this Constitution, I put it upon every man in this country, without coercion from me, without interference

from me, to judge for himself; and therefore I may say that my duty to Australia demands me to record my vote in favour of this Bill.[11]

If he had said that he had decided to vote against the bill, Federation would have been delayed indefinitely.

Reid's chief press supporter, the *Daily Telegraph*, was appalled at his support of the bill, while the *Sydney Morning Herald* was not convinced that he meant it. The *Telegraph* called on the Labor Party to fill the breach; the combination of radical free trade and Labor interests, the paper said, had made Reid 'Australia's most progressive and most successful statesman', and now he had clearly shown that the convention bill would destroy 'one man, one vote', would erect a Senate to be a brake on democratic legislation, and would force New South Wales to shoulder customs duties to save other colonies from bankruptcy. With 'the principle of representative government . . . in deadly peril', it was the duty of the Labor Party to awaken the people to the imminent danger.[12] Lamond followed suit in the *Worker;* Reid, he said, had achieved great things 'for a democratic New South Wales', but his 'apostasy' over the bill had undone it all; the Labor Party would 'have to bear the brunt of opposition to a bill that denies the people the right to govern themselves'.[13] After seven hard years of chipping away, with some success, at the undemocratic parliamentary wall propped up by the middle class to protect their own interests, Labor men observed with deep apprehension the prospect at starting all over again on a stronger and more complex edifice; and they claimed that Reid, the champion of democratic rights, had let the Party down.

Of course, Reid had not let the Labor Party down.[14] He had simply done his duty, hard as it was, by analysing the bill, pointing to its strengths and weaknesses, and finally saying he would support it. He was under no obligation to Labor in respect of Federation. But emotional fervour, noted at the Labor Party's conferences in the 1890s, was part and parcel of the Party's routine, giving it great potency at times, but also occasionally obscuring its vision. The conflict with Reid over the convention bill was the formal beginning of the end of the Party's parliamentary partnership with him. Minor irritations had already prepared the way for dissension that would soon be reinforced by more substantial differences than those over Federation. But a great tension was exerted over the whole colony by the prospect of national union and Labor felt the pressure no less than any other group. There was painful irony in the fact that Reid's honesty, and his continued great service to the Federation cause that included exposing the deficiencies of the proposed constitution, should have aroused Labor against him.

Labor was opposed to the convention bill, but its support of Federation was real. The Party played an important role in the campaign against the bill. Reid's attorney-general, J. H. Want, resigned from the ministry on

4 April and became leader of the 'anti-billites', who were a diverse group indeed, ranging from hard-core provincialists to sincere liberals and radicals who had legitimate fears about a constitution that denied fundamental democratic principles. The 'pro-billites', led by Barton, were similarly variegated, including passionate federationists, who desired union at any price, and capitalists, who coldly calculated the gains of a national as opposed to a colonial economy. The *Worker* continued to fulminate against the bill, reported several Labor leagues strongly opposed to it, and published a carefully argued case by George Black against it.[15] The whole Labor movement stressed the middle class bias of the constitution: the Socialist League argued it was undemocratic;[16] in Melbourne Ben Tillett criticised it as a 'lawyer's' and a 'fatman's bill', and the Intercolonial Labor Conference condemned it.[17] Hughes was active on the platform, and in one of his letters to the press he superbly satirised Wise, one of the pro-billites, as 'Mr. Munchausen Wise';[18] at a Labor meeting, with Watson, Brown and Ferguson also present, Hughes pointed out that Federation would suit the Party because it had sunk the fiscal issue, but argued that the bill would hand the people of New South Wales over to minority rule.[19] McGowen made a strong speech against the bill in the Town Hall at a large meeting organised by Want,[20] and Griffith spoke vigorously in opposition at Waratah and Manly.[21] The Labor campaign certainly was a large factor in the bill's defeat in New South Wales; 71,595 voted for it and 66,228 against it,[22] but the 1897 enabling act required a minimum of 80,000 voters for the bill to be approved. In any case, the slender majority for the bill indicated a deep-seated resistance to it in New South Wales. The bill was carried comfortably in the three other colonies that put it to a referendum, Victoria, South Australia and Tasmania: the total national vote was 219,712 for the bill and 108,363 against it.

The Labor Party had shown conclusively that its voice had to be listened to on all public questions. To confirm its prestige and give it nineteen members in parliament, H. Ross won the north-west seat of Narrabri, chiefly agricultural, at a by-election on the same day that the referendum was held. The parliamentarians' demand for a reorganisation that would restate Labor's traditional role in the colony had been resoundingly vindicated. And the national referendum figures revealed the strength of Labor in New South Wales compared with the movement in other colonies: about 61 per cent of the total 'no' vote was polled in the mother colony. Of course, there were other reasons apart from Labor's opposition to account for the loss of the bill; but Labor's attention to Federation for seven years had helped to define practically all of the major problems associated with union, and its 1898 work had capped its contribution. Essentially, the success of Labor's opposition to the convention bill was related to the whole movement's vital social and political role in New South Wales.

There was no rest for the Labor members of the Legislative Assembly. The *Herald* reported on 14 June that all the talk at Parliament House was about the forthcoming election and that many members were 'hoping against hope' that Reid would lay 'the menacing federal spectre before the time comes to meet their constituents'. The *Herald* had fought hard for the convention bill and now predicted that failure to accept it would postpone Federation for eight to ten years. Ignoring Lyne, and assuming that the protectionist Assembly members had no party cohesion, it looked forward to Barton leading a strong Federationist party of probably forty to fifty members, and argued that such a party would either force the rest of the parliamentarians to form into an anti-federal party or it would become a powerful 'third party'. The *Herald* held the Labor Party up as an example: 'What can be done by a third party holding the balance of power', it stressed,

> is shown by the achievements of the labour party during the last four years. The consideration which has been shown by the present Government has been quite out of proportion to the numerical strength of the party.[23]

The next day the *Herald* was able to announce that Barton, O'Connor, Wise and B. Smith would run at the elections as the nucleus of a federal party. O'Connor had already decided to oppose Watson at Young.[24]

The *Herald's* comment and advice reflected the ultimate decline of the old fiscal groups, especially, of course the protectionists. The fiscal question had had some slight validity in 1887–9 when Parkes had used it consummately as a means of bringing some degree of order into a decadent parliamentary system, but it was never more than a temporary expedient, and when Federation entered public discussion its days were numbered. Nevertheless, its doctrinal accretions and emotional attractions ensured that it would outlast its political reality, even when the Labor Party injected a powerful class and social element into politics in 1891. In 1894 when Labor regrouped its forces and Reid changed Parkes's old free trade group into a liberal reforming group, the Party recognised that 'dropping the fiscal issue' meant support for Reid and that a free trade tariff was an acceptable price to pay for reforming legislation. Meanwhile the protectionists, perforce, became increasingly conservative under Dibbs, Barton and Lyne, and, as Federation forced more and more fiscalists to perceive the emptiness of their faith, the protectionists were left with virtually no policy at all. The year 1898 was the end of the road for them. The *Herald,* the traditional backer of free trade, was patently trying to replace Lyne with Barton to undo Reid; partly to facilitate the implementation of Federation. But Reid, too, was determined to bring about national union, and soon Barton had to agree with him that changes in the convention bill were necessary. The real force

behind the *Herald's* campaign against Reid was deep conservative pressure to try to stop Labor's thrust for radical reform. But it was a tricky
game, in which the great newspaper over-rated Barton and under-rated
not only Reid but also Lyne, who had a few old-fashioned political
trumps to play yet. Above all, the *Herald* surprisingly misread the Labor
Party, and, like the organised socialists, it had a hard lesson to learn; as
did O'Connor, who in his stuffy way and with his Catholic connections
in the Young district, thought that Watson would prove an easy mark.

The top men of the other colonies at the 1897 Federal Convention
had fully accepted Barton, whose classical profile and bland and languid
style certainly gave the impression of profound knowledge, whereas they
were somewhat shocked by Reid's earthy manner. This reception had
confirmed Barton's sense of his own superiority over Reid. When the
cabinet's proposals to amend the draft federal constitution became
known, Barton scouted them and said authoritatively, 'It is plain . . .
that most of the other colonies decline to be played with any longer by
Mr. Reid'.[25] But he was no doubt pleased when the scheme to put him at
the head of the anti-Reid forces got off to a good start with thirty-four
opposition members of the Assembly meeting under Lyne himself, and
agreeing to work with Barton to secure modifications to the constitution;
the meeting also decided that Lyne should move in parliament to censure
Reid over Federation.[26] The *Herald* was pleased that Barton had agreed
to seek some changes in the convention bill, because the decision would
confound many anti-Federation members of the Assembly;[27] and it noted
that

> The labour party, which is about the only body in Parliament at present
> possessing any individuality, has been holding several meetings lately, and
> [its] members . . . will no doubt also take advantage of the opening of
> Parliament to further consider their position.[28]

The newspaper also reported McGowen as saying after a Labor caucus
that the Party would wait to see what Barton's and Reid's proposals
were, and would select the better offer of the two.[29] But first Barton
would have to win a seat in parliament.

The last session of the seventeenth parliament opened on 21 June,
with the government naturally placing a new list of Federation resolutions to the fore, aimed at amendment of several clauses of the draft
constitution, including reduction of the power of the Senate, recasting of
the financial proposals, and asking that the federal capital be fixed by
the constitution (preferably in New South Wales); the government
noted, prematurely, that a severe drought was ending, stressed that its
1895 land legislation had increased agricultural settlement, and projected
fresh laws to solve new problems of selectors; with more direct attention
to the Labor Party, the government proposed the establishment of a
fund to provide for the families of miners killed or permanently disabled

in mining accidents. Lyne, anxious to exacerbate the differences between Reid and Labor moved an amendment to the address in reply to the effect that parliament declined to trust the government with 'the momentous question' Federation.[30]

By this time the Labor members were convinced of the instability of a group whose real leader was not in parliament and whose political program was limited to Federation, on which virtually everyone was now agreed, subject to some changes in the draft constitution. Griffith made the main Labor speech against the motion and paid a tribute to Reid's ministry which 'during the last four years has placed more measures on the statute book than any half-dozen preceding governments'; he regretted the fact that the Legislative Council remained unreformed, but agreed that it was chiefly because Federation had overshadowed all other questions; he accepted Reid's new Federation proposals and conceded that New South Wales should not get all its own way, but argued that it should not make all the sacrifices; he assailed Barton for giving away too much to the demands of South Australia and Western Australia; and wanted the constitution to be amended by a simple majority of all voters irrespective of their state. He accused the protectionists of being the 'mouthpiece of financial institutions'. A highlight of Griffith's speech was his squelching of John Norton, 'Jacko' to his cronies, now feared by many as a result of his blackmailing tactics in his newspaper *Truth*; Norton had continually heckled Griffith, who finally told the speaker of the House, 'I do not think that I ought to be subjected to the bibulous verbosity of this sewer rat'.[31]

Hughes turned his formidable guns on Barton, and, to a lesser extent, on O'Connor for their questionable roles in the Proudfoot case of 1893, in which as attorney-general and minister of justice respectively they had accepted briefs against the Railways Department and thus contributed to the decomposition of the Dibbs ministry. Hughes also pointed out that Barton had had his chance when in government in 1891–3 to further Federation but had done nothing except harm the cause by being a party to the cabinet's protectionist tariff; he derided Lyne for being in the process of being superseded as leader of his group, and praised Reid for being 'the most democratic premier we have had' and for doing things instead of merely talking about them. Hughes attacked the protectionists for going to the country 'arrayed behind the greatest conservative in the colony' (Barton) at a time when 'the fiscal issue is dead'; but he skilfully played Lyne at his own game by admitting that the Labor Party would have had an alternative if Lyne had remained as leader, but as it was, with Barton about to take over, they had no choice but to stick to Reid.[32] Sleath also attacked Barton, and the seventeen Labor men present enabled the government to withstand the censure by 65 to 32.[33]

The whole debate had shown that the Labor Party would have none of Barton, seeing him as a man who had breached his trust when a minister of the crown, who had failed to take the opportunity to help Federation when in office, and who had become obnoxiously conservative: in short, a man whose style was antipathetic to radicalism, who would not take up the slack in reform legislation brought about by Reid's concentration on other issues. On the other hand, Hughes's speech had developed some points he had adumbrated at a Labor rally in January when he had astutely assessed the changes posed by Reid's decline as a reformer and had dangled the bait of Labor support, at the right price, before Lyne.[34] In the political confusion shaped by the consummation of Federation, only the Labor Party had a clear vision of what it wanted, and by the middle of 1898 it had produced the kind of men who could evolve sound policy from efficient analysis of dynamic political problems. The prominent members of the Party, McGowen, Watson, Hughes, Griffith, Dacey and Black were more than a match, in parliamentary tactics and political skill, for any member of the other groups, with the exception of Reid: and his day was drawing to its close. In its review of the debate on the censure motion the *Herald* climaxed its mission to depose Lyne; he was incapable of heading a federal party, it argued, because he was merely a protection leader and Federation demanded the end of the fiscalism issue.[35] With mischievous skill, the *Herald* also played on the growing rifts in the Labor-Reid coalition; the premier, it said, had hoodwinked the Party when he told it he could not have a referendum on the fiscal issue without first bringing in a bill, which would naturally have to pass the Legislative Council.[36]

The general election of 27 July 1898 lacked nothing in complexity and excitement in comparison with any of the three previous elections of the 1890s. Federation dominated the campaign and snapped the meagre links that the existing political groups, except the Labor Party, had with previous electoral organisations. The Reid free traders set up a new body, consisting of a parliamentary wing and a section of outside supporters, and called it the liberal federal party.[37] The *Herald* labelled it the Reid-Wantite or the provincialist party: the *Telegraph* favoured it and called it liberal, free trade and federal party. The protectionists had reached an impasse that was only partially removed by a loose agreement between the pure federationists, mainly in the Federal Association, led by Barton and the protectionist-federationists more or less led by Lyne. The *Herald* termed these groups the Federation or national federal party: the *Telegraph* opposed them and labelled them the conservative, protectionist and federal party. Lyne's personal manifesto for his seat of Hume indicated that he had not renounced protection, and this caused defections of some free traders from the Federal Association.[38] In desperation the *Herald* discussed the great complexity and confusion of issues and parties; the newspaper claimed that the influence of Want (who had rejoined the ministry on 18 June) gave the government an anti-federal stance, and thus it would lose support from federationists; that the ultra-conservatives and staunch provincialists, represented by Sir Julian Salomons, MLC, Sir Normand MacLaurin, MLC, and Sir George Dibbs would support the government, and thus the 'Tories', 'Fossils', liberals and socialists had joined forces; the *Herald* concluded perceptively that once Federation was declared to be above politics, but now it had absorbed politics.[39]

Despite the confusion, the *Herald* had to admit by the middle of July that both Barton and Reid agreed on the amendments needed in the draft constitution: that a simple majority should replace the three-fifths requirement at joint meetings of the Senate and House of Representatives; that the 'Braddon clause' should be omitted to prevent New South Wales being taxed four times more than was necessary; and that the federal capital should be within the mother colony; Reid also wanted the Senate to lose its power to amend money bills.[40] But the *Herald* still affected to believe that the 'Reid-Wantite party' was a real danger to Federation, despites its opinion that the elections were showing that anti-federationists had disappeared from public life.[41] In fact the issue of the elections was crystallising into the question of who was to complete the formalities of Federation in New South Wales: Reid or Barton. And Barton, in effect, accepted this proposition when he said he would oppose Reid in the seat of King, the centre of big business in Sydney.

Barton's decision was partially caused by his acceptance of the validity of his projected image as the great Australian who alone could save national union from the arch-enemy of Federation; but there were also large elements of hard-headed political judgment in it. Barton had topped the poll in East Sydney in 1891, while Reid had dropped to fourth (the last to be elected); admittedly the position had changed in 1894 because of Barton's failure in the Dibbs ministry, and he had left the city core (King) of his old seat to Reid, and retreated to part of its eastern extremity (Randwick), only to be soundly defeated; but in the 1898 Convention bill referendum King was one of the six (out of eleven) city seats to vote for 'yes'.[42] Above all, Barton was responsive to the changed capitalist climate so well reflected by the *Herald,* which from the firm beginning of the Federation movement in 1889 had noted that the nation-wide markets and tariff, which would accompany union, would shape basic changes for the powerful financial interests it largely represented. After Reid's victory in 1894 the *Herald* had observed the blurring of the differences between merchants and manufacturers, previously divided by free trade and protection; and Reid's taxation policy had sharpened this discernment. Of course, the Chamber of Commerce and the Chamber of Manufactures did not rely entirely on the *Herald* to tell them that direct taxation was more painful than indirect taxation. One of the great forces behind the dislike of Reid on the part of the *Herald* and significant segments of powerful capitalist groups, not only in Sydney but also in Melbourne, especially, and in Adelaide, was the possibility that land and income taxation would be the nation's main source of revenue if Reid became Prime Minister of a united Australia. On the other hand Barton had shown convincingly by his conversion in the 1880s from free trade to protection, and by his backing of the Dibbs ministry's customs duties increases in 1892 that any tariff over which he had influence would provide the substantial part of national revenue. Barton's resolve to oppose Reid in King was by no means entirely quixotic.

The events of 1898, culminating in the general election, had dissolved the remnants of the old fiscal political organisations but they actually strengthened the Labor Party. The main task of the Party in the 1898 general election was to maintain its hard-won identity in the turmoil of the determination of great questions. Labor could not hope to gain seats on its radical program at a time when the attention of voters was concentrated directly on the final form of national union and indirectly on the shape of national policy for the first years of a federal parliament. The *Patriot,* a protectionist newspaper, analysed the ethos of Labor after its renewal at the 1898 conference and as the Party prepared for the general election. Despite the fact that 'Laborists' were 'numerically weak', the *Patriot* said, '[they win because they] work, and organise and sacrifice for the principles which they propound'; loyalty to the cause was a mark of the Labor man:

> Everywhere you hear the laborists declare, 'He is the selected man, and if he was a Chinaman or a blackfellow I would vote for him'. Splendid loyalty, misguided though it may be;

enthusiasm was associated with fidelity,

> They leave nothing to chance . . . Voters are raked up by every possible device, and their organisation and sacrifice enable them to poll a much greater proportion of their sympathisers than either of their opposing parties.

The *Patriot* was impressed with the way in which the Party had campaigned for Ross,

> Only the other day, at Narrabri, a couple of voters were on the road with a bullock team, 15 miles from a polling booth. But the laborists had them marked down, and in the end the team was camped and their votes recorded.[43]

What the *Patriot* had done, with sure touch, was to observe 'the Labor man' in action. By 1898 a peculiar aura, produced by an amalgam of comradeship, controlled bickering, and missionary fervour, enfolded the Labor Party and conditioned a special type of colonist. For the most part he was a member of a league, but not necessarily; and generally he was a member of a trade union, but not invariably. But always he voted Labor. A 'Labor man' owed a lot to the trade union tradition of purposeful solidarity, originally shaped in the city by constant pressure to improve working conditions, but effortlessly absorbed by the bush unions from the middle 1880s and given a new dimension by the shrewd inarticulateness and warm generosity that was part of the lonely country life. The Labor Party linked the city with the country, in a way no other organisation could hope to because it was the crown of a movement that held out the prospect of a better life for all people who found life hard. The Labor Party offered a chance to all colonists, irrespective of their background and education, to become significant people as they shared in a common socially curative task. A league president or secretary was a person of local importance, a conference delegate more so, the executive officers of the PLL were colonial figures; Labor members of the Legislative Assembly were men of power and authority. The lowliest league member, or even just a Labor voter, could share in the system that made these men; and he knew that he would not be overwhelmed by them, indeed if necessary he might be able to organise support that could destroy them; and he knew that Jim McGowen or Chris Watson were leaders who belonged to him and were answerable to him, not leaders who had the ascendancy and the will to scorn him, even should one of them become the premier of New South Wales or the prime minister of Australia, as were possibilities for all 'Labor men' looking forward from 1898. The turn of the 'Labor woman' would come early in the twentieth century.

The Labor Party needed men of this spirit at the elections of 1898 because its chances of attracting 'swinging voters' were negligible. The Party ran a total of thirty-five candidates,[44] a decrease from forty-three in 1895; five were run in the eleven city seats, seven in the twenty-nine suburban seats, and twenty-three in the eighty-five country seats. The overall total of candidates rose from 310 (1895) to 316.[45] The biggest reduction in Labor candidates was in the suburban constituencies, in which thirteen were run in 1895. The major electoral problem confronting the Party, the task of converting the suburban middle class, had finally been clarified. Labor was finding it hard enough to form leagues in these areas, and its difficulty was compounded at the election by the withdrawal of Smailes from politics: in 1898 he had been noticeably losing interest in the work of an MLA and decided to concentrate on his clerical duties; in 1902 he went to New Zealand where he died in 1934. C. Dyer took over from him with very little hope of success in the outer metropolitan seat of Granville. As expected, Davis did not run (he died the following year) and was replaced by Samuel Smith. Again Reid's organisation decided not to oppose sitting Labor members, though the

PLL did not return the compliment.[46] Reid spoke at Temora to help Watson, who was working hard to withstand O'Connor; Watson, in turn, praised the premier for taking up Federation 'from where it was left in the gutter and [bringing] it to its present advanced stage'.[47] McGowen at Wallsend emphasised that his Party had always supported Federation and now it intended to 'trust [Reid] to get Federation as they wanted it, rather than trust Mr. Barton, who was a conservative'.[48] Black was fighting a peculiar campaign in Gipps; at Church Hill on 13 July he told his audience that he would not beg for votes and would refuse to canvass house to house.[49]

On 16 July the Labor Party broke new ground in New South Wales politics by issuing a manifesto in which it surveyed its achievements since 1894 and gave its policy for the future.[50] The statement was a moderate and accurate account of the Party's record, even though, naturally enough, it played down the vital co-operative work of Reid. The essence of the manifesto was an affirmation by Labor that it did not depend for its existence and policy on particular events, no matter how important, or on particular personalities, no matter how outstanding. It was a party manifesto, stressing Labor's permanence, hoping to gain votes on the basis of what it had already done and what it promised to do. The Party was giving notice of its confidence that it would press on with its mission when the euphoria engendered by the prospect of national union and the pyrotechnics surrounding the battle of the giants at King had passed away. At the same time, the manifesto was a valuable summary of the great impact Labor had made on the social and political life of New South Wales.

The Party underlined its reformatory work in parliamentary procedure, and on the strength of it claimed to be 'The Watchdogs of the People'; details were given to show that the attendance of Labor parliamentarians in divisions in 1895 was 34 per cent better than the non-Labor ones, 45 per cent better in 1896, and 26 per cent better in 1897. The Party was proud of its role in the introduction of day labour in place of contracts for public works, an administrative change that certainly meant the extension of the principle of the government as an employer; pointed to new laws on electoral reform, land problems, coal mines regulation, metalliferous mining practices, shops and factories control, and exclusion of coloured races, to which it had contributed. Criticism of the Legislative Council was a feature of the manifesto, especially because of the Council's mutilation of the bill to amend the navigation laws, which provided for new safety provisions as part of a general reform of the maritime industry. The use of the referendum in respect of Federation was shown to justify Labor's emphasis on this democratic device. The manifesto summarised Labor's valuable work on Federation and pointed out that flexible amendment of the proposed constitution was vital and should be vested 'in a majority of the whole people without reference to the States in which they reside'; in this way 'no Constitution could long remain inequitable'. Finally the fighting platform approved by the 1898 PLL conference was detailed to show the short term objectives of the Party.

While the Labor manifesto showed the substantial strength and tenacity of the Party, it had little effect on the results of the 1898 general election. Two seats were lost, Gipps (Black) and Granville (Dyer), and two were won Grenfell (Holman) and Cobar (Spence). Spence had been born in the Orkney Islands in 1846 and had come to Victoria in 1853, he was a unionist of vast experience and in 1898 was general secretary of the AWU; his win illustrated the growing significance of that union in Labor affairs especially in country organising, though Macdonnell, to prove a much abler politician than Spence, lost in Barwon. Holman's win in Grenfell was a tribute to his undoubted capacity, now tempered somewhat by a developing resilience shaped by his persistent work over some years in the electorate. Smailes's Methodist ministry in the Granville area and his Christian radicalism had given him a large personal vote that Dyer could not hold against a well-known local identity John Nobbs, who had originally represented part of the seat in 1888.

On the other hand, Black's was a seat that the Party should not have lost; his narrow defeat in Gipps showed that politics was not simply a matter of having a strong candidate and a progressive policy. Electors had to be made to feel that they were part of the democratic process; they could not be taken for granted; electoral campaigns had to be fought. Black's individualism often shaded into vanity, which in turn conditioned a belief that he had a right to represent a seat he had first won in 1891 when it was part of old West Sydney; he had strengthened his hold on it in 1894 when it became the Millers Point area of his original seat. But in 1898, when new methods had to be adopted, so well explained and exemplified by Holman, Black decided to rest his campaign on his past record which he extolled at many street corner meetings; he refused to move with the times and knock on doors. A strong independent, W. J. Spruson, a Roman Catholic, ran against Black, did everything that Black refused to do, and reaped his reward. Black explained his defeat in a letter to the *Worker;* he said his organisation had only twelve members, while Spruson's had 200; that 'muddle-headed and meddlesome body', the New South Wales Alliance (union of temperance societies) had claimed him as one of their own and then dropped him; he had lost the Catholic vote; the Protestant vote had been alienated by stories of his atheism and immorality; he was alleged to have departed from Glen Innes in debt to a baker.[51] These were old-style rationalisations; many of the tales (some of them true) had been spread about Black at all three of his previous elections. The lesson was clear to Labor; modern organisation was necessary all the time, no matter how burdensome. There had been great calls on the time and financial resources of members of the PLL in 1898; but politics required constant attention.[52] Holman, who saw this issue more clearly than any other Labor man, would have a lot to say and do about it now that he was in parliament.

The loss of two metropolitan seats and the gain of two country seats left the Labor Party's strength unchanged at nineteen, but it dramatically bore out Watson's belief that the Party would find it easier to make gains in the country. Counting N. R. W. Nielsen, who won Boorowa at a by-election on 30 September 1899, in the 1898–1901 parliament Labor held fifteen country seats and five metropolitan seats, and the latter consisted of three suburban and two city electorates; Dacey had held Botany which still had its voting strength within five miles of the GPO, and McGowen's and Law's seats were similarly situated. There were twenty-six other suburban seats, many of them awaiting strong organisation by the Party, the inner group being mainly residential areas for white-collar workers who had shown little inclination to vote for Labor, and the outer section chiefly semi-rural inhabited by a type of voter who had revealed virtually no interest in the Party's reforming drive. The placing of early closing on the platform had indicated that the PLL was seized with the need to attract support from the large group of shop and clerical workers who lived in the nine suburban seats of Leichhardt, Petersham, Marrickville, Annandale, Glebe, Newtown (three seats) and Paddington, all in the inner west and south-west suburban belt, except Paddington, which was in the inner east.

Apart from Lang, Pyrmont and Gipps, around Darling Harbour, Labor also had a special kind of problem in the city area: these seats were the old residential metropolitan areas, still in the late nineties providing some of 'the classes' with fine homes, even though workers' habitations, some of them the worst slums in the colony, were dotted among them; and they were seats that tended to attract either outstanding politicians, such as Reid in King and Copeland in Phillip, or well-known community figures such as Dr James Graham in Belmore and Sir Matthew Harris (sometime Mayor of Sydney) in Denison, or 'characters' like 'Jacko' Norton in Fitzroy (though he unexpectedly lost in 1898); these men had large personal followings and enthusiastic groups of supporters who organised the electorates thoroughly. Labor's emphasis on policy rather than candidates went against the traditional political grain of many compact city seats, and would need time and a more settled political climate than that of the nineties to erode old voting habits.

On a percentage basis Labor held some 18 per cent of the total rural electorates, and some 13 per cent of the urban electorates. But the disparity of support was greater than these figures suggest. The problems of distance and communications in relatively primitive living conditions made electoral organising much harder in the country than in Sydney. Labor was, in fact, making a greater appeal in the country, as Watson had foreseen. It was not simply because of the temporary decline of city trade unionism, though that was important, and the effects of unionism's revival would soon be noticed on the PLL in Sydney. Labor's total program related very closely to new country needs headed by demands for revision of the system of land holding, for long-term loans at low interest rates, for closer settlement, for new and improved methods of marketing as agricultural, especially, and dairy products increased in relation to the output of the well-established and controlled pastoral industry. The social changes that accompanied these new economic manifestations reinforced Labor's rural impact: the farmer, the bush-worker and their families were finding themselves and asserting their human rights after decades of arduous pioneering with very few economic rewards and many fewer than the minimum of creature comforts; their hope and determination adjusted nicely to the solidarity of the Labor Party, to its good news of improvement and, above all else, to its spirit of simple humanity.

Labor's policy and emotional appeal had, of course, to be backed up by hard work. But in 1898 they provided the basis of Ross's win in Narrabri, Spence's in Cobar, and Holman's in Grenfell, and the following year would do the same for Nielsen in Boorowa. Holman, Ross and Nielsen represented seats that were mainly agricultural; Spence's had some copper mining, but was mainly pastoral. And Labor's qualities enabled Watson convincingly to defeat O'Connor in Young. Indeed Watson's win typified the great social strength of Labor, for O'Connor was a leading federationist, an ex-minister of the crown, a barrister, who, despite his religion, was eminently one of the 'the classes'; he and his backers were supremely confident of defeating Watson, whom they rightly assessed, on their conservative view of politics, as the most dangerous man in the Labor Party. Before 1891 a man like O'Connor could have had a seat like Young for the asking. But in 1898 Watson increased his 1895 majority. Except for Wise, who won Ashfield by five votes, O'Connor did no worse than the other well-known federationists who expected to get into parliament. Bruce Smith lost in Glebe, Barton lost in King. In an electorate of 2174 in 1895 Reid had polled 608 against Parkes's 478; in 1898 he got 761 and Barton 651 from 3028 electors: at 10 o'clock on election night when the premier's victory was confirmed, unable to address the closely packed crowd from a platform in King Street, he made a short victory speech to the reporters and then 'bowed to the crowd, and retired amidst a tumultuous scene of waving hats, handkerchiefs, umbrellas, and walking sticks, and cheering'.[53]

After the 1898 general election, probably more than any other election of the nineteenth century, it was difficult to allocate precisely all the returned members to recognisable parliamentary groups. With the backing of 'the labour wing of the ministerial party' as the *Sydney Morning Herald* referred to the Labor Party, there was no doubt that Reid had won the contest, though he lost three of his ministers, including two of his best, Garrard and Sydney Smith. Counting the nineteen Labor men, and giving him a doubtful independent, the premier probably had sixty-five supporters. The confusion among the protectionist-federalist group, ostensibly led by Barton but divided into at least two groups, one pledged not to raise the fiscal issue during the life of the parliament (the Federal Association members) and the other pledged not to raise it until Federation had been settled, made it even more hazardous to assess the number of the opposition; and the confusion was compounded by Barton's failure in King, (however, he became the nominal leader of the opposition when he won the seat of Hastings and Macleay on 23 September, after F. Clarke had resigned for him). Subtracting Reid's supporters, there were sixty Assembly members left and it seemed that they formed at least an opposition group, with probably fifty more or less firmly behind Barton and ten independents who seemed as if they preferred him to Reid.

The 1898 general election marked the culmination of Reid's policy to involve the voters of New South Wales in Federation. Practically all members returned were federalists, and eminently because of Reid's work, they agreed substantially on the changes in the draft constitution he would now be required to negotiate on behalf of the colony. But the premier's political support had been considerably eroded. In the metropolitan area he had a net loss of four seats, and twelve in the country. After due allowance was made for the political confusion induced by Federation, it was clear that the wide range of legislative and administrative reforms effected by the government had not been well received by many voters; and Reid had not had the time to counteract this trend in public opinion because of his concentration on Federation. His land and income taxation policy had hit many voters, country and city alike; in the city, conservative propaganda had projected Reid as only a little better than the 'communistic' Labor Party, and public servants could only agree with the assessment. Even on Federation Reid had been a loser; his careful analysis of the convention bill had alienated those who were federationists at any price, while his support of it had antagonised various groups of provincialists, including free traders who believed that Federation would inevitably be accompanied by protection.

To complicate Reid's predicament, the Labor Party had noted his easing of pressure on the Legislative Council, his lapse into an old-style rate of legislation, his failure to back up his new laws with effective administration, particularly in regard to the regulation of the coal mining and the maritime industries. And a knot of superior federationists, headed by Wise and Barton, blinding themselves to Reid's great practical achievements, were appalled that one so unworthy should be receiving plaudits, and might even accede to the national prime ministership, whilst they who had done so much for Federation were out in the cold; and they salved their envy with sweet thoughts of revenge. And Lyne had his own reasons to detest the premier; Reid had done what no New South Wales politician had ever done before, lead a cohesive ministry for four continuous years;[1] any old-style parliamentary leader could only regard this as indecent. Lyne had entered parliament with Reid in 1880 and had experienced no less than nine ministries before Reid took over in 1894; Lyne could at least recognise the form of the bitter and agitated eddies gathering around Reid, and they stirred his ambitions to succeed to the premiership.

Reid's mandate was to complete Federation. After that he would be put to the test under circumstances he had not experienced before. When the new parliament met on 17 August, the governor's speech stressed that its first business would be to consider a new set of federal resolutions. But Reid was aware of some of the other pressing problems: he accepted the great need to reform the navigation laws because of the risk of accidents that current legislation was powerless to cope with; he also indicated that the government hoped to legislate on friendly societies, fisheries, the difficulties of selectors, the extension of local government, and legal changes. Apart from the maritime problem, again he virtually promised the Labor Party that he would amend the Legislative Council, introduce compulsory investigation into industrial disputes, and provide relief for the aged poor. But Reid's main preoccupation was clear: Federation, he said, was 'the greatest of all objects open to Australian patriotism'.[2] Edden said everyone would agree with that, but asserted that 'the sooner we get down to practical work the better'; he brought up the failure of the government to enforce the weighing provisions of the Coal Mines Regulation Act and said that the mining unions were disturbed about it.[3] J. Haynes, an unstable free trader, warned the premier about Wise, whose sole policy, he said, was to destroy Reid.[4] But Watson reflected Labor's policy of giving Reid time to complete Federation, and cheered him by attacking Barton's 'duplicity' and Wise's 'inconsistency'.[5]

Inevitably parliament concentrated on the completion of Federation and the Labor Party was automatically involved. The opposition, instead of co-operating with Reid seized the opportunity to harass the government at every turn. The difficulties of working out the final form of a federal system, given the envy Reid had inspired and the tense parliamentary situation, seemed to offer the motley protectionists-federalists a chance to achieve the power the premier had denied them since 1894. An unwonted unity of purpose soon possessed them, making it possible for the brutality of W. P. Crick, the bitterness of Wise, the selective charity of O'Sullivan, the cunning of Lyne and, after 23 September, the gentility of Barton to form a fine patriotic stew. The Legislative Council was encouraged by the great strife in the Assembly to prepare to settle its own score with Reid. The Labor Party performed by no means its least service to national union by supporting the premier at all stages of his strenuous work to bring Federation to success, both in parliament and in negotiations with the premiers of the other colonies. There were times when several Labor Assembly members, affected by the great confusion, were inclined to overlook the compelling need to dispose of the problem before normal political pressure could again be rationally applied, but they were out-voted in caucus at the important stages: Hughes, Holman, Dacey and Edden were not always so clear-headed about the right order of priorities as were Watson, McGowen, Spence and Ferguson. But the great social value of the solidarity system was revealed when all the Labor members toed the line to help Reid in critical divisions. To have changed the government in New South Wales between August 1898 and March 1899 would have postponed Australian Federation indefinitely.

The opposition tried hard to change the government. On 7 September Lyne moved another censure motion on the grounds that Reid, in submitting a new set of federal resolutions to parliament, was laying down pre-conditions for the negotiations he had to have with the other premiers. In fact these resolutions clarified the position in the light of the results of the general election and the failure of the convention bill referendum, and debate on them was necessary to let the other premiers know what New South Wales wanted. Summarised, the resolutions were:

1. If equal state representation in the Senate were insisted on, then the three-fifths majority at joint sittings should be replaced by a simple majority; or the referendum should replace the joint sitting

2. The Braddon fiscal clause should go

3. The federal capital should be in New South Wales

4. There should be better protection against alteration of state boundaries

5. There should be clearer safeguards for the use of inland rivers

6. The Senate should not have the power to amend money bills

7. Appeals from states' supreme courts should be either to the high court or the privy council, not indiscriminately to one or the other.[6]

In his reply Reid revealed what everyone knew, that Barton and Crick had helped to draft Lyne's motion.[7] Ferguson, emerging as one of the Labor members who saw clearly that the convention constitution was inevitably the substantial basis of Federation, made the main Labor speech and clarified what the Party was, perforce, coming to accept; he said he would not insist on the capital being in New South Wales or on the removal of the 'Braddon blot', but he would demand the abolition of the three-fifths majority for joint sittings; perceptively he prophesied that 'the line of cleavage in a federal parliament will not be on state questions, but on party questions, the same as in any other parliament'.[8] Edden restated the Party's distrust of Barton, reinforced on this occasion by Wise's bitter speech against Reid.[9] The motion finally lost on 15 September 54 to 58, with all of the nineteen Labor men present and voting for the government.

The Legislative Assembly was in committee from 21 September to 3 November on the federal resolutions, a long and tedious process in which virtually every phrase had to be dissected. This obligation on all Assembly members did not prevent the opposition from keeping up their disruptive tactics. On 29 September they reverted to a method well-known to all pre-1891 parliamentarians and redolent of the revival of the old parliamentary game despite the advent of Barton. At 5.13 p.m. Sleath moved the adjournment of the House to discuss the need to remove fallen trees from the Darling River. This was a normal action of a member under strong demands from his electors; in most cases, it would have been followed by a reassuring statement by the minister concerned, with normal business being quickly resumed without a division. The time of the motion suggested that Sleath thought the matter would be finished by the meal break, 6 p.m., and that the House would resume committee discussion of the Federation resolutions at 7 p.m. But the opposition immediately sensed an opportunity to split the Labor Party from Reid and bring down the government; seventeen members spoke on the motion, described by Reid as 'a stonewall', all of them, except Sleath, J. H. Young and Haynes, opposed to the ministry, Lyne, Crick, and O'Sullivan among them. At 10.55 p.m. the opposition ran out of speakers, and forced a division, which lost 25 to 50.[10] Neither the Labor Party nor Reid were deceived by the tactic, though the Party (thirteen of them) had to vote against their own colleague's motion, and Sleath had to absent himself from the division. Barton voted with the opposition.

Within a week Lyne struck again with an artfully worded motion attacking J. H. Young, minister for public works, for his actions in the by-election won by Barton. The censure was debated on 5 and 6 October, and Hughes exposed his restlessness when he said that he had been elected 'on other matters besides federation, and one of them is a bill dealing with the navigation laws of the country';[11] but eighteen Labor men turned up for the division and helped Reid to stay in office by 58 to 52 votes. Barton, himself, responded to the snarl of motives of his following on 15 November by moving the third censure motion in a little over two months. Reid's financial proposals had taken account of reduced rural incomes arising out of the continued severe drought and had included slightly increased revenue duties to bring in £200,000. The plan emphasised once more how the old fiscal question was related to budgetary exigencies, but it shocked Barton, who claimed, in effect, that the government should have kept it decently buried at a critical time when all patriotic citizens should have been intent on consummating Federation. All the Labor men voted for the government in a 40 to 63 defeat for Barton.[12]

Obviously Reid depended on Labor to give him vital assistance in the redemption of his pledge to bring about national union as soon as possible, and the Party was saving Federation from being submerged in critical confusion. But this work did not stop it from trying to have its views on the constitution incorporated in Reid's resolutions. McGowen was able to have an addendum attached to them that would have facilitated future amendments of the constitution, and made it necessary for any transfer of power from the states to the commonwealth to be approved by a majority of electors in the state(s) concerned.[13] The move showed the persistence of Labor's fears that the constitution was weighed against their view of democratic government. But this attitude was adjusting to the force of events and the realisation that a majority of colonists wanted Federation, even if it meant that compromise had to be made that violated the formal requirements of democracy as well as what some regarded as the basic interests of New South Wales. So far as Reid could arrange it, the ordinary activities of parliament were subordinated to the great national issue; but J. L. Fegan managed to have a select committee set up to inquire into accidents in coal mines, and four Labor members of the Assembly, all representatives of mining seats, were appointed to it: Edden, Ferguson, Sleath and Watkins.[14] This committee, and its personnel, indicated the powerful opinion, rapidly growing in the Newcastle area, that urgent and decisive action was necessary to settle the issue of safety in coal mines. Reid was too busy to be fully aware of the parliamentary implications of the feeling.

The Legislative Council did not really need the example of the opposition in the Assembly to do their utmost to torment Reid, but it helped them to see their duty on Federation; clearer, if possible, than in 1897, when Reid's absence in England had left Carruthers in charge of the convention bill in the Assembly, and Barton (appointed on 12 May 1897 at Reid's request) in charge in the Council, and softened the recalcitrant majority somewhat; even so, on 22 July 1897 Barton gave in and resigned. By 1898 the Council had a definite majority, mostly appointed by Parkes and Dibbs, who detested Reid. The premier had hurt both their pockets and their pride when he forced through his direct taxation legislation.[15] At the height of his reforming impetus in 1894–5 he had insulted them by his reference to 'the barnacles' and 'fossils' who were throwing out and mutilating progressive legislation in the Upper House, and had frightened them by his plans to reform the Council. Their feelings had been aggravated by the National Association, which was in the vanguard of the movement to unite all conservative groups against radicalism, now that fiscal divisions among employers, and between them and squatters, were becoming anachronistic. Reid had compounded his sins by his co-operation with a party that not only had driven him on his reforming way but had also marked the Council out for abolition. The final stages of national union gave the reactionary majority in the Upper House a providential opportunity to pay off many rankling accounts with the radicals by doing their utmost to discredit Reid: in the process they augmented incongruously the malevolent forces in several colonies who were feeling increasingly sick at the prospect of Reid becoming the first prime minister of Australia.

In slaking their revenge against Reid the Council die-hards were forced to make a last ditch stand against Federation from the time they received the Assembly's final resolutions on 23 November 1898 to the time they agreed to the Federation enabling bill on 20 April 1899 (after Reid had had twelve new members of the Legislative Council appointed). In this stirring period as their opposition grew in intensity its form changed from blind reaction against the premier to maudlin emphasis on the rights of the mother colony, and came to eject bitterness towards all backers of the final draft constitution; but the substance of the Council's resistance was hatred of Reid and instinctive fear of Labor that transcended political and economic realities.[16]

Federation was also adding to the difficulties of the PLL in keeping all its members' attention on political realities. But the League kept on trying to spread the enthusiasm of the limited number of 'Labor men'. Arthur Rae in August 1898 had analysed the general problem:[17] some branch leagues, he said, were formed at election time, and were very pleased if they enrolled two or three per cent of the electors; then, if the local candidate won they 'fell asleep' until the next election, or 'dropped dead' if he lost; and this fate befell all other kinds of political organisation. Rae went on to say that a minority of leagues tried to avoid *rigor mortis* by 'Debates, smoke concerts and various devices', but few succeeded. A Labor league should do better than this, he argued, because it was not a 'one-idea' political group; yet workers were mean as well as poor, and many 'would sooner buy' the *Dead Bird* than the *Worker*.[18] Rae probed for other reasons for the lack of political awareness among the workers, and concluded, like so many Labor men of the time, that 'Party Government' was to blame, because it put the emphasis on politics rather than basic problems.[19] The way out was to forge closer links between trade union and political action; unions had a continuous existence; if unionists would become more politically minded and other league members more industrially minded, the leagues themselves could take persistent action for increased municipal ownership and control of industries, for equal local government franchise and fair rating.

Rae exposed some of the general obstacles confronting a mass democratic party, especially one that was pioneering new ideas at a time of great national consolidation; and his stress on the invigorating influence of local municipal political action was sound. The *Worker*, a little earlier, had remarked on the difficulty of involving young men in politics; from the ages of twenty-one to twenty-five most were absorbed by sport and 'the girl', and as a result were conservative; though some were radical and erred in thinking that 'reform can be attained at a stroke', this type had to be kept out of control.[20] But great as these human problems were, no other political organisation could match the PLL's awareness of them, or its attempts to alleviate them. They were problems that could never be fully solved, but the significant relative success that the PLL was achieving in the difficult circumstances of 1898 remained a measure of the continuing deep need for an organised radical party. Nevertheless, the vital requirement pressing on Labor as 1899 began, was to maintain its impetus to preserve its identity in unprecedented conditions that were loosening and reshaping political and social groups, not only within New South Wales but also throughout Australia. The Labor Party could have been sunk without trace in 1899. The premiers' conference to decide the final form of the Australian federal constitution met in Melbourne from 29 January to 4 February; Labor's annual conference was postponed from 26 January to 31 March, Good Friday, and met in Woonona, a small town near Wollongong.

The meeting on the south coast was a continuation of the PLL's tactics to instil greater interest among Party members by meeting in country areas. But the hard fact was that Sydney was the most convenient place for a conference of delegates who resided in widely dispersed parts of the colony. Only seventeen leagues were represented, and counting the Assembly members who were present, the total attendance was about twenty-five. The executive's report was adopted;[21] it recorded twenty-six meetings in the preceding fourteen months, sound evidence of purposeful continuity; and listed the attendance of its twenty-seven members (including the nineteen Assembly members, who had a total of five votes), ranging from twenty-five for Riley, twenty-four for Harper, twenty-two for Flowers and twenty-one for S. Smith to nil for Cann, Thomson and Watkins. Fears expressed at the 1898 conference that the Assembly members would dominate the executive had been proved groundless: McGowen nine, and Watson seven, had the best attendance of them. The report showed that the executive had sent a deputation to Reid in April 1898 which stressed the need for further reform of the Navigation Act; recounted Labor's strong efforts to 'democratise' the draft constitution and paid tribute to support in the struggle from 'the liberal press', and especially from the *Worker*, 'which is the special representative of Labor-in-politics and Unionism in the Fourth Estate'; and emphasised the need for stronger organisation and 'for an intelligent and alert democracy' to complement Labor's demand for use of the referendum. The executive noted that it was evident that until the question of Federation was dealt with there was not much 'chance of domestic legislation of any useful character being passed'; and stated proudly that 'The 19 Labor men averaged during last year's session 97 divisions per man' against eighty-eight for government supporters and sixty-six for opposition members: Smith with a total of 130, Watson with 126 and McGowen with 117 were the most assiduous. The executive took up Rae's point on municipal work and welcomed Labor's 'signal victory' at the Broken Hill elections, and progress at Leichhardt; and closed with thanks to the AWU for use of the *Worker* office.

The conference tightened its procedures by appointing a credentials committee and a standing orders committee.[22] Compulsory arbitration was debated at length, supported virtually unanimously and placed on the general and fighting platforms; the need for a properly constituted authority to settle disputes and make binding awards was stressed, although there was some disagreement as to whether the New Zealand method should be adopted in its entirety. Clearly the Party intended to work strongly for a compulsory system, but the precise details remained to be worked out: Reid's conciliation and arbitration bill, which went some of the way Labor wanted, had been sent to the Legislative Council on 19 December 1898, but had not been returned. The increasing renewal of trade union strength in the PLL was reflected in Lamond's motion on behalf of the executive to allow AWU branches direct representation on conference; after G. Henderson had argued that the Miners' Union was entitled to similar treatment, an amended resolution was unanimously approved,

> That each Trades Union which affirms the necessity for a solid Labor Party and endorses the Labor Platform, be entitled to one delegate at conferences of the P.L.L. for each branch of not less than 25 members.

Riley and Dacey tried to have Labor's policy on Federation reopened. The ensuing 'lengthy discussion' indicated how the Party was being affected by the inexorable process by which a majority of Australians were coming to accept a compromise constitution. Hughes argued that conference could do as it liked, but, 'after some heated passages' it was decided that, as the item was not on the agenda, no change could be made in the existing policy 'of opposition to the Bill'. James Wilson (1861–1925), a confectioner, replaced S. Smith as president of the PLL, G. A. Jones remained secretary, and Flowers, Hepher and Riley were among the seven elected to the executive, which was given the task of revising and consolidating the platform.

There were some very significant undercurrents to the conference's discussion of Federation. The *Worker's* report of the whole meeting was discreet and summary, bringing out clearly how the important procedural framework protected the rights of the rank and file when it recorded, in the Federation debate, that 'those who denied the right of Conference to take up important matters without consulting the Leagues were found to be in the majority, the motion being negatived by 7 to 3'. But the *Worker's* reference to 'some heated passages' covered clashes that went to the very heart of Labor's integral social role, both in the narrow colonial parliamentary area and in the wider national field being clarified by Federation. The conference resolution on the debate confirmed actions taken and agreements already made by the executive and the parliamentary Labor Party, although not approved by a minority headed by Hughes, Holman and Dacey among the Assembly members and Riley on the executive. The solidarity structure of the PLL had enabled it, in March-April, to reach decisions that bound all members of the Party, and that were an essential part of the process that brought Federation to final approval in 1899. There is enough evidence to show that Watson was the key man in delicate and complex bargaining both within the Party and between it and the premier; and to reveal that, at least in respect of 1899, he ranks with Reid as a chief engineer of national union.

By 1899 Reid had carried in New South Wales the chief responsibility and burden of Federation for five hectic years. No one knew better than he that its completion depended on mutual compromises between the colonies. At the Melbourne conference he was not able to persuade the other premiers that all of the New South Wales resolutions should be agreed to, but unanimous agreement was reached on eight points that went some way to meet the mother colony's wishes: they included the abolition of the three-fifths majority in joint sittings of the two Houses, the limitation of the Braddon fiscal clause to ten years, the national capital to be in New South Wales (though not within 100 miles of Sydney) and provision for a referendum on constitutional amendments if twice passed by one House but rejected or obstructed by the other. Haggling over the constitution had now come to an end. Federation had to be settled in the 1899 version or postponed indefinitely. And Reid was determined it would be settled.

When he returned to Sydney, Reid arranged for a short parliamentary session (from 21 February to 30 March) to consider a federal enabling bill that would refer the revised constitution to a referendum. This action immediately posed problems for Labor. The constitution was still far short of what the Party considered democratic; only one of the three points of McGowen's addendum to the Assembly's resolutions had been accepted. Against that Party principle, Reid's basic proposal was for a referendum, and the first plank of Labor's fighting platform included 'the introduction of the Initiative and the Referendum'. The more important article of faith superseded the lesser, and the Labor members assisted the passage of the enabling bill, which was brought down on 23 February and sent to the Legislative Council on 3 March. The opposition did not check the bill, though Haynes exposed the basic anti-federal core of some free traders, which had been camouflaged while Federation seemed remote, but was now emerging to increase the great pressures on Reid. But the premier's stamina and shrewdness were equal to the mounting demands. The enabling bill was severely amended by the Upper House; agreement could not be reached on 28 March at a conference between managers from each House; and the premier refused to go on with the bill.

Reid was now determinedly shaping the form in which Federation had to be achieved. Clearly he wanted to bring it about; just as clearly he wanted to stay as premier of New South Wales, and so almost certainly become the first prime minister of a united Australia. He richly deserved that great honour, but there were many obsessed persons whose predominant passion in 1899 was to see that Reid did not get it. The Labor Party was the key to his remaining in power and Reid decided to anchor it more firmly to him by offering it seats in the Legislative Council as part of his plan to force his enabling bill through.

This offer compounded Labor's exquisitely difficult predicament. The first part of the first plank of the fighting platform was 'Abolition of the Upper House', and a simple view was that such an objective precluded membership for Labor men. But it was not a simple problem, though in 1899, and later, fastidious idealists thought that it was. The Legislative Council's great resilience derived from its role in the New South Wales constitution; it could not be wished away, neither could it be shaken by threats; and there were powerful sanctions against swamping it in order to destroy it. The Council was virtually immovable, and Labor, no less than Reid, had to accept it as part of the price of the Party's social adhesion. Indeed, implied in the survival of Labor members of the Assembly in the 1890s was the inevitability that they would be joined by Labor members of the Council. As early as October 1891 the TLC had considered the possibility. In 1899 in Labor's agonising over the problem, the long-term difficulty of abolishing the Upper House yielded to the immediate prospect of implementing the referendum. The Labor Party, both caucus and executive, agreed by majority votes that it should be so. That the executive should have been so involved revealed the powerful position it had now assumed.

This was the essential background to the 1899 conference's discussion of Federation. There had been leaks about probable appointments of Labor members of the Legislative Council. The *Daily Telegraph,* now bitterly opposed to Reid, 'this backsliding premier', because of his acceptance of the Melbourne compromises, published a long article two days before the Labor conference in which it exposed what it called the 'extraordinary tactics' of the [Labor] Party both in parliament and in the PLL executive.[23] The newspaper went further and asserted that there was a close alliance between Reid and 'one or two' Labor men and that therefore he was involved in the general Party intrigue; both the Assembly members and the executive had been preparing lists of likely Labor Council members, 'and the completeness of their arrangements seems to show that they have been working on some understanding, definite and implied'. The *Telegraph* admitted it had no information of what had transpired at the caucus 'probably held on the 28 March', but it stated that some Assembly members were opposed both to the revised federal constitution and Labor appointments to the Legislative Council; and concluded that the whole business was significant and asked its readers to remember 'the commanding position the [Labor] Party assumed on the occasion of the imposition of the tea duties recently'.[24] Events were to prove that the *Daily Telegraph* was very well informed; and there was little doubt that Watson and McGowen were the negotiators with Reid.[25]

The *Telegraph* kept up its pressure on Reid and its attempts to split the Labor Party. It reported a pre-conference public meeting at Woonona on 31 March in which it highlighted a strong attack on Federation by Hughes, supported by Holman.[26] The topic of discussion at this meeting was 'Trade Unionism in Politics', with J. B. Nicholson, MLA, chairman; Nicholson had been an 1891 Labor member and was in process of returning to the fold. McGowen and Sam Smith, retiring president of the PLL, also spoke and kept to the point. Smith pertinently said that 'The pledge bound the Party together, and enabled them to mark traitors', and McGowen revealed the steel that lay beneath his benign exterior:

> In acknowledging the vote of thanks . . . [he] said that the reason the *majority* of the Labor Party opposed the action of the Legislative Council . . . was that they believed that the Referendum should be untrammelled, and they denied the right of the Council to coerce the Legislative Assembly.[27]

Smith had also stressed the essential role of trade unionism in the 'permanence and success' of Labor. The picture was clearing to suggest that if Hughes and Holman were to test their strength at the conference they would face formidable opposition; and that they would find themselves, in effect, arguing both in favour of the reactionary, cramping role of the Upper House and against the referendum as part of their attempt to delay Federation.

Hughes and Holman did try. The conference debate on Federation was really their effort to have Labor's sovereign body reverse decisions already made by caucus and the executive.[28] Superficially, they were defeated on a technical procedural point, and this juridical quality of Labor conferences was of great significance; but, as well, their analysis of the situation was faulty: important principles had converged and were in conflict, but the majority's view of the ordering of priorities was undoubtedly correct; and, above all, Hughes and Holman lacked the supreme 'Labor touch' of Watson and McGowen, and were simply out-manoeuvred. The *Telegraph* gave some more details of what it called the 'weak conference' at Bulli: Riley had been in the minority on the executive in the negotiations with Reid, and his conference motion, supported by Hughes, Holman, Dacey, Thomas and Rosa, was designed to reverse Labor's support for the enabling bill and appointments to the Legislative Council, on the grounds that the Party's policy was opposed to the revised federal constitution. The *Telegraph* reported Watson's strong reaction to the motion, '[he] jumped to his feet in a most excited

manner and in heated tones . . . contended . . . that they should not interfere with the referendum'; and the newspaper went on to say that Watson's statement that Hughes and Holman were seeking self-advertisement
was very much resented, but that Smith, Cann and Griffith supported
Watson; and concluded,

> The Labor party seems to have reached the parting of the ways. With the
> prominent men outside debauched by the prospect of sitting in the Chamber
> they had so often and so blatantly denounced, and some of the members
> inside quietened into submission to any democratic outrage on the part of the
> Premier by present and hoped for reward.[29]

Hughes and Holman were never fully at ease with Watson in the
1890s; though all three were warm friends, mainly because Watson
understood and respected the other two Labor men. His experience at
the very centre of the Labor movement, in both city and country, and
his work in parliament had so consolidated his natural understanding of
people and confirmed his innate generosity that his primacy of achievement and personality was taken for granted by others and ignored by
himself, except when necessary. Watson could be at home with Reid,
Barton and even O'Connor, as well as Andy Kelly, Jamie Moroney and
Peter Brennan. He could down a beer at the Wombat hotel with Mick
Loughnane[30] with the same genuine aplomb that he could sip champagne
with Bernhard Ringrose Wise at the Metropole. While Hughes could only
see the 'Munchausen' in Wise, Watson could see the genuine liberal
trying to burst out of the stifling cocoon that Rugby and Oxford had
spun around him. Hughes accepted his defeat by Watson at Bulli with
a shrug, but Holman exhibited the petulance that never quite left him.
In an interview with the *Telegraph* he revealed that he had been hurt by
Watson's reference to 'self-advertisement'. He said that Watson 'in his
saner moments' would see that the Labor Party had to oppose the federal
constitution; that Watson had been affected by the panic that had lately
seized the Legislative Assembly and that Labor's desires to avoid embarrassment to Reid had jeopardised solidarity. He also said that several
Labor Assembly members were already preparing to enter federal politics.[31] Obviously Holman's injured pride had prevented him from perceiving that solidarity had conditioned all the Labor decisions about
support of the enabling bill and appointment to the Upper House.

Reid spent the 1899 Easter weekend fishing at Lake Macquarie,
supremely confident, as usual, that he would confound his enemies, and
that the way he had chosen to effect Federation was the right one. The
whole colony, particularly Sydney, was bursting with excitement to know
if the lieutenant-governor, Sir Frederick Darley, would agree to 'swamp'
the Legislative Council, and, if so, who the appointees would be. The
Labor movement, if anything, was even more agitated than any other
group. The elements joined in on 4 April with a rocketing southerly

storm in the city that unroofed houses, stopped the Manly ferries, inundated low-lying areas, and silenced political conjecture. On 5 April a conflagration destroyed a large box factory in McGowen's electorate. On 7 April Reid broke the news that the lieutenant-governor had approved all twelve of his recommendations, they were N. J. Buzacott (1866–1933), a wheelwright from Broken Hill; F. Clarke, a surveyor, who had resigned his seat in 1898 to allow Barton to go into the Assembly; J. Estell (1861–1928), a miner from Newcastle; A. J. Gould, a solicitor and defeated cabinet minister in 1898; G. H. Greene, a grazier, defeated by Holman at Grenfell in 1898; N. Hawken, a produce merchant, who had been MLA for Newtown in 1887–91; J. Hepher, a tailor; W. H. Holborrow, a colonel, who had been MLA for Argyle in 1880–94; R. Jones, a businessman; E. D. Millen, a newspaper proprietor, who had lost his Assembly seat in 1898; S. McCaughey, a grazier; and J. Wilson, a confectioner. It was the first time a miner, a wheelwright, a tailor and a confectioner had gone to the Legislative Council; they were all trade union officials and Hepher and Wilson (president) were on the PLL executive. Reid at a banquet in his honour at Lake Macquarie welcomed the Labor men as a sensitive leaven for the Upper House.[32]

Hughes could contain himself no longer; with Haynes on the platform at an anti-federal constitution meeting, he shrilled, 'These appointments have been made to nobble the Labor party'.[33] McGowen and Watson put the matter straight; McGowen said he still opposed the constitution but that had nothing to do with the question of submitting it to the people's decision. Watson paid a tribute to the *Telegraph* for its liberal work in the past, but said it was producing 'mistiness' now; he denied he was at the tail of either Reid or Barton, said he would not swallow all he had claimed for the referendum in the past, and emphatically would not agree with the proposition that, 'We must think for the people, and not let them think for themselves'.[34]

The Legislative Council, now with sixty-nine members, had not been 'swamped', however tremulously it looked forward to sharing the company of four tradesmen. But Reid left it in no doubt that he wanted his enabling bill passed quickly. The new Council members were summoned on 8 April and all but Buzacott took their seats for a new session of parliament three days later. The premier brought down the bill again on 13 April and it was sent to the Council the same day; on 20 April the Council agreed to it with minor amendments which Reid accepted. The date for the second referendum on the federal constitution was fixed for 20 June. The parliamentary session ended on 21 April with the stage set for the final turbulent campaign to bring New South Wales into Federation. This time Reid and Barton combined forces, and, although there were a lively two months ahead, the result was never in doubt.

The 1899 federal constitution referendum campaign provided the *coup de grâce* for the old fiscal groups. Appropriately, the chief executioners were Reid and Barton, as leaders of the 'yes' forces, with Wise not far behind; and Lyne, as a nominal leader of the 'no' ranks, with Haynes, Fegan, Cotton and other free traders backing him up. The Federation movement had at last produced the result that was implicit in it from 1889. But the campaign had even more complex ingredients. The Labor Party was solid for 'no', with two important exceptions, Ferguson and Sleath; and some of the chief reactionaries of the Legislative Council headed by H. N. MacLaurin, L. F. Heydon, C. G. Heydon and C. E. Pilcher condescended to come down into the electoral arena to advocate 'no'. This grand 'no' coalition meant that nearly all of the groups hoping for Reid's downfall had come together: disaffected free traders, the last of the old-style protectionist leaders, Lyne, the mastodons of the Upper House, and an embittered minority in the Labor Party, led by Hughes and Holman. So far as Labor was concerned the position was complicated further by the fact that, while Watson and McGowen were strongly opposed to the constitution, they still thought that Reid should be given another chance once the Federation excitement had subsided. On the 'yes' side, Barton and Wise, stoically bearing their fate of having to associate with Reid, looked forward to the time when they could take advantage of the great build-up of freakish opposition to him. No matter what the result of the referendum, Reid could only lose the premiership of New South Wales; and, should 'yes' win he would also forego his chance to become the first prime minister of Australia. He, unquestionably, had more than an inkling of the difficulties that lay ahead of him, but he fought the greatest campaign of his life, and crowned his incomparable record as the most effective protagonist of Federation in New South Wales.

The Labor Party was probably the best organised section in the variegated combination fighting the federal constitution, and, as a group, the Labor parliamentarians worked harder than any others.[1] Although the Party was on the losing side it emerged from the campaign with its organisation strengthened and its reputation intact. Alone of the political bodies it had consistently supported the idea of Federation; and it was the only one that had undeviatingly insisted that the federal constitution should adhere to the principles of formal democracy, including one man, one vote; one vote, one value; initiative and referendum; the primacy of the Lower House; and ease of amendment. More intangibly, but of great significance, Labor had helped Reid to implement pressing essential social and political reforms that had made it possible for the people of New South Wales to reflect rationally on Federation. Indeed, the very development of the idea of union had strengthened the Labor Party and decomposed the fiscal groups, if only because of the fact that Labor's policy of sinking the fiscal issue fitted in with the growing approval of a federal system. Admittedly, the Party had been forced to modify the details of its policy on Federation, but even this process had kept pace with majority colonial opinion as the intense difficulties of forging a nation from six separate colonies had been clarified. Of great immediate importance in 1899, the Labor Party had clearly been seen as an essential part of the process by which the voters were asked to record their opinion on the final constitution.

Labor gained in stature, too, from its principled, accurate and democratic analysis of a series of intricate party problems associated with Federation, in the six months before the referendum. The whole colony was aware of Watson and McGowen's work and their success in convincing a majority in the Party that they were right. That this was not merely 'machine politics' became manifest when Watson, McGowen and their supporters, to the edification of Hughes and Holman, calmly accepted their duty to oppose Reid on the details of the constitution. In the 1899 referendum New South Wales voters received confirmation of what they already knew, that a party with a new approach to politics was firmly established; a party with a coherent, wide-ranging policy that incorporated Federation, and one that had men capable of precise assessment of complex political problems in relation to that policy, and capable of consistent and determined action based on their analysis. That a majority of voters disagreed with the Labor Party about the federal constitution had no effect on the value of its future either in the New South Wales or in the Commonwealth parliament, for the constitution was above and beyond politics.

The Labor men campaigned throughout the colony, both as a separate group and in association with the anti-Reid coterie.[2] On 28 April Law spoke with Cotton at Marrickville; on 3 May Hughes was with E. M. Clark at North Sydney. Holman was with L. F. Heydon at Leichhardt on 7 May, MacLaurin at Marrickville on 12 May and C. G. Heydon at the Protestant Hall on 15 May. Dacey was at Bungendore on 19 May; McGowen at Newcastle on 21 May, Singleton on 11 June and Bathurst on 15 June; Watson at Young on 12 June. At the Protestant Hall on 13

June the PLL executive organised a demonstration with McGowen, Watson and Griffith the main speakers. With the exception of Ferguson and Sleath, every Labor MLA worked strongly for 'no', and together they covered practically every region of the colony to give the Party the most efficient publicity it had yet had; probably McGowen, Holman and Hughes spoke more than the rest. One of the most interesting 'no' meetings was held at the Protestant Hall on 24 May, with Dibbs chairman and the main speakers H. B. Higgins from Victoria and A. B. Piddington, backed up by Brown, Law, Smith, Thomas and MacLaurin. After the *Daily Telegraph* had asked plaintively 'Where is Mr. Lyne', he emerged to become a main leader of the anti-constitution forces.[3] As the campaign developed most of the 'no' supporters found it impossible to prevent their speeches becoming arguments against Federation rather than against the constitution, and by 20 June the *Telegraph* made no attempt to hide its true feelings. On the other hand, the Labor members of the Assembly, with the exception of Holman and Hughes, based their criticism consistently on the Party policy, the need to reduce the power of the Senate, for greater ease of amendment, and for clearer electoral safeguards to make the whole federal system more democratic. Again Watson excelled in his ordering of priorities and helped to ensure that the Labor Party maintained its traditional support for Federation.

Reid and Barton made certain that the majority of voters favoured not only the abstract idea of union but also the concrete form of the constitution; and, while they encouraged Victoria to agree that Federation was worth a capital, they convinced New South Wales that Federation was worth having the capital in Melbourne for an indefinite period. About 56 per cent of New South Wales voters turned out and 107,420 were for the constitution and 82,741 against it. The *Sydney Morning Herald* gave credit for the victory to Barton, Bruce Smith, Wise and even Copeland, but was generous, if careful, enough to observe that

> The Premier has nobly redeemed his lapse of last year and discharged ably and gallantly the duties which his high position and influence imposed on him.[4]

Watson reflected the true Labor opinion of the result:

> the mandate of the majority will have to be obeyed. This is the view the labour members have always held . . . it must be satisfactory that the matter is now settled beyond dispute.[5]

William John Ferguson and Richard Sleath had served time in prison as a result of their activities in the 1892 Broken Hill strike. They were typical Barrier men, tough, independent and plain-spoken, with Sleath, a huge man, finding it very difficult to mask a streak of violence that had frequently led him to attempt to prove his arguments with his fists. By 1899 both men were senior officials of the AWU, and Ferguson was president and Sleath a member of the Provincial Council of the ALF. Ferguson had been born in Burra, South Australia, and found it even easier than Sleath to endorse the majority border belief that Federation was urgent and necessary. They had readily accepted Labor's policy to push for union on the most democratic basis possible; but Ferguson, especially, from 1898 began to see that the Labor ideal was impossible and that a federal system would have to be based on a compromise constitution. Both men became convinced after the 1899 premier's conference that Federation had to be effected on the revised constitution or held over for an unlimited period. They agreed with Labor's support of Reid's enabling bill and with the associated Party appointments to the Upper House, but would not consent to campaign against the constitution. Their refusal raised a general problem for Labor, the need to bring strong regional opinion into line with Party policy. Labor held four of the five far western border seats. Both Cann, who held the Broken Hill city seat, and Thomas, from the close surrounding seat of Alma, accepted the entire Federation policy, but there were indications of divisions within the local leagues moulded by the general border demand for quick action to achieve Federation. Ferguson sat for Sturt, which surrounded Alma; Sleath held the adjoining seat of Wilcannia, a vast sun-baked electorate filling up the far north-western corner of New South Wales. Their acceptance of the popular viewpoint was divulged at a caucus meeting late in May, and was met by a decision to give members a free hand on the question.[6]

This was the first time that the Labor Party had been confronted with a problem of this type. The platform plank remained as 'The Federation of the Australian Colonies on a National, as opposed to an Imperialistic, basis', but it had been expounded by the conferences of 1896 and 1897, and in 1899 Labor policy sought a constitution that excluded the Senate and included non-party government and the initiative and the referendum. Practically these objectives were futile, and Labor's campaign in 1899 was based on criticism of the constitution because of its particular undemocratic features and fiscal inequalities. Nevertheless, the official policy had not been rescinded and, however eroded it may have been, it could not be interpreted to imply support for the constitution. Moreover, it was hardly feasible that the parliamentary Labor Party could legitimately decide that the referendum was an open question. The executive rightly claimed that it alone could rule on the problem;[7] but, in view of the pressure of the campaign, and the fact that the remainder of the members accepted the need to fight for a 'no' vote, it decided to postpone a final decision on the position of Ferguson and Sleath until after 20 June.

As early as 24 April at Summer Hill, Ferguson spoke with Wise in favour of the constitution.[8] On 4 May the *Telegraph* reported that the

Worker had claimed that he had deserted the Labor Party. The resentment of the rank and file was revealed by the unanimous decision of the associated leagues at Botany, Darlington, Redfern, and Waterloo to ask that the executive expel him.[9] By the end of May news of Sleath's activities had also reached the executive and they asked the Barrier District Assembly for a report on both men.[10] The *Telegraph* seemed to be more upset about them than the Labor Party and, recalling 1893, the newspaper argued that they had earned the same fate as Fitzgerald, Johnston, Kelly and Murphy, who had also heeded Barton's call to defect from Labor. Sleath's answer to that was to speak strongly for 'yes' at Pyrmont, in the city.[11] Subsequently both he and Ferguson worked indefatigably for the constitution in various parts of Sydney and the country. They were joined by a small trade union group, known as the 'Trades Union Federal Committee', headed by John West and J. Dwyer, of the Stewards and Cooks', which had been repudiated by the Sydney District Council of the ALF.[12] At the Trades Hall on 9 June Ferguson and West stressed to a rowdy gathering that the nation had its last chance to federate; but the meeting was taken over by the audience who voted five to one against the constitution.[13] This incident was in keeping with more complaints reaching the executive demanding strong action against Ferguson and Sleath. The half-yearly meeting of the Bourke AWU, and the White Cliffs Labor league both condemned them.

The PLL executive had no intention of ignoring the disloyal actions of the two; but in 1899 it was an experienced and assured body, well versed in the complexities of Labor issues, and Wilson and Hepher could now bring some parliamentary perspectives to bear on the problem. The colony's acceptance of the federal constitution, and especially the overwhelming vote for 'yes' in the far western electorates,[14] had given cause for second thoughts. Moreover, the question was not solely related to the defection of two members, but also raised the topic of the distribution of powers between the executive and the parliamentary caucus. The executive decided to hold a special conference to sit in judgment on the whole problem.

The special conference met at the Labor Centre on 28 and 29 July.[15] The Labor Party had fully recovered from its disappointment at the result of the referendum, and had realised that the joyful effusions of men such as C. E. Pilcher, MLC, who had said that 'the power of the Labor Party is a thing of the past',[16] were not only wishful thinking, but also incompetent political analyses. The parliamentary situation, as a new session proceeded, recalled the tangled confusion of July 1891, when a raw and inexperienced Party was able at least to begin to dictate events; now, exactly eight years later it had the practised skill both to shape affairs and to ensure that they continued more or less as the Party desired. In its sour way the *Telegraph* summed up Reid's impossible

position: the premier, it argued, was the head of a free trade party that
was now committed to financing the commonwealth by customs duties,
and went on to say that in fact the free traders were leaderless and
should elect a new chief and continue to rule with the aid of the Labor
Party.[17] That was not a well-grounded forecast of the immediate future
in parliament; but it did correctly underline the muddle indirectly produced by Reid's dedicated exertions for Federation and his final triumph
at the referendum; and the newspaper's comments accurately distinguished the powerful role that the Labor Party would play in the
resolution of the situation.

The July conference marked the return of the trade unions to the
Labor Party. Since 1897 the AWU had partially filled the gap opened
up in the close connections between Party and unions by the depression
of the early nineties and the consequent temporary dissolution of the
TLC in 1894; and there had been indications that other unions would
rekindle their interest in direct political activity as signs appeared of
brighter economic conditions, despite the persistence of the severe
drought. In addition, the strong interest of the PLL in compulsory
arbitration, with possible formal recognition of unions and associated
help in their operations implied in its implementation, strengthened the
intentions of many unions to resume contact with the Party. A new
phase in the development of the Labor Party had begun, firmly conditioned by the nature and past history of the movement. There were
seven unions represented at the conference, four of them in the AWU-
ALF combination and three belonging to long-established city unions,
the Stonemasons', the United Laborers', and the Furniture Trades'. The
interest of the far western unions in the possible expulsion of Ferguson
and Sleath was shown by the representation of two Broken Hill and one
Bourke union. There were fifteen leagues represented, ten metropolitan,
five country. Wilson presided, and reminded delegates that the conference was the sovereign body of the Labor Party.

W. Brennan, Waterloo league, moved for the expulsion of the two
members of the Assembly; he put forward a salutary solution for the
problem of keeping the caucus under control by arguing that the ten
members who made up the majority in the decision to give parliamentarians a free hand on the referendum should all be disqualified. P.
McGarry (1863–1930) agreed that caucus had acted beyond its powers,
which, he said, were limited to parliamentary matters; and he stressed
the rule that 'the executive was the custodian of the movement from
conference to conference'. Macdonald owned up to having moved the
critical motion in caucus, and admitted a mistake may have been made,
although he said he did it because many members were restless about
support for Reid's enabling bill: during Macdonald's speech, Hughes
made an interesting interjection, 'Where in the pledge is power given to

caucus to decide matters outside?' J. Grant (1858–1928) moved an amendment that while the caucus action was deplorable, it did not justify the expulsion of members who took advantage of it; he exhibited Labor mateship by saying he made it a rule not to denigrate his fellow Party members because 'they got enough of that from their opponents'. Lamond said that the Bourke AWU thought Ferguson and Sleath should go, because they had breached Labor policy, even though caucus had been remiss.

Holman intimated that he spoke in no spirit of vengeance, and he acknowledged the good work of Ferguson and Sleath; but the policy was plain and they had breached it. 'In his judgment they had broken the pledge' and their expulsion would help to maintain solidarity. Watson again opposed Holman; he regretted what Ferguson and Sleath had done, 'but he could trust them in Labor matters just as much as any member of caucus—even Mr. Holman himself, and he disclosed that Holman had opposed the majority on the enabling bill, though caucus had given no freedom on it; he showed that the Labor policy on Federation had been whittled down by events between 1897 and 1899; and pleaded for leniency for the two members, because '[The Party] had a lot of work to do yet, and should not recklessly shatter their forces'. Hughes defended Holman, and showed that a subtle but risky way of attempting to undermine caucus had been discovered; he said that the members had at first not made a decision on the enabling bill, but subsequently resolved to support it, and this action had brought Holman to the point of resigning: 'The temptation to go with one's constituency— that was the great temptation', Hughes mused. But he was firm for expulsion, because the executive was supreme outside parliament and 'If they did not punish them, what would they do with the next man?'

Flowers gathered up the main threads of the debate: the relative powers of caucus and executive, and the fact that Ferguson and Sleath may have acted in good faith, though clearly in breach of basic Labor policy. He insisted that the parliamentarians had no right to assume control of the Party; that they had to conform to the platform and rules just like any other member. But he did not think expulsions were justified in this particular case. Riley reiterated Flowers's arguments. When Ferguson and Sleath addressed the conference, neither of them showed any regret for his action. Both rested their arguments on their assessment of what their voters wanted and their own firm conviction that what they did was right; a dangerous line of reasoning to submit to delegates of a Party which believed that once a policy had been made, after full discussion, all members had to accept it or resign. If the two members had been less frank, probably the vote would have been against their expulsion; but, as it was, the vote was 11 to 10 for it; a nicely judged vote in all the circumstances, asserting the rightful powers of conference and executive against caucus and individual members, but so close as to warrant another examination of the problem.

The vote was taken at midnight on 29 July. In the ensuing excitement Watson tried to have the matter referred to the leagues, and helped to influence delegates to have the decision reviewed. Finally McGarry's motion was agreed to that, 'In view of the small majority for the motion, the matter be referred to the Parliamentary Party for decision'. The *Worker* commented that the tone of the conference debate was excellent, and that the final vote indicated that 'Conference thought that solidarity would be better preserved by allowing the matter to rest where it is, than by the expulsion of Messrs. Ferguson and Sleath'. These opinions were perceptive. At a critical time the conference had clarified some basic principles of Labor's machinery, and had given Party members an opportunity to come together and analyse problems in the light of the new social and political conditions being shaped by the culmination of Federation. Ostensibly the conference was about the expulsion of two members of the Legislative Assembly, but in reality it was related to the reinforcement of the morale of the Labor Party as it was about to face new and potent challenges. No doubt was left now about the ultimate power of conference, and the relationship between executive and caucus had been clearly defined. Ferguson and Sleath had certainly breached solidarity, but under mitigating circumstances that had been revealed to include some aberrant tendencies in the fellowship of the Assembly members, whose idea of solidarity was not quite co-extensive with that of outside members. The two did not deserve expulsion and the final decision was wise. On the other hand, the expressed notion of a possible right of appeal of members to electors was a dangerous conceit, related to the parliamentary experience, that held within it seeds of future conflict. Any Labor parliamentarian who felt inclined to use such a right now knew that he not only would take a risk about re-election, but would also be expelled from the Party.

Reid had called parliament together again on 18 July. He was fully conscious of the need to make up for lost ground in legislation; but he under-estimated the bitter strength of free traders he had alienated and over-estimated the gratitude he had earnt from the superior federationists who had joined him to help him win the referendum. On the other hand, McGowen and Watson were able to maintain a caucus majority to continue Labor's backing of the premier; it was reported many times to be a majority of one. Reid announced through the governor that he had devised a system of 'grand committees' to revise certain bills after their first reading in order to speed up their consideration in committee.[18] He planned to review the reallocation of 8,721,000 acres of leasehold that would soon revert to the crown, in the light of demands for land for agriculture and closer settlement, and the rights of the lessees; he also proposed a short land bill for the reappraisal of conditional purchases and leases. Both these land projects were an attempt to meet probably the most crucial political pressures of late 1899. With his eye more specifically on the Labor Party, Reid promised to restore the Navigation Act amendment bill to the notice paper, to review the early closing bill, and to submit a bill to provide relief for the victims of mining accidents. He also made somewhat vague references to legislation for old-age pensions and extension of the Factories and Shops Act. An air of unreality surrounded those proposals, for it was by no means certain that the ministry had majority support in a House substantially transformed by the referendum campaign. But so long as the Labor Party adhered to the government it seemed safe.

McGowen and Watson's support for Reid was not entirely based on their appreciation of the vital help he had given the Labor Party by bringing down essential reform legislation and effecting necessary administrative changes. They also had some affection for him, and, what was more important, great respect for the way in which he had coped with Federation problems; a corollary of their suspicion of Barton's political incompetency and inert conservatism, and their grave doubts about Lyne's capacity for reform. So, although Reid had virtually stopped reform legislation in 1897, the valuable effects of his administrative innovations continued, and he still was the best premier for the Labor Party. But McGowen and Watson were politicians, and belonged to a confident Party, restless for constant improvement, that decided policy on majority opinion. As the parliamentary session ground on its negative way, the initiative slowly passed to the opposition. Lyne, well aware of Labor's ban on Barton, and observing Reid's inaction, sensed the opportunity so long denied him to become premier of New South Wales.[19] There were limits to the ability and the will of McGowen and Watson to keep Labor with Reid.

Aside from the practical politics of the situation, there was a strong case for the parting of the ways. Reid was losing control and was still absorbed in Federation; he had to push the address to the Queen through parliament praying the imperial parliament to legislate for a commonwealth of Australia; and he had made no secret of his intentions to enter federal politics. The Labor Party could reasonably question whether they had any useful future with Reid as premier; of great significance was the feeling, exhibited most by Holman, that Labor had lost the capacity of independent action in parliament and was in danger of losing its identity. The tangled skein could possibly unravel with Labor taking its leave of Reid, gaining more reform legislation, and at the same time reasserting its parliamentary autonomy.

The debate on the address to the Queen opened up the sores of dissension. Barton wanted a reference included in the address to the

1898 referendum, to which he had been encouraged by his admirers to look back on as one of his great feats, seeing himself as fighting alone for national union; but Reid thought it unnecessary, and Barton's amendment lost 25 to 40, with Lyne voting against him.[20] Several disgruntled free traders seized the opportunity to assail the premier for handing New South Wales over to the protectionists in the forthcoming federal parliament. Haynes, in particular, exposed an animosity that approached the pathological; he moved an amendment to let Her Majesty know that over 82,000 New South Wales voters had protested against a constitution that could not be amended by a majority of the Australian people; it lost 22 to 75 after McGowen had asked him if Dr MacLaurin was one such voter.[21] Law restated the essential Labor objection, that Federation was based on minority rule and accused Reid of joining the conservatives, Barton, Wise and O'Connor.[22] Both Spruson and Holman observed that party lines had disintegrated. In reply Reid excoriated the provincial irrationalities not only of Haynes, but also of Cotton, Fegan, and Law, all his erstwhile supporters, as well as Lyne.[23] His peroration had a desperate nobility about it, because he knew that there was no chance of Barton, Wise and their *claque* sustaining him in the dangerous days ahead; that Lyne had a feeling in his bones that his day was about to dawn; and that the Labor Party was wavering in its co-operation:

> I can only say that in any respect in which I have deflected from the full length of any political principle which I have proposed, I have done it for a much nobler and greater cause than many of the changes which have characterized the public life of the country.

After that the address to the Queen was carried on the voices on 9 August. New South Wales was poised to enter the commonwealth.

The Labor caucus had met the day before. By that time, apart from one finance bill, the ministry had been able to put only one other bill before the House: the Coal Mines Regulation Act amendment. The primacy given to this legislation reflected Reid's great need to appease the Newcastle members, including Edden, especially, Griffith and Thomson among the Labor men and Fegan among the dissident free traders. When on his fishing week-end at Easter, Reid had told a meeting at Wallsend of his 'gratitude to the people of this great district', and that his 'heart [was] full of gratitude to the miners of this district'; as an earnest of this feeling he had had Estell appointed to the Legislative Council. There was no dissimulation about Reid's interest in the region, but parliamentary events were soon beyond his control and he could do nothing for it: in the upshot, the mines amendment bill was the only one cleared by the Assembly before the fall of the Reid government; it was sent to the Council on 24 August and stayed there. The caucus was bitterly concerned about Reid's inaction, and it was becoming increasingly difficult to keep the Party from withdrawing its support from him.

Caucus also considered the special conference's decision in the case of Ferguson and Sleath, and, as expected, resolved not to expel them.[24]

On 22 August Edden asked in the Assembly if any money had been paid to anyone in respect of a report on old-age pensions and state insurance. Carruthers, now colonial treasurer, said yes, £350 had been paid on 19 January to J. C. Neild towards his out-of-pocket expenses in England and on the Continent for the purposes of obtaining information for such a report.[25] From this simple interchange began the chain of crises that culminated in defeat for the Reid ministry on 7 September. With a break in 1889–91 Neild had been MLA for Paddington since 1887, distinguishing himself only as an intolerable bore who had earned the nickname of 'Jawbone' because of his skill in pinioning members in the lobbies and paralysing them in the chamber. He was a colonel, but was often addressed as 'general'; it was intended as derision but he took it as a compliment. His intentions were the best, but his achievements negligible. One of his hobby-horses was old-age pensions, and he was one of several who claimed to be the originator of the idea in New South Wales; but the National Association knew that pensions were safe with him. In 1896 he had told Reid that he was going overseas and would investigate what other countries were doing for the aged and incapacitated; he said he would submit a report, but would not expect payment. The premier gave him his blessing. In November 1898 Neild presented Reid with a report that rivalled a collection of his speeches, and intimated that he would appreciate re-imbursement of his expenses. Reid promised to put £250 on the supplementary estimates, but did not do so because none was prepared in 1898. During the December recess Neild, with a pressing life insurance bill, again importuned the premier who arranged to have him paid £350 in anticipation of parliamentary approval. By 1899 Neild had graduated from a figure of fun to be the most unpopular man in parliament.

On the day after Edden's question about Neild, Barton resigned as leader of the opposition; he said that his following had consisted of two sections, those who had promised, as he had, not to raise the fiscal issue during the life of the current parliament, and those who had promised not to raise it while Federation was in abeyance. With the address to the Queen completed, national union was now imminent, and Barton had discovered that his group was in a minority and hence he could not potentially form a ministry; Lyne had replaced him.[26] The inferences were loud and clear; Lyne potentially could form a ministry, and a possibility existed that he might be asked to do so. As soon as Barton sat down Edden rose again to raise a question of privilege on 'a matter of urgent importance', and moved for Neild's seat to be declared vacant because he had accepted an office of profit under the crown; the debate was concluded with the appointment of a select committee of nine, including Ferguson, to inquire into the matter.[27] The committee reported on 30 August that Neild had not accepted an office of profit, but that it 'was dangerous' for members who held commissions to accept payment without previous consent of parliament.[28] The day before, Lyne had given notice of a censure motion on the government, and as soon as the report on Neild had been received he got up and moved, 'That the present government does not possess the confidence of this House'.[29]

Edden's obsession with the Neild case had three main sources: he shared in the general dislike of the colonel; he perceived the incident as a means of bringing pressure to bear on Reid because of what he saw as his neglect of the Newcastle district; and, of the greatest importance, he reflected Labor's intense determination to ensure that government would be incorruptible. Of course, many other members also stressed the need for purity of administration, especially as it was a time when parliament's rights were regarded as superior to those of the executive government; but no group manifested the earnestness with which the Labor Party sought to ensure that every act of the administration should be subjected to the closest scrutiny. The *Daily Telegraph's* disdainful exaggeration could not disguise its recognition of one of the essential qualities of Labor in the New South Wales legislature: 'the cold, sticky calm of respectability which has lain like a funeral pall on the public life of this country ever since the advent of the Labor Party';[30] and Edden exhibited all the virtues of the Protestant miner, not by any means entirely shared by all the Labor men, but they all agreed that government should be above suspicion.

The Newcastle region returned six Assembly members. The four Labor men Edden, Griffith, Thomson and Watkins shared a close community of interest with the free traders Fegan and W. T. Dick, and they all were under pressure from their electors to obtain a better deal for the district. Fegan had been one of the original Labor members in 1891, and in October 1898 he had sat with Edden and Watkins on a select committee into safety in mining. Fegan was well aware of Edden's feelings about the impropriety of paying Neild £350 without parliamentary approval, and he agreed strongly with them. But the Newcastle Labor members were in the minority in the caucus that met on 30 August to consider how the Party should vote on Lyne's motion: the division was ten for Reid, viz., Brown, Cann, Ferguson, Law, Macdonald, McGowen, Ross, Smith, Spence and Watson, and nine against him, Dacey, Edden, Griffith, Holman, Hughes, Sleath, Thomas, Thomson and Watkins.[31] The McGowen-Watson line prevailed on the simple issue posed by the terms of Lyne's motion. Their view was strengthened by Reid's strong reply in parliament to Lyne's pedestrian speech, in which the premier asked,

> Is it not time to remind these men who have loyally supported me that I
> have set myself one by one against all the great vested interests of the country
> [the public service, the landed interest, and the financial interest]?[32]

Fegan, inspired by Lyne's promise during his speech not to raise the
fiscal issue, got the call immediately after Reid; the debate was adjourned, and next day Fegan dramatically changed its context by moving
an amendment to add to Lyne's motion, 'and [the government] deserves
censure for having made payments of public money to Mr. J. C. Neild . . .
without asking Parliament, and contrary to the assurance given by . . .
the premier'.[33]

Fegan also cleverly emphasised how Reid had failed to redeem his
promises to legislate for, *inter alia,* an accident fund for miners, and
effective compulsory arbitration; and he pointed out how more was
needed than progressive laws, they had to be administered effectively;
for example, the Coal Mines Regulation Act was being nullified in important sections because the government had failed to provide sufficient
skilled staff to make it work.[34] O'Sullivan tried to allay the doubts of
many federalists, who were troubled by Lyne's provincialism, by remind-
ing them that Barton intended to vote with Lyne; and he consolidated
Fegan's line of argument by asking Holman what the premier had done
about his promise to establish a state bank to help farmers; 'nothing'
replied Holman. O'Sullivan pursued this tactic by asking Smith why the
ministry had dropped the navigation bill.[35]

There was little doubt that a combined operation was under way to
detach the Labor Party from Reid and so bring the government down.
A vital part of the strategy was based on exposing the failure of Reid to
sustain reform legislation and efficient administration and the implicit
promise that a new ministry under Lyne would repair the omission. This
was indeed a new situation for the New South Wales parliament. Many
governments had fallen between 1856 and 1894, practically all of them
before their full terms were finished; but none had been removed in
order to allow another to consolidate and continue a program of progressive legislation and administration. In an important sense the censure
of Reid in 1899 was a culmination of the Labor Party's mission to change
the whole basis of the parliamentary system; to transform the narrow,
sterile routine produced by unruly factionalism, in which sparse legislation
was virtually left to the capricious play of random combinations of
individuals and groups; and to replace it with a regular order in which
the government would plan modern, improving legislation and administer
it efficiently. The adherence of Fegan to the plot and O'Sullivan's revitalised radicalism suggested strongly that Lyne might be made into a
reformer.

Labor, of course, had been critically aware of Reid's decline for a long
time. The Party was prepared to respond to the great pressure being

exerted on it. 'How can the Labor Party, pledged before all things to maintain purity of government, ignore [the Neild case]?' demanded the *Star*.[36] Correspondence between Griffith, who was secretary of caucus, and Lyne was published. Griffith wrote on 30 August,

> I think there can be no impropriety in my asking you to tell me if you would be willing . . . to 'immediately' undertake legislation on the subject of old age pensions, a miners' accident fund, and the early closing of shops;

Lyne replied the same day,

> I am strongly in favor of the first and second named in your letter, but the Closing of Shops bill, I don't think is good, and I want to have one much more in accord with the wishes of the people than that introduced by the government.[37]

The Melbourne *Age*, knowing that Lyne had no chance of becoming Australia's first prime minister, and hoping for a Victorian to win the great prize, said that Barton had quitted the leadership of the opposition because he was unacceptable to the Labor Party, which was now 'ripe for revolt' against Reid.[38] The premier was well aware of what he termed the 'violent intrigue' between Lyne and certain Labor members, and he knew that if he went down he had no chance of becoming prime minister. Reid fought back vigorously. But the scales were heavily weighed against him when the *Worker* finally denounced him, on the grounds that he would be so involved with federal politics in the immediate future that he would not have enough time to prepare legislation and force it through the Legislative Council.[39]

The Labor caucus met at 11 a.m. on 5 September to reconsider its decision to support Reid in the light of Fegan's amendment. Only sixteen could attend and Watson was chairman in McGowen's absence. Apparently no detailed account of the discussions has survived, but both the *Herald* and the *Telegraph* gave useful reports.[40] The meeting went on until 7 p.m., over-lapping with the continuation of the debate on Lyne's censure motion, during which strong efforts were made to keep Labor with Reid. The premier found an unlikely but powerful ally in Meagher, a fervent federalist who recognised Reid's primacy in the success of the movement, but also an unshakeable protectionist, embittered by Lyne's renunciation of the faith in order to become premier. Meagher was a superb, if somewhat fruity, orator, and he decided to pay off some old scores as well as help Reid. First he excoriated 'the stiletto party', the renegade free traders, Haynes, Fegan, E. M. Clark, Cotton, and J. C. L. Fitzpatrick,[41] whose hatred of Reid over Federation, he claimed, had led them to embrace both Lyne, a protectionist, and Barton, a federalist. Next he argued convincingly that the prime ministership of Australia was at stake, though he did not foresee that Barton would slip in along the rails; instead, Meagher quoted the *Age* to show that Victoria wanted

Reid out and the Victorian premier, Sir George Turner, in: at which stage Reid interjected that the *Telegraph* and the *Age* were working together against him; and Meagher quoted the *Australasian* and the *Argus* to indicate that Lyne had no chance of becoming prime minister. Finally he made a direct appeal to the Labor Party to see who their friends really were; Reid was 'the first practical politician to make the wealthy classes pay their due share of the expenses of government', and the first to bring in day labour in place of contracts for public works; Lyne, he argued, had no policy; if he became premier he would have the 'stiletto party' on one flank and the 'Kilkenny cat brigade' (Crick and his friends) on the other.[42]

As well as Meagher's eloquent advocacy for Reid, the Labor Party had also to weigh up an impassioned defence of the premier by W. H. Wilks, who alleged that Barton and Wise 'have stated that [Reid] will not be the first premier of a federated Australia', and ended with an amendment that tried to separate the Neild case from Lyne's general censure motion.[43]

Caucus had made up its mind before the end of Wilks's speech. The *Herald* reported that several Labor members had threatened to leave the Party and vote against Reid, if the meeting had gone against them. The *Telegraph* went somewhat further and said, 'It is confidentially believed that five or six members are prepared to resign their seats rather than condone the payment to Mr. Neild'. Both newspapers agreed that the majority opposed Reid; the *Herald* gave the division (including the votes of absentees) as: eight for the premier, Brown, Cann, Law, Macdonald, McGowen, Ross, Smith and Spence; and eleven against him, Dacey, Edden, Ferguson, Griffith, Holman, Hughes, Sleath, Thomas, Thomson, Watkins and Watson. H. V. Evatt has surveyed the reversed caucus decision and ascribed it chiefly to Holman.[44] Evatt also stressed the plotting of Wise, Crick and Lyne, with Barton, whose 'chief ambition lay elsewhere', a willing accomplice. Holman certainly was active in the campaign to bring the premier down, but, on the death of Dacey on 11 April 1912, he recalled that Dacey 'was practically the leader of that group [the "solid six"]', which prevailed on caucus to end the alliance with Reid in 1899.[45] The evolution of events following Edden's question of 22 August about Neild strongly suggested that there were guiding hands behind them: the resignation of Barton on 23 August, with Edden moving at once for a select committee into the Neild case; the *Star's* disclosure on 24 August that a censure motion was imminent; Lyne's notice of motion on 29 August; the reading of the select committee's report on 30 August, followed immediately by Lyne's motion; and Fegan's amendment of 31 August, which brought the Neild case specifically into the censure debate and put intense pressure on the Labor Party in one of its most sensitive areas.

Nevertheless, Labor's objections to Reid were deeply rooted, and it was only the urgent need to settle Federation in the first half of 1899 that had enabled McGowen and Watson to keep the caucus behind the premier, almost certainly only by a majority of one. In purely political terms the case for a change was very strong, and there is little reason to doubt that a meeting of various minds was probable, with the interests of Labor Assembly members coinciding with the ambitions and vindictiveness of Lyne, Barton, Wise, Crick, Fegan and Haynes, amongst others, and helping to condition a new *modus vivendi* in parliament with Labor settling the issue. The available evidence indicates that, on the Labor side, the prime mover was Edden, who was being subjected to special demands from his Newcastle electors. But it is not necessary to try to isolate the chief men in the episode. Labor was a party seeking wide-ranging and non-stop reforms; Labor members had a collective feeling that the Party's institutional nature should determine important matters of policy, rather than personal relationships such as those that had naturally developed between Reid and some of their colleagues. In the caucus discussions it was easily possible that supporters of Reid could have been convinced of the need for change. Watson and Ferguson were the two men who voted for Reid at the caucus of 30 August and reversed their opinion on 5 September. There was nothing in the record of either man to suggest that they would be swayed by anything other than reasonable assessment of an intricate problem. Watson, especially, would not have been bluffed by Holman, or any other member of the 'solid six', Hughes, Edden, Dacey, Thomas and Thomson. Indeed, the fact that Watson finally voted against Reid invested the premier's final defeat with the dignity of reasoned political judgment as opposed to the humiliation sought by his chief non-Labor opponents.

It is probable that the 'solid six' did threaten to resign their seats. Evatt has said that 'The rules of the Labour Party forbade a dissentient member from refusing to vote as caucus had decided. But the rules were silent on the question of resignation'.[46] It was a little more complicated than that. At the July conference Hughes had revealed that both he and Holman had hit upon this loophole; but the conference stamped the authority of the executive and so defined its relationship with caucus that any member who did resign would certainly have been expelled, and would have provoked the full weight of Labor retaliation. Resignation of six men would have been a blow to the Party, but it would have been fatal to the men concerned. Of the four members expelled in 1893, only Kelly and Fitzgerald had remained interested in politics, and both had failed in attempts to re-enter parliament (they were subsequently readmitted to the Party, and Kelly won Sydney-Denison for Labor in 1901). Watson and McGowen would have known how to deal with threats of this kind in 1899, and neither would have been intimidated,

especially with the trade unions in process of resuming their close contacts with the Party. The caucus deliberations on the fate of the Reid government were far too momentous to be determined by petty tricks, and Watson would have made sure that the final decision was made on the political merits of the case irrespective of Hughes's and Holman's artfulness. That McGowen's vote was counted in caucus for Reid and Watson voted against him was important evidence of how the Labor Party had so moulded conditions in parliament that great decisions could now be made on rational instead of partisan grounds.

McGowen consolidated this position when he got up in parliament on 6 September and announced what was already known, that Labor had sealed Reid's fate.[47] He began by denying reports of the unruliness of the caucus meeting, and went further by saying that nearly all accounts of Labor Party discussions were inaccurate; Labor had no feeling of revenge towards Reid or of anti-federalism, although he said that the Party would continue the fight in the commonwealth parliament to democratise the constitution; but Labor could not condone 'the action with regard to [Neild]', for the Party firmly believed that no one, even members who were barristers, should get fees from the crown. McGowen paid a

9 The Unkindest Cut of All.
Lyne: 'Now then, M'Gowen, cut away, it's cruel to keep the poor beggar in suspense. Ta-ta, George, old man.'
The Bulletin, 30 September 1899

great tribute to the government, 'there is something I desire publicly to refer to . . . that is even beyond their progressive legislation, and that is [their] progressive administration'; which had resulted in the employment of 6000 artisans on day labour and in the appointment of Samuel Smith to the Marine Board where he had done essential work to improve the safety of sea travel; perhaps, he went on, a new ministry would bring down improved legislation on marine matters; but Reid's 'administration will live even when its progressive legislation is overshadowed'. McGowen left no doubt about Labor's intention to put the ministry out, but at the same time he instinctively shaped his speech to reflect his own personal regret and his Party's appreciation of Reid's outstanding premiership. In order to avoid recriminations the caucus had decided that only McGowen would speak for Labor on the censure motion.[48]

Hughes, Holman and Griffith made statements to the press. All said there was nothing personal in their actions. Hughes pointed out that Lyne had approved all the pending reform legislation, that he would introduce an amended navigation bill and a new early closing bill, and had promised the kind of compulsory arbitration legislation required by Labor. Hughes also stressed that Reid's proposal to enter federal politics meant that he would not have been serious about future domestic reforms, including old-age pensions; Hughes, himself, said that he had given up objections to Federation, and he confirmed McGowen's declaration that Labor would seek amendments to the constitution in the federal legislature. Holman emphasised that the Party's action had rehabilitated it as an independent factor in parliament. Griffith said that caucus had based its decision on 'conscientious conviction', and warned Lyne not to take 'unacceptable people' into his ministry. Great rejoicing was reported from Newcastle.[49] The *Herald* commented that political observers were well aware that once Federation had been removed from parliament the influence of the Labor Party would be felt.[50]

The debate continued in the Assembly. The general opinion about the payment to Neild was that while, it was 'an unwarranted executive act', it did not involve any question of corruption.[51] But Barton thought otherwise. He said he had no intention of reflecting on Reid's personal integrity, but insisted that in a parliamentary sense the transaction implied corruption.[52] When he arose to make his main speech on 6 September he found it very difficult to maintain this distinction; and, aided by Crick's interjections, his arguments were seasoned with language that belied his reputation as a gentleman, and degenerated into a mawkish defence of his Federation record in contrast with Reid's 'tortuousness and shiftiness' on the question.[53] Barton revealed the abject blindness of the superior federationists when they looked at Reid's work for national union; he said he had always been an opponent of the government,

> except . . . when [Reid] absolutely changed his policy with regard to feder-
> ation, and adopted . . . the policy I had laid down at the general election;

and that

> we need not recall many instances to be satisfied that there is ample ground
> for fault-finding with the Government in respect of their federal policy and
> their parliamentary conduct generally.

Reid relished the opportunity to confirm Barton's own revelation of
what lay behind his formal facade; 'I only want to show' said the
premier, 'how this Lord Chesterfield of high politics can use the
language of the pot-house when it suits him'; Barton, he said, was the
shifty one, who had 'never yet touched a large interest except with a
velvet glove'; in contrast, Reid, himself, whose 'personal associations
were with the classes', had 'risked and earned [their] hatred in performance of [his] public duty to the masses of this country'.[54] And the premier
showed that his acknowledgment of the triumph of the Barton-Wise axis
did not erase his sardonic contempt for them. Wise supported him
against Haynes and Crick on a point of order; 'May I say', commented
Reid,

> in grateful acknowledgment of the long lost generosity of the hon. and
> learned member for Ashfield, that when [he] is inclined to show me generosity
> I feel a cold shiver, and I really do begin to believe that I am approaching a
> final extinction.

But the defeated premier could still find reserves of generosity: thanking
all his friends and supporters, including the Labor Party, he said: 'I can
assure them . . . that I shall never cease to remember with a feeling of
pride the loyal support which has enabled this Government to make so
many lasting reforms'.[55]

Before the end came on 7 September Carruthers complimented Mc-
Gowen on his 'manly speech', but pointed out that it was the Labor
Party that would bring the government down.[56] That was undeniably
true, and the fact lifted Reid's downfall far above the petty mixture of
ambition, vengeance and envy that motivated most of Reid's other
opponents on the final vote. McGowen, Edden, Hughes and Ferguson
had been mentioned as possible members of the new ministry, but the
institutional nature of the Labor Party, which had conditioned the
Labor decision to oust Reid, prevented any individual from gaining
personally from the change in government. But Wise, Fegan and Crick
were naturally promoted to the ministry. Barton's much greater elevation
would come in due course. The Legislative Assembly finally resolved

> That the present Government does not possess the confidence of this House,
> and deserves censure for having made payments of public money to Mr. J. C.
> Neild, member for Paddington, without asking Parliament, and contrary to
> the assurances given by the right hon. the Premier.

While the division was being taken Crick unavailingly drew the Speaker's attention 'to the fact that [the premier] who is personally under censure is voting to whitewash himself. I ask if that is in accordance with parliamentary usage?' The vote against Reid was 75 to 41, with all nineteen Labor members opposing him.[57]

With some irony, and with personal pain to some of its members, the Labor Party had parted from the man who, in 1891, had foreseen as an individual what the TLC had envisioned as an institution: that New South Wales ought not to continue under an outmoded political system. Reid's aspirations included the insight to analyse the existing system and the determination and stamina to change it: partly, he strove to do this to save his beloved free trade by harnessing its reforming strand to modern social impulses; partly, to prepare his beloved colony for Federation by exposing the dangers of a protection policy that could only be regarded as retaliatory by Australians in the other colonies. The Labor Party was strong on reform, and it was not weak on Federation: by sinking the fiscal issue it helped Reid indispensably in both objectives. Indeed, on reform, it complemented his basic ideas on direct taxation with a multitude of separate improvements, several of which were implemented. But Reid never had a comprehensive and long-range reform program, and his failure to defeat Dibbs in 1892 over the Broken Hill strike had revealed the limits of his radicalism; moreover, the growing importance and complexity of Federation had come eventually to absorb virtually all his energies. The Labor Party could only remain restlessly with him until his plans for union were consummated. Then its powerful thrust for continued reform simply disintegrated a partnership that had revealed Reid as the greatest reforming politician in New South Wales in the nineteenth century and the most significant federationist in Australia in the 1890s.

Throughout these vital five years the *Sydney Morning Herald* was almost always bemused by the Labor Party. In September 1899 the great newspaper had learnt to its mortification that in the last resort the Party controlled parliament; it agreed that the new political position had resulted from Labor's action, and looked at the Party reflectively:

Since [it] emerged into parliament . . . [it] is entitled to credit for fidelity on its own part to the objects which it set out to gain or to further. It has abstained from seeking office in the Government which it has supported; it has shown such regularity in attending to business that there is hardly a sitting day when Parliament does not meet; at all hazards it has kept together, and in that way has managed to secure a greater influence in legislation than its numbers would have entitled it to . . .

Labor, the *Herald* went on, had escaped decomposition, which was the usual fate of parties; but it rebuked the Party because of its caucus system, which demanded sacrifices from its members and, worst of all, in a sense injured parliament itself.[58]

On 30 September 1899 Niels Rasmus Wilson Nielsen (1869–1930) won the seat of Boorowa, which adjoined Watson's electorate on the east. He had been selected for the by-election by the PLL executive because the local league had collapsed. Nielsen was a bush carpenter with advanced views on land tenure, fully conscious of the problems of country people. A member of the AWU, he had been born in Copenhagen and had come to Australia when five years old. A Roman Catholic, he was the twentieth Labor MLA to join the parliamentary caucus. Earlier in the month the executive had begun the tasks of forming a federal Labor Party and drawing up a federal platform; it decided to correspond with parties in Victoria, Queensland, South Australia and Western Australia with a view to a preliminary conference in Sydney in 1900.[59] The Interstate Conference on the formation of the federal Labor Party was held on 24 January 1900 at the Trades Hall, Sydney, with Wilson president and Jones secretary. Ten delegates from Victoria, South Australia and Queensland were present; in addition, eleven members of the New South Wales Legislative Assembly attended, plus the PLL executive. The conference drew up a federal platform.[60] Two days later the 1900 PLL conference approved the platform and 'rules and regulations for the guidance and control of the Federal Section of the Labor Party', and drafted a federal pledge for the approval of 'the Interstate Labor Parties':

> I hereby pledge myself not to oppose any selected Labor candidate. I hereby pledge myself if returned to the Commonwealth Parliament to do my utmost to ensure the carrying out of the principles embodied in the Federal Labor Platform, and on all such questions to vote as a majority of the Federal Labor Party may decide at a duly-constituted caucus meeting.[61]

Selected Bibliography

Manuscript Sources

The records of the Trades and Labor Council of New South Wales 1871–94, including general minutes, executive minutes and parliamentary committee minutes.

The general minutes of the Sydney District Council of the Australian Labor Federation, which replaced the TLC in 1894–1900.

These records are in ML. Micro-film copies are held in the Archives Section, Research School of Social Sciences, Australian National University.

ALF, LEL, PLL material, ML.

George Black papers, ML.

Coonamble Labor League minute book, NL.

Denison Labor League minute book, ML.

Official Sources

The *Parliamentary Debates* of the New South Wales Parliament 1891–9, Series I.

First Intercolonial Trades Union Congress, Oct. 1879, Sydney, Report of Proceedings, Sydney 1879.

Reports of similar congresses published as follows:

Second, Melbourne 1884.

Third, Sydney 1885.

Fourth, Adelaide 1886.

Fifth, Brisbane 1888.

Sixth, Hobart 1889.

Proceedings of the First National Protection Conference, October 1889, Sydney 1889.

Report of the First Annual Conference of the Free Trade and Liberal Association, Sydney 1889.

A Note on Newspaper Sources

The *Sydney Morning Herald,* founded in 1831, was the leading daily newspaper in New South Wales in 1870–1900. It was edited by A. Garran from 1873 to 1885, thereafter by W. M. Curnow, until 1903. The *Herald* represented the familiar colonial values of liberalism and free trade; but under Curnow it had a strong conservative tinge. It gave sustained support to the Sydney bankers, importers and shippers, and necessary backing as required to the pastoralists. The paper was very well written and produced, and, because of its quality, gave fair and reasonable coverage to the Labor movement and to selectors, but opposed them when the interests of 'the classes' were threatened. It was very well-informed on political affairs. In general, it backed the free traders and opposed the protectionists, hence was for Parkes and Reid, and against Dibbs and Lyne. But it became a very powerful supporter of Federation, and, as Reid lost the favour of 'the classes' from 1895, it affected to see him as a threat to national union and opposed him bitterly in 1898; as a corollary it gave uncritical praise to Barton. The *Herald* certainly played a part in Reid's downfall.

The *Daily Telegraph,* founded in 1879, was similar to the *Herald* in that it supported liberalism and free trade. But it lacked the quality of the *Herald,* though it was a very good newspaper. The *Telegraph,* with L. J. Brient as its editor in 1891–1901, was a partisan free trade organ and strongly supported Reid in 1895–8. But it was more of a Sydney than a colonial newspaper and its bias led it to become anti-Federation, though almost to the last it claimed to be against the 1899 constitution and for union. As a result of its sectional character it turned fiercely on Reid when he campaigned for the 1899 federal referendum and for a while rivalled some newspapers in Melbourne and Adelaide as a strident provincial rag. Generally its news and analysis of political matters were first class, and there is some reason to believe that W. M. Hughes, especially, and W. A. Holman leaked Labor information to it. Because Labor supported Reid, the *Telegraph* was usually very fair to the Party.

The *Australian Star,* an evening newspaper founded in 1887, was the organ of the Sydney manufacturers' clique in the protectionist group. Generally it was poorly produced, and was partisan and unreliable, though occasionally it scooped the other newspapers on protectionist news. It was anti-Labor whenever the Party was opposed to the protectionists.

The *Evening News* founded in 1875 was the afternoon echo of the *Herald* and *Telegraph* so far as free trade was concerned. It generally gave more space to current events than comments or analyses of politics. It took a poor view of the Labor Party.

The chief Labor newspapers were the *Australian Worker* and the *Australian Workman* both founded in 1891. The *Worker* developed from the *Hummer,* which was produced by the Wagga Wagga shearers, to become in 1892 the official organ of the Australian Shearers' Union (the Australian Workers' Union from 1894). The *Workman* was first published by the TLC, but in 1891 it provoked a libel suit and passed out of the Council's control; in 1897 it was published by T. J. Houghton and on 2 October 1897 it amalgamated with the *Worker* (which had ceased publication on 27 August and resumed on 2 October 1897 under the editorship of H. Lamond). The *Worker* always represented AWU/ALF (Provincial Council) opinion; the *Workman* fluctuated with its control, sometimes supporting the TLC, sometimes the Labor leagues against the parliamentarians, sometimes the reverse. Late in 1891 it was 'the recognised organ of the Labor Electoral League'. In 1895–7 it was the official organ of the Sydney District Council of the ALF. Frank Fox (born in 1874 in Adelaide, died 1960 in England) was its talented young editor for a time from 1891. Fox was later editor of the *Lone Hand;* he went to England in 1909, became a distinguished soldier, journalist and author and was knighted in 1926.

The *Liberty* was the organ of the National Association and consequently represented the most conservative views in New South Wales and bitterly opposed the Labor Party; but it was very well informed on Labor affairs, and apparently had someone on its staff who read all the small socialist and anarchist news sheets, as it often published large extracts from them.

Books, Pamphlets and Articles

Australian Dictionary of Biography (general editor, D. H. Pike), 4 vols, Melbourne 1966, 1967, 1969, 1972.

G. Black, *Labor in Politics,* Sydney 1893.

—— *A History of the N.S.W. Political Labor Party,* Sydney 1926–9.

T. A. Coghlan, *Labour and Industry in Australia: from the First Settlement in 1788 to the Establishment of the Commonwealth in 1901,* 4 vols., Oxford 1918.

Brian Dickey, 'Parliament and the Trade Unions', *JRAHS* 47 (4), 1961.

—— 'The Broken Hill Strike, 1892', *Labour History* (11), 1966.

H. V. Evatt, *Australian Labour Leader, The Story of W. A. Holman and the Labour Movement,* Sydney 1942.

J. D. Fitzgerald, *The Rise of the N.S.W. Political Labor Party,* Sydney 1915.

L. F. Fitzhardinge, *William Morris Hughes: A Political Biography,* vol. 1, *That Fiery Particle, 1862–1914,* Sydney 1964.

Patrick Ford, *Cardinal Moran and the A.L.P.: a Study in the Encounter between Moran and Socialism, 1890–1907,* Melbourne 1966.

R. Gollan, 'The Trade Unions and Labour Parties, 1890–4', *HS* 7 (25), 1955.

—— *Radical and Working Class Politics,* Melbourne 1963.

A. Griffith, *The Labor Platform: an Exposition,* Sydney 1893.

G. S. Harman, 'G. S. Beeby and the First Labour Electoral Battle in Armidale', *Labour History* (2), 1962.

P. Loveday and A. W. Martin, *Parliament, Factions and Parties: the First Thirty Years of Responsible Government in New South Wales, 1856–1889,* Melbourne 1966.

—— and —— 'The Politics of New South Wales, 1856–1889: a Reply', *HS* 13 (50), 1968.

Catherine B. Mackerras, 'Dibbs versus Duff. The Sad Story of a Colonial Governor', *JRAHS* 56 (4), 1970.

B. E. Mansfield, *Australian Democrat, the Career of Edward William O'Sullivan 1846–1910,* Sydney 1965.

A. W. Martin, 'Freetrade and Protectionist Parties in New South Wales' *HS* 6 (23), 1954.

W. G. McMinn, 'George Reid and Federation: the Origin of the "Yes-No Policy" ', *HS* 10 (38), 1962.

—— 'The Federal Policy of G. H. Reid: a Rejoinder', *JRAHS* 51 (1), 1965.

John N. Molony, *An Architect of Freedom: John Herbert Plunkett in New South Wales 1832–1869,* Canberra 1973.

N. B. Nairn, 'The 1890 Maritime Strike in New South Wales', *HS* 10 (37), 1961.

—— 'Some Aspects of the Social Role of the Labour Movement in New South Wales in the 1870s', *Labour History* (1), 1962.

—— 'J. C. Watson in New South Wales Politics, 1890–1894', *JRAHS* 48 (2), 1962.

—— 'The Role of the Trades and Labor Council in New South Wales, 1871–1891', *Historical Studies Selected Articles,* second series, Melbourne 1967.

—— 'The Political Mastery of Sir Henry Parkes: New South Wales Politics 1871–1891', *JRAHS* 53 (1), 1967.

—— 'A Note on a Colonial Treasurer's Resignation', *HS* 13 (49), 1967.

—— 'The Politics of New South Wales: a Note on a Reply', *HS* 13 (52), 1969.

P. J. O'Farrell, 'The Australian Socialist League and the Labour Movement', *HS* 8 (30), 1958.

—— *Harry Holland: Militant Socialist,* Canberra 1964.

F. Picard, 'Henry George and the Labour Split of 1891', *HS* 6 (21), 1953.

T. R. Roydhouse and H. J. Taperell, *The Labor Party in New South Wales,* Sydney 1892.

W. G. Spence, *Australia's Awakening,* Brisbane 1942.

Ian Turner, *Industrial Labour and Politics: The Labour Movement in Eastern Australia 1900–1921,* Canberra 1965.

R. B. Walker, 'Australia's Second Arbitration Act', *Labour History* (19), 1970.

J. C. Watson, 'The Labor Movement', *Handbook of the British Association for the Advancement of Science,* Sydney 1914.

P. Weller, 'Disciplined Party Voting: a Labour Innovation?', *Labour History* (21), 1971.

Notes

Introduction

1 For Plunkett's career, see John N. Molony, *An Architect of Freedom, John Hubert Plunkett in New South Wales 1832–1869*, Canberra 1973.
2 For a study of the Church Act, see Naomi Turner, *Sinews of Sectarian Warfare? State Aid in New South Wales, 1836 to 1862*, Canberra 1972.

Chapter 1

1 For a survey of the nineteenth century work of the TLC see N. B. Nairn, 'The Role of the Trades and Labor Council in New South Wales 1871–1891', *Historical Studies, Selected Articles*, second series, Melbourne 1967.
2 The minute book of the League is in ML; it has references to the success of the working men's clubs' in England.
3 See article by Bede Nairn on Dixon in *ADB*, vol. 4, Melbourne 1972.
4 See minute book of Sydney Society of Progressive Carpenters and Joiners, 1871–80, meeting 13 March 1871. ML.
5 See article by Audrey Ferguson on Daniel Cameron Dalgleish in *ADB*, vol. 4.
6 TLC minutes, 1 May 1872.
7 Ibid., 15, 22 October 1873.
8 An outline of the strike is in Nairn, op. cit.
9 TLC minutes, 10 June 1874.
10 See articles by Bede Nairn on Cameron and Garrard in *ADB*, vols. 3 and 4.
11 TLC minutes, 24 June 1874.
12 Ibid., 28 July, 5 August 1874.
13 Ibid., 18 August 1874.
14 *SMH*, 18 October 1874, p. 2. The circular was signed by W. Miller, president, C. Hurley, vice-president, and F. B. Dixon, secretary.
15 TLC minutes, 16 September 1874.
16 Ibid., 3 February, 18 March 1874. The coalmining unions joined the TLC before 1879.
17 *SMH*, 5 December 1874, p. 5.
18 Ibid., 7 December 1874, p. 5. Dibbs and J. Sutherland, MLA, gave donations to the TLC's elections fund, TLC minutes, 31 December 1874.
19 *SMH*, 10 December 1874, p. 5. See article by Bede Nairn on John Davies, in *ADB*, vol. 4.
20 *SMH*, 10 December 1874, p. 6.
21 Ibid., 15 December 1874, p. 7.
22 Ibid., 17 December 1874, p. 5.
23 *Witness*, 3 April 1875, p. 5: newspaper in ML.
24 TLC minutes, 14 January 1875. The balance sheet was adopted 18 to 3.

231

25 Ibid., 20 January 1875. As a carpenter Cameron would have earned between £2 and £3 per week when he had constant work in 1874.
26 *Evening News,* 10 February 1875, p. 2.
27 *SMH,* 22 April 1875, p. 4.
28 TLC minutes, 8 April 1875.
29 Ibid., 1 July 1875. The unions were the Coachmakers', the Shipwrights' and the Quarrymen's: the latter refused to pay.
30 Ibid., 23 September 1875.
31 Ibid., 14 October, 11 November 1875.
32 Ibid., 30 December 1875.
33 Ibid., 17 February 1876.
34 Ibid., 23 March 1876.
35 *SMH,* 3 April 1876, p. 3.
36 Ibid., 4 April 1876, p. 4.
37 An account of the seamen's strike is in Bede Nairn, 'Some Aspects of the Social Role of the Labour Movement in New South Wales in the 1870s', *Labour History* (1), 1962.

Chapter 2

1 *SMH,* 14 June 1877, p. 5.
2 Ibid., 16 October, p. 5; 17 October, p. 3; 18 October 1877, p. 7.
3 *Echo,* 28 December 1878: newspaper in ML.
4 See *First Intercolonial Trades' Union Congress, Oct. 1879, Sydney. Report of Proceedings,* Sydney 1879, p. 64.
5 TLC minutes, 4 March 1880.
6 Ibid., 19 August 1880. The Stonemasons' notified their withdrawal on 16 September. Roylance was one of their delegates, but the Seamen's Union made him their delegate in order to keep him on the Council.
7 Ibid., 2 November 1880. The parliamentary scheme may best be followed in the general minutes of the Council from April to November. The executive minutes give an over-optimistic and defective account of Cole and Roylance's planning.
8 See B. E. Mansfield, *Australian Democrat, the career of Edward William O'Sullivan, 1846–1910,* Sydney 1965.
9 TLC minutes, 21 May 1885.
10 *SMH,* 3 August 1885, p. 11; TLC minutes, 13 August 1885. About this time the TLC received many requests to sponsor lectures.
11 Ibid., 27 August 1885.
12 For the parliamentary drama see Mansfield, op. cit., pp. 66–77; P. Loveday and A. W. Martin, *Parliament, Factions and Parties,* Melbourne 1966, pp. 129–34; and N. B. Nairn, 'The Political Mastery of Sir Henry Parkes: New South Wales Politics 1871–1891', *JRAHS* 53 (1), 1967.
13 TLC minutes, 21 October 1886.
14 Ibid., 18 November 1886.
15 Ibid., 27 January 1887.
16 Ibid., 14 February 1887.
17 *SMH,* 19 January 1889, p. 11.
18 TLC minutes, March–June 1887, *passim.*
19 Five Intercolonial Trade Union Congresses were held in the 1880s. See *Reports* as follows: Second, Melbourne 1884; Third, Sydney 1885; Fourth, Adelaide 1886; Fifth, Brisbane 1888; Sixth, Hobart 1889.

20 Aware of its position, the Council presumed to ask Parkes in December 1887 for 'its fair share of the money to be spent in the [1888] Centennial festivities', TLC minutes, 15 December 1887; but in vain.

21 *Report,* Brisbane 1888, p. 64.

22 TLC parliamentary committee minutes, 21 November 1888.

23 TLC executive minutes, October 1888 to September 1889, *passim;* general minutes, 19 December 1889.

24 Ibid., 2, 9 August 1889.

25 At 21 December 1889 thirty unions were affiliated; at 1 July 1890 there were fifty-three.

26 TLC executive minutes, 3, 6, 10 September 1889. The meetings were held on 7 and 15 September; neither Moran nor Salomons attended.

27 TLC minutes and executive minutes on dates indicated.

28 TLC minutes, 7 November 1889.

Chapter 3

1 See article by Bede Nairn on Brennan in *ADB,* vol. 3.

2 *Evening News,* 25 October 1889, p. 6.

3 There are differences of opinion about this: see P. Loveday and A. W. Martin, 'The Politics of New South Wales, 1856–1889: a Reply', *HS* 13 (50), 1968; and Bede Nairn, 'The Politics of New South Wales, 1856–1889: a Note on a Reply', *HS* 13 (52), 1969.

4 *Trades and Labour Advocate,* 21 December 1889, p. 4. ML.

5 TLC minutes, 5 December 1889.

6 Ibid., 30 January 1890.

7 TLC executive minutes (parliamentary committee) 11 March 1890. In the circular of 14 April 1890 sent by the Council to trade unions, it was pointed out that 'Only those candidates who are members of recognised labour organisations and accepted by the Trades and Labour Council shall be entitled to receive monetary assistance in their candidature'.

8 Ibid., 8 April 1890.

9 See *Report of the Proceedings of the First Annual Conference of the Free Trade and Liberal Association,* Sydney 1889; and *Proceedings of the First National Protection Conference, October 1889,* Sydney 1889.

10 There are useful but sanguine articles on these leagues by F. Picard, 'Henry George and the Labour Split of 1891', *HS* 6 (21), 1953 (the League was originally called the Land Nationalisation League, but changed its name at a conference in 1889, see *SMH,* 27 April 1889, p. 8); and P. J. O'Farrell, 'The Australian Socialist League and the Labour Movement', *HS* 8 (30), 1958. Patrick Ford gives valuable details of the various sects of socialists in *Cardinal Moran and the A.L.P.,* Melbourne 1966.

11 See article by Bede Nairn on Henry George in *ADB,* vol. 4.

12 J. D. Fitzgerald, *The Rise of the N.S.W. Political Labor Party,* Sydney 1915, pp. 16–19.

13 G. Black, *A History of the N.S.W. Political Labor Party,* Sydney 1926–9, No. 1, p. 21.

14 TLC minutes, 27 August 1891.

15 Ibid., 10 April 1890.

16 See Bede Nairn, 'The 1890 Maritime Strike in New South Wales', *HS* 10 (37), 1961.

17 See TLC general and executive minutes, April–August 1890, *passim.*

18 The great volume of work may be gauged from secretary Houghton's half-yearly report; see *SMH,* 4 July 1890, p. 3.

19 Houghton, ibid., gives the figures as at 30 June as '65 societies were approached . . . [and] not more than a third . . . [have replied] of which . . . only four were favourable'; it seems he took a pessimistic view of some conditional replies; but there is no doubt that the response was disappointing. The Tinsmiths' and Sheet-Iron Workers' Trade Society decided not to participate in the scheme because 'the Society, being a non-political one, could not entertain the proposal', minutes, 2 May 1890 (ANU Archives).

20 See Bede Nairn, 'J. C. Watson in New South Wales Politics 1890–1894', *JRAHS* 48 (2), 1962.

21 The committee consisted of C. Hart, James Watson, J. Riddell, T. E. Colebrook and J. C. Watson. P. Ford, op. cit., p. 59, favours Hart as the principal behind the scheme, though he accords J. C. Watson an important role. But Hart had no special knowledge of newspapers and seems to have been too much of an eccentric protectionist (e.g., see his letters in *AS,* 13 May 1891, p. 3, 1 June 1891, p. 3, and TLC minutes, 4 June 1891) to have been able to influence unduly the calm, persuasive and up-to-date tone of the circular. Riddell, a stonemason, was a single taxer who in July 1891 defeated J. C. Watson in a ballot to replace Houghton as TLC secretary (TLC minutes, 16 July 1891). A copy of the newspaper circular is appended to ibid., 27 June 1890; 20,000 copies were printed. The TLC had first considered starting a newspaper in 1871 and had looked into the matter several times after that, without result.

22 TLC minutes, 7 August 1890.

23 See Bede Nairn, 'A Note on the Colonial Treasurer's Resignation', *HS* 13 (49), 1967. Earlier in the year at Broken Hill Parkes had laid the foundation stone of the Amalgamated Miners' Association Hall.

24 *Trades and Labor Council Secretary's Report for the Half-Year ending 31.12.1890,* Sydney 1891, p. 3. In August 1890 there were about fifty-three unions affiliated to the TLC. At 31 December there were eighty-five, ibid., p. 4. The Labour Defence Council raised £37,000 for the strike, of which £24,000 came from unions affiliated to the TLC.

25 TLC minutes, 28 November 1890.

Chapter 4

1 The manifesto is in W. G. Spence, *Australia's Awakening,* Brisbane 1942, pp. 106–11.

2 TLC minutes, 9 October 1890.

3 TLC parliamentary committee minutes, 14 October 1890.

4 Ibid., 17 October 1890.

5 TLC minutes, 20 October 1890.

6 *Secretary's Report for the Half-Year ending 31.12.90,* p. 12.

7 TLC parliamentary committee minutes, 27 October 1890.

8 Ibid.

9 TLC minutes, 12 June, 29 July 1890.

10 Ibid., 27 November 1890. At the same time the TLC decided to go on with plans for a newspaper. Council had helped to issue a few numbers of the *Australian Workman,* during the strike, and took it over officially on 23 December 1890 (minutes); but a costly libel suit ended the association in August 1891.

11 TLC parliamentary committee minutes, 24 February 1891.

12 See, e.g., *SMH*, 2 April 1889, p. 4, report of meeting of Liberal Association.

13 Picard, op. cit., pp. 51–2, quotes a misleading statement from George Black and a letter from Cotton to Parkes that seriously exaggerate Cotton's work.

14 TLC parliamentary committee minutes, 10 March 1891.

15 Ibid.

16 See letter from T. J. Houghton to *SMH*, 5 March 1891, p. 4, in which he explains how important freedom was to the working class.

17 *AS*, 19 May 1891, p. 7. Houghton's letter is a valuable document, making explicit Labor emphasis on unity that would gather up diverse elements to facilitate pragmatic advance. He was defending Cotton and the Labor platform against editorial attack in the *Star*, which was the protectionists' organ.

18 TLC minutes, special meetings on 17, 24, 31 March 1891.

19 TLC parliamentary minutes, 3 April 1891; *SMH*, 7 April 1891, p. 8. The sixteen planks are in T. R. Roydhouse and H. J. Taperell, *The Labour Party in New South Wales*, Sydney 1892, pp. 15–18.

20 *SMH*, 23 March 1891, p. 4.

21 *SMH*, 26 February 1891, p. 5, full report of speech.

22 Ibid., p. 6.

23 TLC parliamentary committee, 25 March 1891; *SMH*, 26 March 1891, p. 8.

24 TLC parliamentary committee, 26 March 1891.

25 *SMH*, 27 March 1891, p. 7.

26 Ibid., p. 6; TLC minutes, 26 March 1891.

27 *SMH*, 30 March 1891, p. 3.

28 Ibid., 27 March, 1891, p. 6.

29 TLC parliamentary committee minutes, 3 April 1891.

30 TLC minutes, 23, 30 April 1891.

31 *Australian Workman*, 30 May 1891, p. 4.

32 *AS*, 5 May 1891, p. 6. The Miners' and other unions formed the Lithgow league, *SMH*, 28 April 1891, p. 5.

33 TLC minutes, 2 April 1891; parliamentary committee minutes April-May, *passim*; *SMH*, 7 April 1891, p. 8. For example of advertisements see *AS*, 13 April 1891, p. 1.

34 *SMH*, 6 April 1891, p. 3. As early as 19 March the TLC had given the Balmain Labourers' Union permission 'to inaugurate a branch . . . under the auspices of the Council', TLC minutes, 19 March 1891.

35 Ibid., 9 April 1891.

36 TLC parliamentary committee minutes, 6 April 1891.

37 See, e.g., *SMH*, 7 April 1891, p. 8; 8 April 1891, p. 1: the latter advertisement listed eleven meetings and said: 'Members of the Parliamentary Committee . . . will attend and explain the rules and objects of the League. Members of the Council and Union officers are respectfully invited to occupy seats on the platform.'

38 TLC parliamentary committee minutes, 5 May 1891; *SMH*, 6 May 1891, p. 8.

39 Ibid.

40 TLC parliamentary committee minutes, 2 June 1891.

41 *SMH*, 9 April 1891, p. 8, report of interview.

42 *SMH*, 14 April 1891, p. 4. The *Herald* was referring mainly to objections to plural voting.

43 Ibid., 5 March 1891, p. 4.

Chapter 5

1 *SMH,* 17 April 1891, p. 5.

2 *PD,* vol. 51, p. 31 ff.

3 Specific duties still remained on, e.g., bacon, butter, cheese and kerosene, indirect taxes that affected the poorer classes more than other groups. For a critical review of the work of the 1889–91 parliament, see *SMH,* 6 June 1891, p. 5.

4 *PD,* vol. 51, p. 327; the disordered state of parliament was shown by the fact that five protectionists voted for Parkes, and three free traders voted against him.

5 *SMH,* 6 June 1891, p. 5.

6 Ibid., 14 April 1891, p. 4.

7 Ibid., 5 June 1891, p. 6.

8 See, e.g., TLC parliamentary committee minutes, 2 June 1891.

9 *SMH,* 6 June 1891, p. 7.

10 Ibid., 8 June 1891, p. 6.

11 *AS,* 10 June 1891, p. 3.

12 *SMH,* 12 June 1891, p. 8. There are numerous reports of league meetings and the selection of candidates in the daily press; see *DT, AS, Evening News,* and *SMH,* May, June 1891, *passim.*

13 *Western Herald and Darling River Advocate,* 3 June 1891. H. Langwell was president and T. H. Hall secretary of the league.

14 Ibid., 13 June 1891.

15 Ibid., 27 June 1891.

16 Ibid., 1 July 1891; *SMH,* 27 June 1891, p. 10. Langwell was elected but was not allowed into the Labor Party caucus.

17 Doubts were cast on the importance of plural voting in 1891 and some historians have considered it a false issue. But radicals at the time thought otherwise, and they were right. Houghton calculated that there were 450 plural voters in Glebe electorate (*DT,* 2 July 1891, p. 6) about 10 per cent of the voters (4752). A return to the Legislative Council gave January 1892 figures as follows (Legislative Council *Journal,* vol. 49, 1891–2, p. 405) (the figures of voters are from *SMH,* 13 June 1891, p. 10):

Seat	Plural Voters (13 January 1892)	Voters on Roll (June 1891)
East Sydney	3388	10,041
West Sydney	2261	10,821
South Sydney	1034	9862
	6683	30,724
St Leonards	1544	7379
Newtown	1360	8163
Canterbury	3767	18,704
Central Cumberland	2264	9914
Paddington	1343	10,397
Redfern	862	9960
Glebe	472	4752
Balmain	2019	9780

Parramatta	....	....	....	....	212	2165
Camden	....	....	....	....	750	5815

14,593	87,029

These figures show that 18 per cent of all voters in the city and suburban seats had more than one vote.

18 Fitzgerald, op. cit., pp. 14, 15.
19 TLC minutes, 28 May 1891.
20 Ibid., 9 June 1891.
21 Ibid., 4 June 1891. Grey presented the Council with a large photograph of himself in recognition of their help during his Sydney sojourn, *SMH*, 9 June 1891, p. 7.
22 TLC minutes, 28 May; 9, 11 June 1891.
23 *SMH*, 11 June 1891, p. 6.
24 Ibid., 10 June 1891, p. 8; TLC minutes, 11 June 1891.
25 Ibid.
26 *SMH*, 13 June 1891, p. 7.
27 *AS*, 16 June 1891, pp. 3, 4, report of meeting. Advertisements also stressed the platform and the aim to operate the balance of power, see, e.g., *SMH*, 10 June 1891, p. 3.
28 Ibid., 13 June 1891, p. 6.
29 See daily reports of meetings throughout New South Wales in *SMH, DT, AS* and *Evening News*, June-July 1891, *passim*.
30 See analysis of the columnist, 'S', *SMH*, 8 June 1891, p. 7.
31 See, e.g., ibid., 15 June 1891, p. 5.
32 Ibid. Of course this was part of Parkes's rhetoric, in fact he had always been interested in helping some candidates get elected whom he thought would support him. But this was old-fashioned factional politics in 1891. See ibid., 8 June 1891, p. 2, for his personal statement; he helped some free trade candidates in 1891, see ibid., 18 June 1891, p. 3.
33 Ibid., 11 June 1891, p. 4. Two days before, the *Herald* had isolated a third policy of the protectionists simply as 'allegiance to Mr. Dibbs on the fiscal policy' and concluded, 'Who could give serious consideration to ephemeral and ever-varying changes of a party . . . [which verifies its lack of a policy] by the desperate and versatile efforts it is making to find one?', ibid., 9 June 1891, p. 6. A Forsyth, a leading protectionist manufacturer, complained because no policy had been enunciated, *AS*, 11 June 1891, p. 7.
34 *SMH*, 10 June 1891, p. 2. In October 1889, when the protectionists had been making probably their most determined effort to start a political party, an effort was made to replace Dibbs with Barton as leader, see *Proceedings First National Protection Conference*, pp. 71–5.
35 *SMH*, 8 June 1891, p. 7.
36 The 'cocktail party' was the name given to the five protectionists who voted for Parkes in Dibbs's censure motion on 28 May 1891; they were B. B. Nicoll, T. T. Ewing, W. W. Davis, J. Perry, and O. O. Dangar, see *AS*, 3 June 1891, p. 5. This was an example of a common contemporary use of the word 'party' to convey contempt for a backsliding section of a wider group, but the word had a variety of other meanings.
37 Ibid., 17 June 1891, p. 6.
38 Ibid., 18 June 1891, p. 4. Dibbs was defeated in South Sydney; he later won his old seat, Murrumbidgee. See TLC minutes, 18 June 1891 for enthusiastic reception of election results.

39 These successes were gained almost entirely at the expense of the free traders, who in 1889, had won thirty-six of the forty-one metropolitan seats, see electoral map *DT,* 18 February 1889. Two of the suburban seats were almost entirely semi-rural, Central Cumberland with four seats, where Labor ran two candidates, including J. T. Gannon, and lost, and Parramatta with one seat, where no candidate was run.

40 *SMH,* 6 June 1891, p. 6; 7 June 1891, p. 5.

41 Ibid., 12 June 1891, p. 7; 13 June 1891, p. 7.

42 There are many letters in the newspapers to support this interpretation, see e.g., *DT,* 14 July 1891, p. 2; *SMH,* 25 June 1891, p. 6; and ibid., 20 July 1891, p. 6, a letter that argued 'as a plain matter of fact . . . 99 out of every 100 of the 70,000 or so electors who voted for labour . . . did so to show their profound dissatisfaction at the unprogressive and irritating see-saw of party government'.

43 The number elected and their leagues are known, but from the available sources the exact number of country leagues established and the exact number of candidates run in 1891 cannot be precisely stated. One of the major problems in the variable practice of the newspapers showing most candidates as either M (ministerialist, nearly all free traders) or O (oppositionists, nearly all protectionists). The figures shown are estimates based on an examination of most city and a sample of country newspapers. This problem will be considered again in connection with details of the elected Labor members.

44 *AS,* 25 June 1891; *SMH,* 20 June, p. 10; 1 July 1891, p. 3 (letter).

45 All the daily city newspapers gave progressive totals as the various elections were held and final totals 4–10 July 1891. See *SMH, DT, Evenings News, AS, passim.* Roydhouse and Taperell, op. cit., and Black, op. cit., also give details of the Labor members. T. J. Houghton gave the official figures in his half-yearly report to the TLC, 30 June 1891. '42 candidates were run . . . [by] the league, of whom 31 were elected. In addition . . . 10 candidates [ran] on the rules and platform of the league in electorates where it was impossible to start branches previous to the dissolution of Parliament . . . and four of these were returned making a total of 35 elected out of 52 who stood solely in the interests of the league'. *SMH,* 18 July 1891, p. 7. It is not possible to reconcile fully Houghton's figures and statements with my calculations, based on a variety of sources. The minutes of the TLC parliamentary committee are incomplete, indicating the great rush and volume of work in June and July. There is no doubt about the thirty-five elected members, but my calculations show fifty-four candidates (counting E. M. Clark and excluding H. Langwell). Personal details of the Labor members are chiefly from *DT,* 29 June, p. 6; 30 June, p. 3; 2 July, p. 3; 3 July, p. 3; 7 July 1891, p. 3.

46 C. M. H. Clark, *Select Documents in Australian History 1851–1900,* Sydney 1955, p. 667.

47 *Bulletin,* 18 March 1893, pp. 6, 7. 'One of Them' was probably either J. D. Fitzgerald or G. Black.

Chapter 6

1 *SMH,* 3 July 1891, p. 4.

2 Roydhouse and Taperell, op. cit., p. 20.

3 *AS,* 16 June 1891, p. 3.

4 *DT,* 19 June 1891, p. 5; see also *SMH,* 20 June 1891, p. 10.

5 Ibid., 27 June 1891, p. 10.

6 See, e.g., letter from 'W.G.', *DT,* 30 June 1891, p. 6.

7 Ibid., 2 July 1891, p. 6. Houghton also said there were thirty-six Labor members; he included D. C. J. Donnelly, Carcoar, who appears in some lists, but he was a protectionist who never associated with the Labor Party.

8 This account is based on Black, op. cit., No. 2, pp. 12–14; Roydhouse and Taperell, op. cit., p. 66; and *DT,* 6 July 1891, p. 4. J. T. Gannon as convenor was present at the second caucus on 13 July, *SMH,* 14 July 1891, p. 6, and he was almost certainly present on 4 July. There are some minor discrepancies in the various accounts and it is possible that both Roydhouse and Taperell as well as Black telescope some of the decisions arrived at the two caucus meetings.

9 Black, op. cit., No. 2, p. 13.

10 Ibid.

11 Ibid., p. 14.

12 *DT,* 14 July 1891, p. 4.

13 *SMH,* 14 July 1891, p. 6, 16 July 1891, p. 4; Roydhouse and Taperell, op. cit., p. 66.

14 *DT,* 9 July 1891, p. 4.

15 Henry Parkes, 'The Labour Party in New South Wales', *Contemporary Review,* July 1891, postscript dated December 1891; pamphlet in NL.

16 *PD,* vol. 52, pp. 28–9.

17 Roydhouse and Taperell, op. cit., p. 53.

18 *PD,* vol. 52, p. 53 (15 July 1891).

19 Ibid., p. 201.

20 *SMH,* 21 July 1891, p. 6.

21 *PD,* vol. 52, pp. 126–30.

22 Ibid., pp. 358–9.

23 The lapsed ones were Edden, Gough, Kelly, Scott, Sheldon, Vaughn, Morgan and Mackinnon who all voted for Garvan's amendment, and Fitzgerald, Kirkpatrick and Newton who abstained: the latter three, however, could have argued that they had not breached the caucus rule by not voting, although if all the Labor members had done that Parkes would have been beaten. Mackinnon, of course, was no longer in the Party, and Kelly, Morgan, Vaughn and Gough, by voting for Dibbs's censure, seemed to be on the way out of it.

24 *PD,* vol. 53, p. 1284.

25 Ibid., p. 1299.

26 Ibid., pp. 1315–17.

27 Ibid., p. 1344. The seven backsliders on Barton's amendment were Edden, Gough, Hutchinson, Morgan, Scott, Sheldon and Vaughn. Kelly did not vote in this division, but he voted for the final motion, and Hutchinson changed sides.

28 *PD,* vol. 54, pp. 2517–21.

29 Ibid., p. 2537.

30 Ibid., p. 2538.

31 Ibid., p. 2638 (15 October 1891).

32 Ibid., pp. 2639–45.

33 Ibid., pp. 2655–84 (15 October); 2685–6 (19 October 1891).

34 Ibid., p. 2693 (21 October 1891), a perceptive speech by Black answered Parkes's assertion that the 'third section' had recklessly brought down the government.

35 Ibid., p. 2716 (18 November 1891).

36 Ibid., p. 2714.
37 Ibid., pp. 3199–204.
38 Ibid., p. 3388.
39 *SMH,* 10 December 1891, p. 5; Roydhouse and Taperell, op. cit., p. 76.
40 *PD,* vol. 55, pp. 3526–31, 3544.
41 Ibid., 3544–99.
42 Ibid., p. 3599. Murphy, free trader, and Vaughn, protectionist, did not vote.

Chapter 7
1 See *SMH, DT, AS,* December 1891 to January 1892, *passim.*
2 Notice, LEL—The Approaching Conference, in PLL handbills, etc., ML.
3 TLC minutes, 17 September 1891.
4 *SMH,* 14 December 1891, p. 6.
5 TLC minutes, 22 October 1891, 18 February 1892.
6 Ibid., 5 November 1891.
7 Ibid., 14 January 1892.
8 Ibid., *DT,* 15 January 1892, p. 3. In November Watson used his dual
  position as president of the TLC and chairman of the LEL to prevail on the
  Council to urge unionists to join the leagues, in order to strengthen them,
  TLC parliamentary minutes, 14 November 1892.
9 *SMH,* 19 January 1892, p. 5.
10 Ibid., 8 January 1892, p. 4.
11 Ibid., 30 January 1892, p. 10.
12 *DT,* 27 January 1892, p. 3.
13 *SMH,* 30 January 1892, p. 10.
14 Ibid.
15 Ibid., 29 January 1892, p. 6.
16 Ibid.
17 TLC minutes, 28 January 1892.
18 Ibid., 9 February 1892; TLC parliamentary committee minutes, 24 February
   1892.
19 TLC minutes, 9 February 1892; *DT,* 9 March 1892, p. 6.
20 Ibid., 4 February 1892, p. 3.
21 TLC minutes, 25 February 1892.
22 Roydhouse and Taperell, op. cit., pp. 84, 99; Black, op. cit., *passim.*
   Gough, Kelly, Mackinnon, Morgan and Vaughn had virtually joined the
   protectionists; Edden, Scott and Sheldon were more or less independents.
   But there was much looseness in all these classifications, judging by voting in
   parliament.
23 Roydhouse and Taperell, op. cit., p. 83.
24 *Report and Balance Sheet of the TLC,* 30 June 1892, p. 3. Affiliations fell
   from 85 on 31 December 1891 to 67 on 30 June 1892, and continued to fall
   to 34 on 6 July 1893 (TLC minutes).
25 TLC minutes, 5 July 1892; TLC parliamentary committee, 15 August 1892.
26 Ibid., 4 August 1892.
27 *PD,* vol. 59, pp. 242–92.
28 Ibid., p. 185.
29 Ibid., p. 392 (15 September 1892).
30 TLC minutes, 15 September 1892.
31 *PD,* vol. 59, p. 432.
32 Ibid., p. 491.
33 TLC minutes, 29 September 1892.
34 *PD,* vol. 59, pp. 869–70.

35 TLC minutes, 6 October 1892.
36 *AS,* 10 October 1892, p. 7. Italics supplied.
37 The settlement had also revitalised the central executive committee; see secretary's circular urging strengthening of existing leagues and reformation of defunct leagues, October 1892, in PLL handbills, etc. ML.
38 *SMH,* 27 January 1893, p. 7.
39 Ibid., and 28 January 1893, p. 7.
40 Ibid., 27 January 1893, p. 7.
41 Ibid., and 28 January 1893, p. 7.
42 TLC parliamentary committee minutes, 12 September 1892.
43 *The Liberal,* 22 October 1892, p. 1.
44 *Bulletin,* 18 March 1893, pp. 6, 7.
45 In March the central committee of the LEL advised the parliamentary Party to support the government if additional Labor legislation was promised, T. A. Coghlan, *Labor and Industry in Australia,* Oxford 1918, vol. 4, p. 1866.
46 TLC parliamentary committee minutes, 20 February, 10, 17 April 1893.
47 TLC minutes, 9 March 1893.
48 Ibid., 18 May 1893; see also 27 April 1894.

Chapter 8
1 TLC minutes, 15 June 1893.
2 *Worker,* 22 July 1893, p. 1.
3 TLC parliamentary committee minutes, 14 August 1893.
4 *Worker,* 19 August 1893, p. 4.
5 *SMH,* 21 April 1893, p. 4.
6 Ibid., 6 April 1893, p. 4.
7 *SMH,* 13 October, p. 4, 18 October 1893, p. 4.
8 TLC minutes, 14 September 1893.
9 G. Black, op. cit., No. 2, p. 30.
10 TLC minutes, 14 September 1893.
11 *SMH,* 10 November 1893, p. 3.
12 H. V. Evatt in *Australian Labour Leader,* Sydney 1942, p. 270, states 'in 1893 the actions of Holman and Hughes gave to the political Labour movement a foundation without which it could never have been built'; there is virtually no substance in this judgment; W. M. Hughes was possibly at the November conference, but there is no available evidence of it. Holman was secretary of the Amalgamated Railways Association in 1894.
13 *Bulletin,* 11 February 1893, p. 4.
14 TLC minutes, 8 November 1893.
15 *SMH,* 10 November 1893, p. 3. The connection of this pledge with those of 1891 and 1892 is apparent. Evatt, op. cit., p. 52, quoting the *Worker,* 16 December 1893, has Holman moving the pledge in its finally amended form. The press were debarred from reporting the conference, but the *SMH* published verbatim accounts, referred to at the conference on 10 November as 'an accurate report of the whole proceeding', an opinion reinforced by the fact that the *SMH* gave the central committee's draft of the pledge in the exact words used by Watson at the TLC on 8 November. The *Herald's* reports are in issues of 10 November, p. 3, and 11 November 1893, p. 7.
16 *SMH,* 10 November 1893, p. 3.
17 The final form of the pledge is in Black, op. cit., No. 2, p. 32 and T. A. Coghlan, op. cit., p. 1870. *SMH,* 10 November 1893, p. 3, shows the amendments, but not the consolidated motion passed.
18 *DT,* 10 November 1893, p. 6.

19 Black (op. cit., No. 2, p. 31) is very much astray in his judgment that 'With the Central Committee pulling the strings, its puppets naturally danced to its time and tune'.

20 *SMH,* 10 November 1893, p. 3.

21 Ibid., 11 November 1893, p. 7.

22 Ibid.

23 Black, op. cit., No. 2, p. 32. Evatt (op. cit., p. 52) states that Holman moved the original motion in the form that Black and the *SMH* report as the amendment.

24 Evatt seems unaware of this fact in his analysis of Holman's role in the expulsions, ibid.

25 *SMH,* 13 November 1893, p. 4. In the long editorial the *Herald* expressed the hope that 'the coming intercolonial conference of Labour members' would put things to rights. This meeting was held in Sydney in January 1894, it had no constitutional status, and had no effect on New South Wales Labor development, see *Worker,* 27 January 1894, p. 2, for report.

26 Cook in a letter of 26 April 1894 to the TLC (*SMH,* 27 April 1894, p. 6) indicated that these three were in favour of conference rulings; this applied specifically to the April 1894 situation, but it was probably the same in November-December 1893, almost certainly for McGowen.

27 Ibid., 21 November 1893, p. 6.

28 *Worker,* 16 December 1893, p. 3. The *Worker,* controlled by W. G. Spence at the time, reflected his hopes to erect the ALF into the main political agency. Before the November conference Spence had written, 'I think it would be a mistake to say that the party should be guided by the majority in all cases', ibid., 4 November 1893, p. 4.

29 Ibid., 3 February 1894, p. 4.

30 *SMH,* 20 November 1893, p. 6.

31 Ibid., 13 November 1893, p. 4; other country delegates had gone home by this time.

32 TLC minutes, 21 December 1893. Hall's opinions are a useful corrective to W. G. Spence's mischievous summary, 'A large conference held in Sydney on November 9, 1893, did much harm to the cause . . . As the Central Committee was naturally composed of city men, the question of town versus country was raised', op. cit., p. 187.

33 See Australian Federation of Labor, Rules and Platform of the Riverina District Council, Political Section, Sydney 1894. ML.

34 Coonamble Labor league minutes, 7 February 1894. NL.

35 'Union! Solidarity! Cohesion!', conference manifesto no. 1, Labour Federation of Australasia. ML.

36 *SMH,* 24 May 1894, p. 5.

37 The executive first planned a conference for 26 January 1894, but two months' notice had to be given; see minute book, Denison Division, LEL (1893–5), 29 December 1893, 12 January, 16 February 1894. ML.

38 *SMH,* 12 March 1894, p. 6; other accounts put the number of delegates at seventy-six, see ibid., 21 March 1894, p. 8 (letter).

39 Ibid., 12 March 1894, p. 6; and 10 May 1894, p. 5.

40 Ibid., 14 March 1894, p. 6. For Hughes, see L. F. Fitzhardinge, *William Morris Hughes: A Political Biography,* vol. 1, Sydney 1964.

41 *SMH,* 13 March 1894, p. 6.

42 Ibid., 14 March 1894, p. 6.

43 Ibid., 12 March 1894, p. 6.

44 Ibid., 13, 14 March 1894, p. 6.

45 Ibid., 13 March 1894, p. 6.
46 Ibid., 13 March 1894, p. 4; this was a typical editorial opinion, see also *Bulletin*, 18 November 1893, p. 5; *Freeman's Journal*, 17 March 1894, p. 13.
47 *SMH*, 9 April 1894, p. 4.
48 The manifesto is in ibid., 21 April 1894, p. 5. The signatories were Bavister, Black, Cann, G. D. Clark, Cook, Cotton, Danahey, Darnley, Edden, Fegan, Fitzgerald, Gardiner, Hollis, Houghton, Hindle, Langwell, Nicholson, Rae and Williams, ibid., 27 April 1894, p. 6.
49 Ibid., 21 April 1894, p. 8.
50 Ibid., 23 April 1894, p. 5; see also 30 April 1894, p. 6.
51 Ibid., 23 April 1894, p. 6. Watson also explained patiently to the *Bulletin* the novel nature of the Labor Party, 3 March 1894, p. 7.
52 See also letter from Rev. Philip Moses in *SMH*, 24 April 1894, p. 6.
53 TLC minutes, 22 February 1894.
54 Ibid., 28 June 1894.
55 The pledge is in ibid., 10 May 1894; its only important difference from the official pledge was the omission of the words relating to monopoly and class privilege; at least one league saw some merit in it, Denison league, minute book, 14 May 1894.
56 See, e.g., exchange of letters between Brennan and Cook, *SMH*, 16 May 1894, p. 4.
57 TLC minutes, 17 May 1894.
58 *SMH*, 24 May 1894, p. 5. Cook's pledge made no provision for the caucus.
59 TLC minutes, 7 June 1894.
60 Ibid.
61 Ibid., 14 June 1894.

Chapter 9
1 See Catherine B. Mackerras's article 'Dibbs Versus Duff: The Sad Story of a Colonial Governor', *JRAHS* 56 (4), 1970.
2 Black was the most vocal and publicity conscious of the 1891 Labor members; the statements are taken from his pamphlet *Labor in Politics* (1893) in NSW Political Labour League collection, ML. Under the 'old regime' much legislation was lost by the absence of quorums.
3 *SMH*, 24 April 1894, p. 6; in May fifty-nine branches had conformed, ibid., 15 May 1894, p. 6.
4 Ibid., 11 May 1894, p. 6; the time was later extended by fourteen days, ibid., 24 May 1894, p. 5.
5 Ibid., 7 June 1894, p. 5; by 18 June, seventy-five leagues had conformed, ibid., 19 June 1894, p. 6.
6 Ibid., 18 June 1894, p. 6; minutes, Denison league, 11 June 1894.
7 *SMH*, 22 February 1894, p. 6; minutes, Denison league, 2 February 1894. At the 1894 (February) Amalgamated Shearers' Union conference, Toomey supported Holman and other LEL members who came in a deputation to try to get the ASU to use its influence to keep the bush unions united with the LEL, pp. 54, 55, *Report of the 1894 A.S.U. Conference*, Sydney 1894.
8 *DT*, 25 June 1894, p. 6, letter from Hughes.
9 *SMH*, 3 May 1894, p. 6.
10 Ibid., 5 June, p. 6, 23 June 1894, p. 7.
11 *DT*, 5 July 1894, p. 5.
12 *SMH*, 2 July 1894, p. 8.
13 *DT*, 16 July 1894, p. 6; see ibid., 4 July 1894, p. 6, for report of Watson in Wyalong.

14 The account of Beeby's campaign, but not the references to his personality, is based on G. S. Harman's article 'G. S. Beeby and the first Labour electoral battle in Armidale', *Labour History*, (2), 1962.

15 Both of Beeby's opponents were sitting members for Armidale.

16 Willard was helped by the temporary presence of railway workers in the electorate. On 15 November 1894 he was disqualified by the Elections and Qualifications Committee because he had obtained an elector's right (i.e., been placed on the roll) improperly; see *DT*, 16 November 1894, p. 6; *AS*, 16 November 1894, p. 5.

17 In May, Toomey had tried without success to get the general election held before July. He told the TLC, which sent his request to Cook, that '75 per cent of the shearers would be hundreds of miles away from their electorates long before July', *DT*, 24 May 1894, p. 6.

18 *SMH*, 8 August 1894, p. 7.

19 In the available sources, chiefly newspapers, varying totals of non-solidarity candidates are given. The figure of sixty is based on an analysis of the information in relation to connections of the candidates with 'bogus leagues' and fiscal groups; in many cases it is virtually impossible to decide whether a candidate was independent Labor, independent or one or other of the fiscalist groups. E. M. Clark, Gough, Mackinnon, Sheldon and Vaughn, who all ran and lost, are not included in the sixty. T. H. Williams was the only one of the original thirty-five Labor Assembly members who did not run.

20 The thirteen non-solidarities were, T. Bavister (Ashfield), G. Black (Sydney-Gipps), T. Brown (Condobolin), J. Cook (Hartley), A. Edden (Kahibah), J. L. Fegan (Wickham), A. Gardiner (Ashburnham), L. T. Hollis (Goulburn), J. Morgan (Dubbo), H. W. Newman (Orange), J. B. Nicholson (Woronora), W. F. Schey (Darlington), W. H. Wood (Eden-Bombala).

21 *SMH*, 3 August 1894, p. 6.

22 Ibid., 8 August 1894, p. 7. The old rule still applied that all ministers had to go back to their constituents for approval.

23 Ibid., 15 August 1894, pp. 4, 5.

24 *PD*, vol. 72, p. 9.

25 *DT*, 2 August 1894, p. 5.

26 E.g., the Illawarra Miners', Wool and Leather Workers', Boot Trades' Unions, TLC minutes, 8 February, 3 May, 7 June 1894.

27 *DT*, 21 July 1894, p. 11.

28 A. Griffith, *The Labor Platform: an Exposition*, Sydney 1893.

29 *DT*, 21 July 1894, p. 11.

Chapter 10

1 TLC minutes, 28 June 1894.

2 Sydney District Council minutes, 13 September 1894.

3 Ibid., 22 November 1894.

4 TLC minutes, 7 April 1894.

5 Ibid., 5 May 1894.

6 Sydney District Council minutes, 16, 30 August 1894.

7 *Daily Post*, 18 January 1895.

8 *SMH*, 28 January 1895, p. 3.

9 Ibid., 1 April 1895, p. 3.

10 Ibid., 24 May 1895, p. 6.

11 Ibid., 25 May 1895, p. 7.

12 Ibid. This pledge was the seventh since 1891, starting with J. D. Fitzgerald's rudimentary form at the TLC on 31 March 1891.

13 Summary based on 1895 rules of PLL in the ML; see also *SMH*, 24 May, p. 6; 25 May, p. 7; 27 May 1895, p. 3.
14 Ibid.
15 Black, op. cit., No. 4, p. 11.
16 Not all free traders did support Reid. Parkes was still in parliament and loathed the man who had not only succeeded him but was also clearly determined to inaugurate a new era in free trade-liberalism. Wise, McMillan and Bruce Smith (no longer in parliament) were not in Reid's cabinet. Wise strangely thought Reid was not going far enough in his policy of direct taxation. McMillan and Smith, wealthy representatives of powerful business interests, thought he was going too far. But a majority of free traders, plus some radical protectionists, and, of course, the Labor Party solidly supported Reid. In his article 'Disciplined Party Voting: a Labor Innovation?' *Labour History* (21), 1971, P. Weller seeks carefully to equate the solidarity of Reid's supporters with that of the Labor Party; an argument that suggests that the unexampled attempts of the whole Party in 1891–5 to secure unity were futile, and that the Labor caucus and pledge were unnecessary. It is rather the case that Reid's dominance in a single, vital and extraordinary parliamentary session produced conditions that rallied unwontedly consistent support to him, and it was support that could always rely on fifteen solid Labor votes when needed. It should be noted that the solidarity Labor pledge did not require, nor did it produce, a solid vote on *every* question; nor had the problem of absenteeism been fully adverted to by 1895. For additional study of the free traders' groups see A. W. Martin, 'Freetrade and Protectionist Parties in New South Wales', *HS* 6 (23), 1954.
17 *PD*, vol. 72, pp. 373, 380.
18 Ibid., vol. 77, pp. 6572–3 (30 May 1895, J. H. Want, MLC, attorney-general).
19 Ibid., vol. 78, p. 7126.
20 *SMH*, 19 July 1894, p. 5.
21 *PD*, vol. 78, p. 7509.
22 Ibid., p. 7604 (J. N. Brunker, colonial secretary).
23 The majority of bills, public and private, were introduced by private members, who had them drafted the best way they could; there were part-time parliamentary draftsmen, but they were chiefly engaged on government legislation.
24 E.g., Sir Alfred Stephen had begun in the Legislative Council his great work on divorce law reform, see Martha Rutledge's unpublished M.A. Thesis 'Sir Alfred Stephen and Divorce Law Reform in New South Wales, 1886–1892', Australian National University, 1966; and Sir Frederick Darley had originated the trade union bill there in 1881.
25 *PD*, vol. 78, p. 7508 (25 June 1895).
26 *SMH*, 27 May 1895, p. 3.
27 Black was in constant touch with individuals who had a view of a comprehensive Labor appeal; e.g., W. Astley wrote to him on 12 May 1891, 'The thoughtful, cultured advocate of labour interests . . . is wanted in the House even more than the labourer himself,' George Black papers, ML.
28 *PD*, vol. 77, p. 6126 (16 May 1895), Parkes, quoting from Reid's financial statement.
29 Ibid., p. 6122.
30 Ibid., p. 6149.
31 *DT*, 8 July 1895, p. 6. The St George league came to a similar decision, ibid.

32 *PD*, vol. 77, p. 6235 (22 May 1895). Reid retorted that it would be 'a
   degradation' to have Griffith's vote, ibid., p. 6236. The incident indicated the
   delicate nature of the Labor-Reid relations. Griffith also ridiculed the
   Parkes-Dibbs coalition, saying that only he and E. W. O'Sullivan could
   describe it and he would term it 'a homogeneous conglomeration of hetero-
   geneous inconsistencies', ibid., p. 6237. O'Sullivan's own peculiar position
   was shown by his vote for Parkes.
33 *DT*, 10 July 1895, p. 4.
34 Ibid., 11 July 1895, p. 5.
35 Ibid., also 12 July 1895, p. 4.
36 Ibid., 17 July 1895, p. 6.
37 Ibid., 18 July 1895, p. 5; also 19 July 1895, p. 6.
38 Ibid., 23 July, p. 6; 25 July 1895, p. 7.
39 Ibid., p. 4.
40 Ibid., 22 July 1895, p. 6.
41 *SMH*, 23 July 1895, p. 4.
42 *DT*, 17 July 1895, p. 4.
43 *SMH*, 18 July 1895, p. 5.
44 *DT*, 13 July 1895, p. 10.
45 Ibid., 19 July 1895, p. 6.
46 Biographical details of Dacey are mainly from obituaries published after his
   death on 11 April 1912, especially the *Freeman's Journal*, 18 April 1912;
   samples of his election addresses are in the *Suburban Times*, 30 December
   1893, and the *Australian Workman* (special edition), 11 July 1894. The five
   Labor Roman Catholics in the 1891 parliament hardly stayed long enough in
   the Party for any judgments to be made of any reciprocal effects, if any,
   between them and the Party. Loughnane, the only Catholic among the 1894
   Labor members, was not really suited to the political life.

Chapter 11

 1 *SMH*, 26 July 1895, p. 5.
 2 Ibid.
 3 Ibid., 27 July 1895, p. 10.
 4 *PD*, vol. 79, pp. 6, 7 (14 August 1895).
 5 Ibid., p. 132 (15 August 1895).
 6 Ibid., vol. 81, p. 2897 (13 December 1895).
 7 Ibid., p. 3406 ff. (17 December 1895).
 8 *Worker*, 1 February, 1896.
 9 *SMH*, 27 January 1896, p. 3.
10 Ibid., 28 January 1896, p. 7.
11 Ibid.
12 Details of planks are taken from 1896 Platform of PLL. ML.
13 Edgar Dunsdorfs, *The Australian Wheat-Growing Industry*, Melbourne 1956,
   p. 533.
14 E.g., *First Congress Report*, 1879, pp. 29–39; *Second Congress Report*, 1884,
   pp. 45–9; *Third Congress Report*, 1885, pp. 16–19.
15 TLC executive minutes, 4 March 1890. The *Shearer's Record*, 15 April 1890
   said the Chinese were admitted 'under exceptional circumstances' but this
   does not affect the point.
16 *Report of the Royal Commission on Alleged Chinese Gambling*, Sydney
   1892, p. 434, question 16097.
17 *Western Herald and Darling River Advocate*, 3 June 1891. The word 'inferior' was used at the time in an industrial sense to describes all groups who

would, or could, not adhere to union conditions of hours and wages; it covered 'scabs', 'blacklegs', women and children, as well as Chinese and Afghans.

18 *Rules and Platform of the Riverina District Council (ALF) Political Section,* Sydney 1894. ML.
19 See A. T. Yarwood, *Asian Migration to Australia,* Melbourne 1964, chapter 1, especially pp. 6–7.
20 E.g., see Reid's speech on the coloured race restriction bill, *PD,* vol. 85, p. 3945 ff. (13 October 1896); it is relevant to mention that on 18 November 1897 a record crowd attended the cricket match between England and New South Wales, chiefly because Ranjitsinghi, the classical Indian batsman, was playing, *DT,* 20 November 1897, p. 8; and in 1897 the champion school-boy swimmer of the colony was Ophir Kong Sing, 'a popular boy at Cleveland Street Superior School', ibid., 2 April 1897, p. 7; see also ibid., 25 November 1897, p. 4, editorial on the alien immigration bills; and article 'In Defence of John', ibid., 7 August 1897, p. 13.
21 *SMH,* 28 January 1896, p. 7.
22 Ibid., p. 4.
23 *Liberty,* 22 February 1896, p. 3.
24 Patrick Ford, op. cit., elucidates in detail the socialist groups to which most of these men belonged, see especially chapters 17–25.
25 *Worker,* 14 March 1896.

Chapter 12

 1 *DT,* 21 February, p. 3, 22 February 1896, p. 4.
 2 *Liberty,* 23 September 1896, p. 1.
 3 *DT,* 13 October 1896, p. 3.
 4 Quoted in Evatt, op. cit., p. 93; see ibid., chapter XIII, for details of Holman's imprisonment.
 5 *DT,* 13 October 1896, p. 4.
 6 *Liberty,* 23 October 1896, p. 1.
 7 Quoted in ibid., p. 10.
 8 *DT,* 15 October 1896, p. 5.
 9 *Northern People,* 23 January 1897, p. 6.
10 Ibid., p. 4.
11 *Worker,* 14 November 1896.
12 Ibid., 30 January 1897; *DT,* 27 January 1897, p. 6.
13 Ibid., 30 January 1897, p. 7.
14 *Worker,* 30 January 1897; *SMH,* 27 January 1897, p. 9.
15 E.g., *DT,* 28 January 1897, p. 8; *SMH,* 28 January 1897, p. 4.
16 *Worker,* 30 January 1897.
17 *PD,* vol. 82, p. 2.
18 Ibid., vol. 86, p. 5113 (12 November 1896).
19 Ibid., vol. 83, p. 1008 (24 June 1896); *Worker,* 4 July 1896.
20 Ibid., 14 November 1896; *PD,* vol. 82, p. 750 (10 June 1896). This vote did not involve solidarity in terms of the caucus pledge, and Black showed his streak of independence by voting against his colleagues.
21 Ibid., vol. 86, p. 4987 (11 November 1896).
22 Ibid., pp. 4991–2. In June Reid, with Watson's help, had rebuffed Griffith's attempt to stop New South Wales convention delegates from sitting with Queensland delegates, who were to be nominated instead of elected. Reid said it was essential for Queensland to be represented; ibid., vol. 83, pp. 1185–8 (30 June 1896).

23 Ibid., pp. 1577 ff.
24 Ibid., pp. 1589 ff.
25 Ibid., vol. 86, p. 5121 (12 November 1896).

Chapter 13

1 *DT*, 3 February 1897, p. 6; *Worker*, 13 February 1897.
2 *DT*, 30 January 1897, p. 11.
3 Ibid., 20 February 1897, p. 5.
4 Ibid., 24 February 1897, p. 5.
5 Ibid., 9 March 1897, p. 5.
6 Ibid., 17 March 1897, p. 9.
7 *Australian Workman*, 24 July 1897; the *Workman* approved the Assembly's censure, stressed the weakness of the leagues and considered the only way out was 'to wind up the PLL'; on 20 March, the *Workman* had a strong editorial on the need for reorganisation of the PLL. For proposals of the Sydney District Assembly to reorganise the PLL, and attempt to censure the Labor members, see ibid., 8 May 1897.
8 *Worker*, 4 September 1897.
9 Printed document in N.S.W. Political Labour League material. ML.
10 *Australian Workman*, 8 May 1897.
11 See Evatt, op. cit., chapter XIV.
12 *Worker*, 2 October 1897.
13 Minutes, Sydney District Council, 18 November 1897.
14 *Liberty*, 24 February 1898, p. 2. Although the 1898 conference did not discuss Moroney's letter, it carried a motion of regret over his resignation and noted his 'long and honourable service with the League', *Worker*, 5 February 1898, p. 7; Moroney responded by telling the PLL executive that he would not work against the Labor Party, ibid., 5 March 1898, p. 3.
15 Minutes, Sydney District Council, 26 August 1897.
16 *Worker*, 30 October 1897.
17 *PD*, vol. 90, p. 4266. In the debate, to p. 4397 (3 November), details emerged of the activity of the Labor members at Lucknow.
18 Ibid., p. 4314 (3 November 1897).
19 Ibid., pp. 4330, 4431. Hughes repeated his charge against Victorian 'black-legs' in a letter to the *DT*, 26 January 1898, p. 11; see also *Australian Workman*, 25 September 1897.
20 *PD*, vol. 90, p. 4349.
21 *Worker*, 30 October 1897.
22 *Australian Workman*, 15 May, and 22 May 1897 (letter from H. Stuart). The AWU's renewal of interest in the PLL was also indicated by the fact that it had made available to the League executive a room in the *Worker* office, see executive's report for 1897, *Worker*, 29 January 1898, p. 6.
23 *Liberty*, 24 February 1898, p. 3.
24 Except for Henderson's speech, details are from *DT*, 27 January 1898, p. 6; the report of the *SMH*, 27 January 1898, p. 5, shows Hepher's motion as carried 14 to 7, which is incorrect, and the *Herald* repeated the error in its editorial on 28 January 1898, p. 4.
25 Quoted in full in *Liberty*, 24 February 1898, pp. 9, 10.
26 *Worker*, 5 February 1898, p. 5.
27 *DT*, 27 January 1898, p. 6.
28 *Worker*, 12 March 1898, p. 7, Rules of the PLL; also ibid., 5 February 1898, p. 7.
29 *DT*, 27 January 1898, p. 6.

30 *Worker,* 26 March 1898, p. 7.
31 *SMH,* 28 January 1898, p. 4.
32 *DT,* 28 January 1898, p. 4.
33 Ibid., 11 April 1898, p. 6; among the delegates were Barlow, Moroney, Keniry, H. E. Holland and P. Bowling. The anarchists had held their conference in January; see ibid., 18 January 1898, p. 5.
34 *Liberty,* 24 February 1898, p. 10.

Chapter 14

 1 *Liberty,* 24 August 1897, pp. 4, 8, 9.
 2 *SMH,* 21 June 1898, p. 6.
 3 *Worker,* 29 January 1898, p. 6; 1897 report of PLL executive. Griffith had moved the resolution, which aimed to bring nurses under the Workshops and Factories Act, see *PD,* vol. 89, pp. 2765–92 (10 August 1897).
 4 In 1897, e.g., the Council rejected Reid's probate duties bill and Griffith's Public Instruction Act amendment bill, which provided for completely free education; see *Worker,* 29 January 1898, p. 6, 1897 report of the PLL executive.
 5 *DT,* 14 January 1898, p. 6.
 6 *Worker,* 5 March 1898, p. 4.
 7 Ibid., 19 March 1898, p. 4.
 8 E.g., see ibid., 26 March, reports of 6 meetings; 2 April 1898, reports of 7 meetings.
 9 Holman addressed the club on 'The English Race' in February, ibid., 12 February 1898, p. 5; in 1897 there had been several discussions on the Federal Convention proceedings, e.g., Von Hagen's paper, *Australian Workman,* 1 May 1897.
10 Evatt, op. cit., p. 97; *Worker,* 14 May 1898, p. 4.
11 *DT,* 29 March 1898, pp. 5–6. Reid's political enemies, of whom there were many in 1898, immediately labelled him 'Yes-No Reid'; the smear has remained despite effective rebuttals by Evatt, op. cit., chapter XV; and W. G. McMinn, 'George Reid and Federation' *HS* 10 (38), 1962, and 'The Federal Policy of G. H. Reid: A Rejoinder', *JRAHS* 51 (1), 1965.
12 *DT,* 30 March 1898, p. 6.
13 *Worker,* 2 April 1898, p. 2.
14 Griffith was one Labor man who saw this clearly; see his letter in *DT,* 31 March 1898, p. 6.
15 *Worker,* 16 April, pp. 4, 5; 23 April, p. 1; 30 April 1898, pp. 6, 7.
16 *DT,* 1 April 1898, p. 6.
17 Ibid., 13 April, p. 3; 23 April 1898, p. 10.
18 Ibid., 11 April 1898, p. 6.
19 Ibid., 7 April 1898, p. 10.
20 *Worker,* 7 May 1898, p. 4.
21 *DT,* 23 April, p. 10; 29 April 1898, p. 6.
22 Less than 50 per cent of the voters went to the poll, and the *Worker,* 11 June 1898, p. 4, commenting on the low proportion, suggested penalties for non-voters: compulsory voting had been considered at the 1898 PLL conference, but not adopted.
23 *SMH,* 14 June, 1898, p. 6.
24 Ibid., 15 June 1898, p. 8.
25 Ibid., 20 June 1898, p. 6.
26 Ibid., 22 June 1898, p. 4.
27 Ibid., 21 June 1898, p. 5.

28 Ibid.
29 Ibid., p. 6.
30 *PD,* vol. 92, pp. 2, 27.
31 Ibid., pp. 124–7 (23 June 1898).
32 Ibid., pp. 138–47.
33 Ibid., p. 251.
34 *DT,* 15 January 1898, p. 11.
35 *SMH,* 23 June 1898, p. 4.
36 Ibid., 25 June 1898, p. 9.
37 Ibid. Later in the campaign it was known as the Free Trade and Liberal Association and the Liberal Federal Association.
38 *DT,* 19 July 1898, p. 4. Lyne also claimed he was not bound to Barton as leader, ibid., 18 July 1898, p. 6.
39 *SMH,* 11 July 1898, p. 4.
40 Ibid., 16 July 1898, p. 9.
41 Ibid., 18 July 1898, p. 6.
42 Of course, Reid had said he would vote for the convention bill and this had certainly influenced the King electors, but Barton and his admirers and advisers, especially the *SMH,* were not impressed by anything that Reid did for Federation.
43 *Patriot,* 16 June 1898, p. 130. ML.
44 The official list is in the PLL executive's report for the year 1898, *Worker,* 1 April 1899.
45 *SMH,* 16 July 1898, p. 9.
46 Ibid., 9 July 1898, p. 9; *DT,* 15 July 1898, p. 4.
47 Ibid., p. 5; *SMH,* 15 July 1898, p. 6.
48 *DT,* 13 July 1898, p. 8.
49 *SMH,* 14 July 1898, p. 8.
50 The manifesto is published in full in *DT,* 16 July 1898, p. 11.
51 *Worker,* 6 August 1898, p. 2.
52 Ibid., p. 4.
53 *SMH,* 28 July 1898, p. 8.

Chapter 15

1 Parkes headed a ministry from 21 December 1878 to 4 January 1883, but it was a coalition with John Robertson, and differed in other important respects from Reid's 3 August 1894 to 13 September 1899 government.
2 *PD,* vol. 93, pp. 6, 7.
3 Ibid., pp. 63, 64.
4 Ibid., p. 109 (18 August 1898).
5 Ibid., pp. 176–7 (24 August 1898).
6 Ibid., pp. 441–2. Clause (1) of the resolutions was incorporated at the instigation of the Labor Party; J. H. Want's statement in Legislative Council, *PD,* vol. 95, p. 2516 (24 November 1898).
7 Ibid., vol. 93, pp. 453–4 (8 September 1898).
8 Ibid., p. 504 (13 September 1898).
9 Ibid., p. 631 (15 September 1898).
10 Ibid., vol. 94, pp. 956–90.
11 Ibid., vol. 94, p. 1215 (6 October 1898).
12 Ibid., vol. 95, p. 2267 (16 November 1898).
13 Ibid., vol. 94, p. 1863 (26 October 1898).
14 Ibid., p. 1269 (11 October 1898).

15 Reid, of course, realised this fully; see his speech at Lake Macquarie, 9 April
   1899, *DT*, 10 April 1899, p. 6.
16 The Legislative Council debated the Assembly's Federation resolutions from
   23 November to 13 December 1898 when they were adopted after substantial
   amendments. Reid had made it clear he would not attempt to harmonise
   the Assembly's and the Council's resolutions; both were submitted to the
   premiers' conference in Melbourne from 29 January 1898 to 2 February
   1899, but Reid naturally based his case on his own resolutions. Dr (later Sir)
   Normand MacLaurin, Sir Julian Salomons, C. G. Heydon, L. F. Heydon,
   Alexander Brown and C. E. Pilcher emerged as the anti-Reid spearhead in
   the Council: see *PD*, vol. 95, pp. 2405–518 (23, 24 November), 2702–946
   (30 November); vol. 96, p. 3149 (13 December 1898).
17 Letter in the *Worker*, 27 August 1898, p. 2.
18 The *Dead Bird* was a slightly bawdy publication, on which Norton had
   modelled *Truth*.
19 'Party Government' meant government by a 'single-party ministry' in contrast with a ministry chosen from the whole parliament; the latter was, of
   course, a practical impossibility, but office seemed so far away for Labor
   men and the abuses of the times seemed so incurable, that many of them
   took refuge in the idea that if only the most talented men could get into
   power, including some Laborites, then all would be well. The initiative and
   referendum were favoured for much the same reasons. All three, i.e., non-
   party government, initiative and referendum, were taken very seriously as
   essential features of ideal democracy.
20 *Worker*, 20 August 1898, p. 1.
21 The report is in ibid., 1 April 1899.
22 A report of the conference is in ibid., 8 April 1899; the *Worker* places the
   meeting at Woonona; other sources, including the PLL notice of the conference (in PLL material in ML) put it in Bulli, which adjoins Woonona.
23 *DT*, 29 March 1899, p. 5, see also editorial on p. 4. At Wallsend on 31
   March 1899, Reid divulged that he had offered appointments to Labor men,
   SMH, 1 April 1899, p. 9. Additional appointments to the Legislative Council
   had been mooted in January, when the *Worker*, 14 January 1899, p. 4,
   argued that although Labor was fighting for more perfect institutions, the
   Party should not leave the Council entirely to the privileged classes.
24 The Labor Party had forced Reid to reduce his duties on tea from 3d to 1d
   per pound; see executive report for 1898, *Worker*, 1 April 1899.
25 The *Telegraph* named McGowen on 3 April 1899, p. 5. There is much less
   ground on which to infer the Labor informant of the *Telegraph*, but it was
   probably Hughes. In the Assembly debates on the enabling bill, the *Telegraph* noted the reticence of McGowen (and Barton and Lyne) in contrast
   with 'the free criticism of the Premier by members of the Labor party', and
   reported Reid as inviting the three 'Hs', Hughes, Holman and Haynes to take
   up the completion of Federation if the bill failed, *DT*, 3 March 1899, p. 5;
   4 March 1899, p. 8.
26 Ibid., 31 March 1899, p. 5.
27 *Worker*, 8 April 1899 (italics supplied). The *Telegraph's* report barely
   mentions McGowen and omits Smith. McGowen's reference to opposition 'to
   the actions of the Legislative Council' referred to the Council's amendments
   which included the fixing of a minimum number for a 'yes' vote at the
   referendum.
28 *DT*, 3 April 1899, p. 5, reported that caucus 'last week' had revised a decision
   not to recommend any names for the Legislative Council; that a speech of

Reid at Wallsend had 'added color' to the reports; and listed the names of four Labor men who would become members of the Legislative Council, J. Estell, N. Buzacott, J. Hepher and G. Black. The newspaper was wrong about only one, Black.

29 Ibid.

30 Wombat was a town in Watson's electorate; Loughnane was born there.

31 *DT*, 3 April 1899, p. 5.

32 Ibid., 10 April 1899, p. 6.

33 Ibid., 11 April 1899, p. 6.

34 Ibid.

Chapter 16

1 This was Hughes's opinion, and, judged on reports of meetings in the *DT* and *SMH*, it is correct: see *DT*, 22 June 1899, p. 6.

2 Reports of the meetings listed will be found in either the *Telegraph* or *Herald* on the dates following each one.

3 *DT*, 26 May 1899, p. 4. On 2 June, p. 5, the *Telegraph* reported that Lyne had a full list of engagements right up to the referendum.

4 *SMH*, 21 June 1899, p. 4.

5 Ibid., 22 June 1899, p. 7.

6 *Worker*, 27 May 1899, p. 4.

7 Ibid.

8 *DT*, 25 April 1899, p. 6.

9 Ibid., 11 May 1899, p. 7.

10 Ibid., 27 May 1899, p. 10.

11 Ibid., 1 June, p. 6; 2 June 1899, p. 6.

12 Minutes, Sydney District Council, ALF, 1 June 1899.

13 *Worker*, 17 June 1899, p. 5.

14 The figures were:

	Yes	No
Broken Hill	1249	438
Alma	732	333
Sturt	476	174
Wilcannia	747	183
Wentworth	725	71

15 The following account is based on the report in the *Worker*, 5 August 1899, pp. 2, 5.

16 *DT*, 21 June 1899, p. 5.

17 Ibid., 30 June 1899, p. 4.

18 This, and the following points from the governor's speech, are from *PD*, vol. 99, pp. 2, 3 (18 July 1899).

19 So far, no direct evidence has emerged of Lyne's plotting with members of the Labor Party before 23 August 1899 when he replaced Barton as leader of the opposition. But the circumstances suggest the possibility of some communication with Labor members, probably either Holman or Hughes, or both of them. Of course, the inexorable logic of events may have made formal planning unnecessary.

20 *PD*, vol. 99, pp. 468, 484 (2 August 1899).

21 Ibid., p. 631 (9 August 1899).

22 Ibid., p. 603 (9 August 1899).

23 Ibid., pp. 621–31 (9 August 1899); exchanges between Reid and Lyne in this debate (2–9 August) were extremely bitter, and indicated the possibility of Lyne's resurgence and Reid's knowledge of it.
24 *DT,* 9 August 1899, p. 7.
25 *PD,* vol. 99, p. 879.
26 Ibid., pp. 928–9 (23 August 1899).
27 Ibid., pp. 931–82. On 24 August the *Star* reported that a censure motion was in the offing, *AS,* 24 August 1899, p. 5. The *Herald* reported Reid as saying that certain members of the opposition would not support a censure motion moved by Barton and that the Labor Party favoured Lyne against Barton, *SMH,* 24 August 1899, p. 5.
28 *PD,* vol. 100, p. 1043 (30 August 1899).
29 Ibid.
30 Quoted in the *Worker,* 9 July 1898, p. 2.
31 *AS,* 1 September 1899, p. 5; *SMH,* 1 September 1899, p. 7.
32 *PD,* vol. 100, p. 1070 (30 August 1899).
33 Ibid., p. 1084 (31 August 1899).
34 Ibid., p. 1077.
35 Ibid., pp. 1093–5.
36 *AS,* 1 September 1899, p. 4.
37 *DT,* 31 August 1899, p. 4.
38 Quoted in *DT,* 31 August 1899, p. 6.
39 Quoted in ibid., 2 September 1899, p. 3.
40 Ibid., 6 September 1899, p. 5; *SMH,* 7 September 1899, p. 7.
41 Other speakers referred to them as the 'bashi-bazouks' and the 'red indian party'.
42 *PD,* vol. 100, pp. 1152–62 (5 September 1899).
43 Ibid., pp. 1162–76.
44 Evatt, op. cit., chapter XVIII, 'Holman puts Reid out'.
45 *DT,* 12 April 1912, pp. 9, 10.
46 Op. cit., p. 121.
47 *PD,* vol. 100, pp. 1192–5.
48 Law spoke in the debate, see ibid., p. 1290 (7 September 1899), and claimed that he had not been told of the caucus decision. Griffith (ibid., p. 1252) admitted that he had not told Law of it.
49 *DT,* 7 September 1899, pp. 5–6. A further report added that Edden and Fegan returned to Newcastle on 8 September to enthusiastic congratulations, ibid., 9 September 1899, p. 6.
50 *SMH,* 7 September 1899, p. 6.
51 This is how Cotton put it on 7 September 1899, *PD,* vol. 100, p. 1293; and he was certainly correct.
52 Ibid., pp. 1141–2 (5 September 1899).
53 Ibid., pp. 1213–17.
54 Ibid., pp. 1226–7 (6 September 1899).
55 Ibid., pp. 1233, 1236.
56 Ibid., p. 1273 (7 September 1899).
57 Ibid., p. 1308.
58 *SMH,* 8 September 1899, p. 4.
59 *Worker,* 2 September 1899, p. 4.
60 Ibid., 3 February 1900, p. 5.
61 Ibid., p. 8; 10 February, p. 2; 17 March 1900, p. 7.

Index

Anarchism, 35, 153
Arbitration and conciliation, 69, 76, 89, 106, 117, 126, 168, 194, 200, 211, 223
Australasian Labor Federation, 82, 90-1, 97, 101-2, 120-3, 146, 149, 166, 168, 211; *see also* Sydney District Council
Australian Workers' Union, 82, 101, 109-10, 120-2, 143, 169, 177, 200, 208, 211, 226

Backhouse, B., 49, 91, 151
Balmain, 59
Barlow, C. M., 150, 151, 156, 160, 166, 171-3
Barton, Edmund, 7, 57, 58, 71, 73, 74, 106, 129, 133, 161, 163, 178, 180, 181-2, 183-4, 185-6, 191-2, 193, 194, 195-6, 197, 204, 205, 206, 208, 210, 214-15, 216, 219, 220, 221, 223-4
Bavister, T., 60, 61, 82, 89, 92, 134
Beeby, George S., 47, 91, 96, 111-12, 120
Black, George, 34-5, 56, 57, 63, 67, 70, 85, 88, 91, 92, 95, 96, 103 104, 106-7, 109, 124, 128, 151, 155, 163, 164, 169, 170, 171, 172, 174, 180, 184, 188, 189-90
Boxall, R., 41
Brennan, Peter Joseph, 28-31, 35, 37, 39, 40, 79, 83, 103-5, 121, 129, 173
Brennan, W., 211
Broken Hill strike (1892), 84-7, 225
Brown, T., 113, 124, 168, 169, 170, 180, 208, 217, 220
Brunker, J., 163
Bulletin, 34-5
Burt, T., 13
Bush unions, 13, 42, 48-9, 55, 64, 90-1; *see also* Trade unions (unionism)
Butler, Edward, 9
Butler, F., 170
Buzacott, N. J., 205

Camb, W., 9
Cameron, Angus, 10, 11, 12, 20, 22, 27, 31, 63, 84, 96; East Sydney campaign, 13-14; in parliament, 15-18
Cann, J. H., 63, 74, 85, 112, 113, 131, 157, 162, 199, 204, 209, 217, 220
Capitalism, 4, 5, 6, 32, 51, 153, 185
Carruthers, J. H., 137, 143, 163, 197, 216, 224
Caucus, 66, 67, 68, 70-1, 74, 76-7, 87, 96, 124, 129, 147, 157, 158, 201, 210-13, 215-16, 217, 219, 220, 221, 223, 225, 226
Caucus of Trades, 21
Central executive committee, 47, 48, 49, 54, 55, 56, 66, 78-9, 80-4, 89, 91-2 93, 95, 97, 99, 100, 103, 109-11, 113, 122, 123, 131, 141, 173, 199-200, 202, 208, 210, 226
Chapman, M., 9
Clark, E. M., 60, 63, 85, 207, 219
Clark, G. D., 59, 63, 89, 92, 96, 103, 115
Clarke, F., 192, 205
Coal mines regulation bill, 73-5, 89, 106, 125-6, 188, 194, 197, 214, 215, 218
Cochran, J. P., 122
Cole, W. B., 21
Colonial society, 1, 2, 24, 37-8, 161
Coloured immigration, 138, 144-6, 157-8, 188
Conference, 78, 82, 84, 96, 97, 100, 104, 146, 172; (1892) 80-1, 145; (1893, Jan.) 87-8; (1893, Nov.) 91-7; (1894) 98-9; (1895) 121-4, 146; (1896) 141-4, 146; (1897) 153, 155-7; (1898) 169-75; (1899, March) 199-204; (1899, July) 210-13; (1900) 226
Conference of All Trades, 25
Constitution, 1, 3, 6, 23, 125; and Labor, 9, 50-1
Convicts, 1, 2
Cook, J., 73, 74, 91, 92, 93, 100, 103, 115-16, 134, 172

255